OXFORD LIBRARY OF
AFRICAN LITERATURE

General Editors
E. E. EVANS-PRITCHARD
G. LIENHARDT
W. H. WHITELEY

THE DINKA AND
THEIR SONGS

—

FRANCIS MADING DENG

OXFORD
AT THE CLARENDON PRESS
1973

Oxford University Press, Ely House, London W. 1

GLASGOW NEW YORK TORONTO MELBOURNE WELLINGTON
CAPE TOWN IBADAN NAIROBI DAR ES SALAAM LUSAKA ADDIS ABABA
DELHI BOMBAY CALCUTTA MADRAS KARACHI LAHORE DACCA
KUALA LUMPUR SINGAPORE HONG KONG TOKYO

ISBN 0 19 8151381

© *Oxford University Press 1973*

*Printed in Great Britain
at the University Press, Oxford
by Vivian Ridler
Printer to the University*

TO
GODFREY LIENHARDT

CONTENTS

PART ONE: INTRODUCTION

   I. The People, their Country, and their Orthography   1

  II. Social Organization   6

 III. Moral Values   12

 IV. Marriage, Kinship, and Family   18

   V. Property and Economy   30

 VI. The Age-set System   41

 VII. Religion and Spiritual Well-being   48

VIII. Power and the Law   58

 IX. The Impact of Alien Cultures   67

   X. The Role of Songs in Dinka Society   78

PART TWO: TRANSLATIONS

   I. Ox Songs   96

  II. Cathartic Songs   159

 III. Initiation Songs   185

 IV. Age-set Insult Songs   199

   V. War Songs   202

 VI. Women's Songs   218

 VII. Hymns   238

VIII. Fairy-tale Songs   243

 IX. Children's Game Songs   247

   X. School Songs   250

CONTENTS

PART THREE: SELECTED TEXTS

I.	Diet ke Mior	262
II.	Diet ke Tɔc	279
III.	Diet k'Agar	285
IV.	Diet ke Tod	287
V.	Diet ke Diaar	292
VI.	Diet ke Nhialic	297
VII.	Diet ke Köör	299
VIII.	Diet ke Gat	300

PART ONE · INTRODUCTION

I

THE PEOPLE, THEIR COUNTRY, AND THEIR ORTHOGRAPHY

THE Dinka are a tall, slender, and fine-featured Nilotic people, living in the Republic of the Sudan, who, though thought to have non-negroid elements,[1] are among the blackest people in the world. Occupying a vast area of about 150,000 square miles and numbering over a million in a country of only fourteen million people and over five hundred tribes,[2] the Dinka are by far the most numerous people in the Sudan. Thus, large in numbers and widespread in settlement, they are a 'congeries' of tribes falling largely under the administration of Bahr el Ghazal and Upper Nile, two of the three Southern Provinces. The Ngok, from whom most of the songs in this volume were collected, are administered as part of Kordofan, one of the six Northern Provinces.

Despite their disunity, the Dinka show striking cultural uniformity. The fact that they have maintained such uniformity notwithstanding centuries of contact with other peoples is evidence of their intense pride in themselves and in their culture. They call themselves *Monyjang*, which for them has the connotation of *the* people. Non-Dinkas are referred to as 'the others', or *juur* (sing. *jur*), 'foreigners'. The Dinka thus take themselves as the standard of what is normal. Their ethnocentricity has often been stressed as a factor behind their conservatism and therefore backwardness in

---

[1] Professor Seligman maintains that although the non-negroid element may not be obvious in the Dinka and the Nuer, there is no doubt that it exists. He considers it to be Hamitic–Caucasian. See Seligman, *Pagan Tribes of Nilotic Sudan* (1932), 4, 20; also id., 'Some Aspects of the Hamitic Problem in A. E. Sudan', *JRAI* xliii (1913), 610–24.

[2] According to the 1956 census, there were 572 tribes.

modern terms.[1] Their conservatism has not been altogether one of
rejection, but rather one of selection and assimilation of alien
elements. A remarkable example is the integration of the concept
of the Islamic Messiah, the Mahdi, into Dinka religion. The Dinka
resisted both Islam and the rule of its nationalist leader, Mohammed
Ahmed, the Sudanese Mahdi, but his miraculous leadership and
victory against the Turko-Egyptian rule impressed them and inspired their recognition of his religious quality, though they conceived of him as the son of divinity Deng, and even prayed to him
for help in their resistance to Mohammed Ahmed, the Mahdi himself. In one Dinka song, swearing by 'Mohammed, Mohammed,
the Prophet of God' is included in Arabic preceding a swearing by
'Abuk, Abuk, the Girl in the River', a Dinka riverine Spirit. In
many other songs, Arabic words and ideas are incorporated to form
part of the whole, which remains distinctly Dinka. Although it has
been argued that male circumcision among some Dinkas came
from the Arabs in the North and that the Dinka practice of training the horns of oxen from early calfhood must have been imported
from Ancient Egypt, no Dinka would question their authenticity
as elements of Dinka culture. These are only examples of a more
pervasive process of conservative or selective adoption and assimilation. Indeed, the fact that the Dinka have remained among
the least touched by modernization is due less to their resistance to
change than to the colonial policy of indirect rule and cultural
preservation, which, though not entirely without merit, ill pre-
pared them for the modern world.

With education and increasing exposure to other cultures, they
are undergoing a rapid change in which they are attempting to
adapt themselves to the new circumstances. For the vast majority
the experience is bitter, the cost is high, and the ultimate result,
though still uncertain, seems to be the disintegration of the traditional order without any adequate substitute. The Dinka now find
themselves less a people assimilating alien ideas than a people
being assimilated by alien cultures. The most conspicuous aspect
of this process is what is known as the 'Southern Problem' with
roots in the South–North dichotomy. Although tribalism still
threatens broader loyalties throughout the Sudan, ethnic multiplicity is overshadowed by that division. While the racial factor is

[1] See Seligman, op. cit. (1932); also Butt, *The Nilotes of the Anglo-Egyptian
Sudan and Uganda* (1952), 41.

not clear-cut, the South is negroid and the North is culturally and, to a lesser extent racially, Arab. Different and isolated from one another until about a century ago when decades of hostility arising out of slave-raiding marked their initial contacts, and administered separately until the dawn of independence in 1956, the two see little in common. The North is dominant; and because of its dominance, the Sudan is an active member of the Arab League.

The British left the country with the problem of disunity unsolved. Their successors' policy for fostering national unity was to reverse the colonial trends of separate development and promote Islamization and Arabization. The Southerners, for the most part unfavourably disposed to Muslim-Arab culture by bitter history and colonial influence, saw subjugation in this form of unity and opposed it. Violent upheavals were first generated in 1955, a year before independence, when a battalion of the Southern Corps mutinied, sparking off a revolt in the South during which several hundred Northern Sudanese and an equal number of Southerners lost their lives. The insurgence continues and, in an attempt to quell it, the Government is still engaged with the Southern rebel army, the Anyanya. In this internecine warfare, many innocent people fall victims and scores of thousands have fled into the neighbouring countries of the Congo, Uganda, Kenya, Ethiopia, and the Central African Republic. Needless to say, this book is not an account of the political or of any other problems confronting the Dinka except in so far as these elucidate the songs.

The songs included here were selected from several hundred songs from three sources. Most of them were tape-recorded in Abyei, the administrative centre of the Ngok Dinka, during a short visit in September 1962. Others were later tape-recorded in England and the United States of America from students and visiting Dinkas of various tribal backgrounds. Yet others are from my memory. As might be expected, those from my memory and from the memory of the educated in general tend to be only extracts. The guiding principle of translation was to be as literal but as clear as possible.

The role of songs in Dinka society will later be discussed in greater detail, but it is worth stating at this stage that songs are intimately associated with all aspects of Dinka life. While traditional order is still the subject-matter of most songs, contemporary songs have already entered the realm of current experience to articulate the deep sentiments connected with the social, economic, political, and other aspects of their accelerated change. Indeed, so rapid is the change that there is reason to believe that what is recorded now may well be at the brink of extinction. A man who goes into the city no longer sings about the past but about the new confrontation of the past with the present. A singer for Omdurman Radio and TV sees his modern medium as incompatible with pure tradition and the content of his songs is of necessity an amalgam of tradition and modernity. There are, of course, many reasons for recording Dinka songs, but that their present content may soon be unavailable is not too romantic a reason.

To guide the reader, I give a few principles about Dinka letters and sounds, and some variations in the construction of words. While Dinka orthography is used in the text, the closest English orthography is used in the translations to facilitate smoother reading:

1. All vowels have their Latin (new pronunciation) values.
2. The letter 'c' is always pronounced as 'ch' in 'change', and not as in 'care'.
3. The nearest English sound to the Dinka letter 'dh' is 'th', but in the Dinka letter the tongue is drawn further back than in the English 'th'.
4. The letters 'ŋ' 'ɣ' 'ɛ' (i.e. open 'e'), and 'ɔ' (i.e. open 'o') are added to the Roman alphabet. 'ŋ' equals the English 'ng' when the latter occurs at the end of a word. 'ɣ' has no equivalent in English, but approximates to the English 'h' with the middle of the tongue pressing the roof of the mouth, leaving a much smaller space for air than is the case with the sound of the letter 'h'. 'Gh' is used in the translation as the closest to 'ɣ'. 'ɛ' and 'ɔ' have no equivalents in English, but, though very inadequate, 'e' and 'o' have been doubled ('ee' and 'oo') to approximate to their respective sounds in the translations.
5. The letter 'ny' is pronounced as in the Italian 'gn', never as in the English 'many'.
6. When a vowel is doubled, the letters are an elongation of the vowel: 'oo' is pronounced something like the 'oa' in 'goal' and not as in 'pool'; 'ee' is pronounced like the 'a' in 'scale'; 'ii' is pronounced like the 'ee' in 'geese'; 'aa' is pronounced like the 'a' in 'car'; 'uu' is pronounced like the 'oo' in 'pool'.

7. The letter 'g' is always as in 'gain' and not as in 'George'.

8. When a vowel is single, 'a' is pronounced like the 'a' in 'what'; 'e' approximates to the 'e's' in 'every'; 'i' is like the 'i' in 'kill'; 'o' is like the 'o' in 'poll'; 'u' is like the 'u' in 'bull'.

9. Among the Agaar, the Bor, and the Ngok Dinkas, 'de' is used to indicate 'of'. Thus, Bol de Deng would mean, Bol, son of Deng, with 'son' implied. Other Dinkas use 'e' or nothing. When certain nouns, proper or common, precede a possessive noun, with or without a 'de', they change their ending. It is not the intention to examine all occasions when this occurs and certainly not to formulate any rules, but merely to warn the reader that a noun may change its form according to the context and yet remain essentially the same. Thus, names which end with the letter 'c' used in a possessive sense would end with 'ny'. For example, Akoc son of Majok would be Akony de Majok. When nouns end with an 'i', a 'y', or a 't', the ending is changed to 'n'. Thus Anai son of Bol is Anan de Bol, Ayiiy son of Kuel is Ayin de Kuel, and kot (i.e. shield) belonging to Tong is kon de Tong. Nouns ending with 'k' change ending to 'ng'. Thus Mijok son of Bol is Mijong de Bol. The same rules apply when the nouns with the above endings are followed by adjectives, for in Dinka, adjectives always follow the nouns.

10. When 'de' precedes a possessive noun beginning with 'a' it changes to 'd' pronounced as one word with the noun following it. Thus Majok son of Akoc becomes Majong d'Akoc.

11. In the case of a double vowel or two vowels preceding the last letter or combination of letters of a noun, the possessive form turns the double vowel into a single one. For instance, Akook son of Akot becomes Akong d'Akot and Ajuong son of Col becomes Ajong de Col.

It must be stressed that the above are merely guidelines and many problems of orthography and pronunciation for which these guidelines present no answers will certainly confront the reader.

II

SOCIAL ORGANIZATION

A DESCRIPTION of the Dinka social system is important for appreciating the roles and the interrelations represented by the songs. Dinka society comprises territorial groups, descent groups, sex groups, age groups, the individual, the ancestors and the spirits, and, now, the educated.

While blood ties are highly revered among the Dinka, social and political organization is largely territorial and comprises tribal groups, tribes, sub-tribes, and sections. There are some twenty-five tribal groupings, each with its own name, territory, and distinctive cultural traits; for, as already indicated, there are minor cultural variations despite a striking homogeneity. Since they are so numerous and so widespread in an area of very difficult communications, most Dinkas do not know all the Dinka tribal groups. Indeed, the Ngok, who are somewhat isolated from the rest, sometimes refer to themselves as *the* Dinka. Sometimes, tribes which have been separated for centuries still have the same names, but are not considered to be the same tribe. Thus, apart from the Ngok of Kordofan and the Tuic of Bahr el Ghazal, there are the Ngok and the Tuic of Upper Nile who have little present connection with their namesakes in the other provinces.

Since most of the songs that follow are of Ngok Dinka origin, I describe Dinka social organization primarily from the Ngok viewpoint. It should be remembered that what is applicable to the Ngok is not always applicable in detail to other tribal groups. The Ngok, though divided into nine sub-tribes, all recognize political unity under the leadership of a 'great chief' (*benydit*, or *nazir* in Sudanese Arabic) of Pajok lineage 'whose history', as P. P. Howell reports, 'is essentially bound up with that of the Ngok'.[1] The great chief is assisted by two chiefs from Pajok and Dhiendior lineages. Also known by the Arabic title *nazir* (or *wakil* sing.) these assistants, like their senior, are expected to transcend sub-tribal

[1] Howell, 'The Ngok Dinka', *SNR* 32 (1951), 239, 265.

loyalties. Howell lists the following as characteristic of a Ngok sub-tribe which he terms 'section':[1]

(a) A common name.

(b) A distinct and effective sentiment of a common purpose for both offence and defence. This was a reality, for sections often combined against each other, and there is still an active attitude of political rivalry.

(c) A common area of permanent habitation, though nowadays the boundaries are far from distinct.

(d) A common grazing area which includes rights in fishing and hunting. A section would combine to protect their rights to this area and would fight if necessary.

(e) A common system of nomenclature in age-sets, e.g. age-set names run through the section and not beyond.

To this list we add the recognition of a sectional chief known by the Sudanese Arabic title *omda*, which, like the terms *nazir* and *wakil*, suggests that the Ngok emphasis on centralization, greater than that of other Dinka, is the result of Arab contacts with their political concomitants. Their early contact with the Arabs seems to have resulted in considerable influence on their political theory and practice.

Sub-tribes are further divided into sections with the same structural characteristics. Within the section, classification is based on descent even though descent transcends territorial boundaries. Descent comprises kin groups, clans, sub-clans or lineages, families, and, within large polygynous families, 'houses' composed of wives and children. Kin (*alaraan* in Ngok and *ruai* in Rek and Tuic) comprises all those related by blood and marriage, including patrilineal kin (*waar*) and matrilineal kin (*naar*). The largest component of kinship is the clan, *dhien* (Ngok) or *gol* (Rek), literally, 'cattle-hearth', an agnatic group composed of people descended from a common ancestor. The exact genealogical link may not be traceable. The intermediate ancestors may be confused or forgotten, and a jump of several degrees may be made to reach the alleged founder.[2] Although the male line is more important,

---

[1] Ibid. 255.

[2] 'The agnatic genealogical structure of his whole clan . . . is not known to a Dinka; he knows that there are likely to be many sub-clans of his clan, all descended from wives or sons of the clan-founder whose name and existence have been forgotten long ago by members of his own sub-clan.' (Lienhardt, 'The

the female line is highly regarded and the totemic and exogamous requirements of clans are observed with respect to both the father's and the mother's clans. The sub-clan is the fragment of the clan within which descent is accurately traced; it may be fragmented into 'main lineages' and 'sub-lineages'. All the descendants of a man constitute a lineage. The length of the lineage differs according to its political importance. Ordinary lineage is traced to approximately ten generations, whereas it would be more in the genealogies of chiefs.

Within the lineage is the family, in effect a degree of the lineage. The Dinka family may be polygynous with its size largely depending on the wealth and the social esteem of the family head. Whereas a commoner (*kic*) or a poor man (*abur*) usually has only one wife, a rich man (*raan bany*) will have several, and a chief may have over a hundred.[1] When there are two or three wives, each *ghot thok*, literally 'the doorway or the mouth of the house', includes a wife and her children. When there are many wives, each *ghot thok* includes a senior wife, her children, junior wives, and their children. There may be two or three of these with the senior wife as the head of the senior house, and the second wife of the second house, and the third of the third house.

While the Dinka are an egalitarian people with no class distinction in the conventional sense, descent carries with it a certain amount of social classification. The main difference is between chiefly clans (*bany*) and commoner clans (*kic*). *Bany* applies to all those members of the clans from whom chiefs, also called *bany*, are descended, though some individuals outside these groups may today acquire power. Because fishing-spears are their symbols of authority, chiefly clans are referred to as the 'masters of the fishing-

Western Dinka', in Middleton and Tait (eds.), *Tribes Without Rulers* (1959), 105–6.) See also Howell, op. cit. 256.

[1] According to the 1955/6 census for the whole Sudan, there were just over 2,000 people with five wives, a few hundred with six wives, and only 405 with ten wives or more. A census authority writes, 'We may, therefore, conclude that the sensational stories about households with dozens and dozens of wives can be put among travellers' tales.' (Krotki, *21 Facts about the Sudanese* (1958), 39.) Polygyny must not be conceived of only in terms of the immediate family. Even if such a family is monogamous, kinship ties bring wives of brothers, cousins, or the like into a kind of relationship akin to polygynous relationship. The term for any agnatic kinsman of the same degree is 'son of my father'. Since one's full brother is not referred to as 'son of my father', half-brotherhood, which among the Dinka implies polygyny, is envisaged.

spear', but among the Ngok they are known as 'Chiefs of the flesh'.[1] Indeed, the Head Chief's symbol of office among the Ngok is not a fishing spear-alone, but two large spears, one an unbarbed fishing-spear and the other a bladed fighting-spear. They are both of very ancient origin. Among the Ngok, the term 'Chief of the spear' is applied only to more specialized religious functionaries. They wear leopard skin and have a purely priestly function, unless they become prophets, when they acquire charismatic authority. *Kic* denotes members of the non-chiefly clans, who, on the whole, wield political power at a lower level of social organization. Class distinction among the Dinka must be seen in the context of a fundamentally egalitarian society which does not permit barriers to social relations. To achieve influence through power or wealth, for instance, the society expects one to be socially conscious, kind, and hospitable. The Dinka word for 'Chief' or 'rich' is also translated as 'kind', 'generous', 'gentle', or 'virtuous'. These words emphasize the relations of a person with other people and determine his potential for winning prestige.

Another distinction and one with important consequences in day-to-day life is that between males and females. The Dinka themselves would not dispute the allegation that they regard women as inferior to men. Paradoxically, Dinka women nevertheless occupy an important and highly respected position. The attitude of domination-with-respect shown to women by the Dinkas has sometimes led to exaggerations. The imputation of slavery is one.[2] The other is exemplified by those who assert that 'the position held by the [Dinka] woman is a high one, and she is considered man's equal'.[3] This, like the allegation of slavery, is inaccurate. Women provide the means to the more male-oriented goals of agnatic continuity and their destiny is almost universally marriage.

Age is another basis of distinction. Age-set system among the Dinka plays a much more important role than anywhere else in the Sudan. Initiation takes a person out of social infancy which carries certain duties and incapacities. Every Dinka longs to get away from this status. When initiated, one becomes 'a gentleman' (*adheng*).

[1] Implying that spiritual power is inherent in them. For the general significance of the divinity Flesh see below, p. 65.

[2] The Dinka themselves say that 'the woman is a slave' (*tit k'alony*), though this is more figurative than literal.

[3] Titherington, 'The Raik Dinka', *SNR* 10 (1927), 153, 159.

Dinka age-sets are essentially sub-tribal, and are divided into male and female sets. Female age-sets are added to for ten or more years; a new male sub-set is created every four years, creating sub-divisions within the set.

It is often alleged that the individual has little importance in traditional African societies.[1] This is based on misconceptions of the intricate balances between the individual and the community in traditional society. The importance of the Dinka individual is particularly true in songs, for while collective songs and choral singing tell much about the emphasis the Dinka place on group spirit, individual songs deal largely with the particular interests of individuals. Indeed, individual and group interests do not always agree. It is precisely in this context that most cathartic songs which criticize the attitude of relatives to the intended marriage of the singer should be understood.

Apart from the ordinary categories of participants already discussed, the Dinka are deeply concerned with spirits, ancestors, and other dead.

The Dinka believe in a supreme being, *Nhialic*, God, but their belief in a complex of spirits, *yeth* and *jak*, tends to blur their monotheistic conception of God.[2] To the Dinka there is only one *Nhialic*, but in their practical life they are more concerned with ancestral spirits and what Dr. Lienhardt calls 'clan-divinities' and 'free divinities'[3] than with the one *Nhialic*.

Associated with divinities are the dead. The relationship between them and their living kin is not merely a sentiment. Indeed, the demands of the dead have priority over the demands of the living. This is the immortality that gives meaning to Dinka religion.

A significant group which has emerged in today's Dinka society is the educated class, who may be distinguished in cultural terms. Education for most Dinka was initially acquired through missionary schools, for it was not until about 1944 that government education

[1] See Elias, *The Nature of African Customary Law* (1956), 82. The author quotes S. Hartland as saying, 'The unit is not the individual but the kin. The individual is part of the kin.'

[2] As Lienhardt puts it, the Dinka 'assert with a uniformity which makes the assertion almost a dogma that "Divinity is one". They cannot conceive of Divinity as a plurality and, did they know what it meant, would deeply resent being described as polytheistic', *Divinity and Experience: The Religion of the Dinka* (1961), 156.

[3] See Lienhardt, op. cit. (1961), Chaps. II and III.

began; and even then, missionary education continued to pre-dominate. Consequently, these Dinkas call the educated *mith abun* ('children of the missionaries'). Among the Ngok, where education was initiated by the state, they are known as *agat wal* ('those who write'). But it is neither the fact of having been to a missionary school nor that of writing and reading that alone classifies a person as 'educated'. Implicit in 'children of the missionaries' is the new culture which education introduced to them and the fact that the Dinka consider them culturally changed. It is rather significant that the educated are sometimes called *juur*, that is, 'foreigners'. There are boys and girls who drift back into traditional ways, but all have something in common which distinguishes them from their fellow Dinkas who have been brought up in the village and the cattle-camp. Despite the diversity of their family backgrounds and their varying ages the educated feel a sentiment of unity and a common purpose. In many ways, they assimilate themselves to the notion of an age-set and it is noteworthy that they are referred to, and they refer to themselves, as *ric* (age-set). In this regard there is a tendency for educated people, whatever their age, all to repre-sent the 'younger generation', since among the Dinka, even though some of the educated have now become elders,[1] education is associated with school and school with children.

The Dinka of course interact with non-Dinkas. Apart from the Nuer, whom they call 'Nuer', other non-Dinkas are referred to as *juur*, and are further distinguished by their colour. Thus the Luo are 'black foreigners'; the Arabs are 'brown foreigners', or 'foreigners with horses'; and the Europeans, who are also referred to as Turks (*Turuk*),[2] are 'pink foreigners'. Among the Ngok, *jur*, unless otherwise qualified with reference to colour, merely means 'Arab'. The Dinka apply to Sudanic and a number of other peoples such opprobrious terms as *nyamnyam* or *nyinyam* which bring to mind the sound of a chewing mouth and indicate the Dinka belief that they are cannibals.

[1] They seem to consider themselves members of one age-set even when there is an age discrepancy between them. There is reason to believe that this will continue as long as they remain a minority. It is also reinforced by the notions of equality which education introduces.

[2] A word which came down from the Turkish period and has been used throughout the Sudan in reference to the British.

III

MORAL VALUES

'DINKA fear to die without issue, in whom the survival of their names—the only kind of immortality they know—will be assured.'[1] Even when dead, a man demands the expansion and the continuation of his lineage. This is the idea behind such institutions as levirate by which a widow continues to bear children to the name of her dead husband with his living kinsman as the genitor, and ghost-marriages by which a man who dies before marriage is married to a wife who bears children with a kinsman in the dead man's name.

This concept of immortality, which aims at a permanent identity and influence, demands more than child-bearing and rearing. *Kooc e nom* (literally 'standing the head' but meaning 'taking the place of a father') is more than *dhieth*, birth. A man may complain about his son by saying that he, the father, has not given birth, *akic dhieth*, implying that he is not proud of his son as a prolongation of himself. The idea of permanent identity and influence is here more evident in *kooc e nom*, which can be achieved also by adoption or by substitutive procreation, than by actual begetting. 'Taking the place of' the father becomes symbolic of a much deeper and more pervasive representational continuity. For the dead, it is in essence a transmission of this world into the hereafter or of the hereafter to this world through the memory of the dead and their experience. The vitality of this memory lies in the maintenance of conditions as the dead left them, otherwise they cease to reflect him. Since the degree to which one is remembered is relative to the significance of one's experience, the memory of the ancestors, who have lived longer and done more, is greater than that of the ordinary dead. The intensity of lifetime relations is also an important

[1] Lienhardt, op. cit. (1961), 26. The importance of procreation was emphasized by Professor Radcliffe-Brown with respect to Africans in general. He wrote, 'An African marries because he wants children . . . the most important part of the "value" of a woman is her child-bearing capacity.' (Radcliffe-Brown, 'Introduction to the Analysis of Kinship', *A Modern Introduction to the Family* (1960), 13.)

determinant. Hence the smallest social unit, the family, is the primary means to immortality.

To emphasize the continuance of one's identity and influence in this world even after one's death does not necessarily mean that the Dinka have no sense of some form of existence in the unknown world of the dead, though their beliefs on this matter are complex and unclear. They emphatically reject the Muslim and Christian concepts of life hereafter as introduced to converted Dinkas, and insist that once a person is dead he cannot live again and be judged in his second life; but they call upon the dead in prayers, which implies a recognition of some form of existence, and some Dinkas will speak of joining their dead and of reporting to them significant information from among the living.

The existence in the next world, and the continued participation of the dead with the living, are not in conflict. People die and dis-appear. The reality of their existence remains but they also are part of the unknown. Their continued participation in human affairs through their descendants proves their immortality, which thus becomes both biologically and socially explicable.

The survival of every individual through a lineage is significantly illustrated by the system of naming. The Dinka do not apply one family name to successive generations. Instead, each man bears his own name, which is equivalent to the first or Christian names in the Western system. His father's first name is then added to his own name for further identification. This addition of the names of forebears continues according to the degree to which they are neces-sary to identify individuals. Allor de Biong de Kwol d'Arob means Allor, son of Biong, son of Kwol, son of Arob, with 'de' or 'd' standing for 'son of'. (Some Dinkas use 'e' to denote 'son of', though, in writing, the mere combination of names may imply it.) Every child is taught from a very early age to recite his father's genealogy to the most distant ancestor remembered.[1] Each ancestor's oral biography is related to the present status of his lineage. The identity of the lineage and its influence are thus explained in terms of the achievements of its founder which are often recalled and dramatized in songs. In this system of naming, people trace their genealogy through individuals, but the clan, the lineage, or the family, as the case may be, is collectively called by the name of its founding father, that is, by adding a prefix to the

---

[1] This is one of the ways in which a child's intelligence is tested.

name of the founder such as 'Pa-jok' for the clan founded by Jok. The effect of the preservation of individual and clan and lineage names from generation to generation is to suggest an unchanging order, which would imply (as indeed often happens) that the conflicts as well as the co-operation of one generation are transmitted to the next. Within each generation too, the segmentation of the social organization, balancing as it does the identities of groups and individuals, produces mutual, competitive, and even conflicting interests at the various levels of the society.

In this balance of interests, what the Dinka emphasize more is the goal of unity in harmony. The characteristics of this goal can best be described and analysed by examining a concept called *cieng*. Dr. Lienhardt writes: 'The Dinka . . . have notions . . . of what their society ought, ideally, to be like. They have a word, *cieng* or *cieng baai*, which used as a verb has the sense of "to look after" or "to order", and in its noun form means "the custom" or "the rule".'[2] Father Nebel translates 'morals' as 'good *cieng*', and 'benefactor' as a man who knows and acts in accordance with *cieng*. He also translates *cieng* to mean 'behaviour', 'habit', 'nature of', or 'custom'.[1] As a verb, *cieng* also means 'to inhabit', 'to live together', 'to treat' (a person), 'to dominate', or 'to wear' (clothes or ornaments), and as an intransitive verb it means 'to last long'. As a noun, it means 'law', 'conduct', 'human relations', 'way of life', or 'culture'. This is in addition to the noun form of the verbs above. These usages represent a multiplicity and a unity which may be either descriptive or normative. In the latter case, an appropriate adjective is sometimes added. 'To *cieng* badly' and 'bad *cieng*' are standard negative evaluations, while 'to *cieng* well' and 'good *cieng*' are positive. Without an adjective *cieng* usually implies the positive. This is the case in such common expressions as 'This is *cieng*' and 'This man does not know *cieng*'. Each aspect of Dinka life has its own *cieng*, which is a component of the over-all Dinka *cieng*.

In its various meanings, *cieng* emphasizes human relations. Even when referring to abstract rules, *cieng* is seen as what the Dinka actually do, though with an emphasis usually on what it is fitting for a Dinka to do. 'Human' values such as the power of persuasiveness, respect, rectitude, and loyalty are at the heart of *cieng*. Traditional education, rather than emphasizing knowledge for its

[1] Lienhardt, op. cit. (1959), 106–7.
[2] Nebel, *Dinka Dictionary* (1954), 315.

own sake, puts emphasis on what makes for good human relations—
good *cieng*. In Dinka economy, *cieng* stresses sharing the produce,
and not the maximization of resources. Sharing labour is stressed
only to help the owner of the field to produce his normal yield, not to
increase production for its own sake.

Dinka perspectives about good human relations appear in the
demand for unity and harmony among men and the attuning of
individual interests to the interests of others.[1] This goal is more
than avoidance of conflict and violation of other people's rights; it
imposes a positive obligation to foster a solidarity in which people
co-operate in shaping and sharing values. Coercion is contrary to
good *cieng*, for solidarity, harmony, and mutual generosity are
more fittingly achieved voluntarily and by persuasion. In this
process of persuasion, the participation of the divinities and the
ancestors is essential as representing the best in tradition: what has
lasted and proved its worth for the Dinka over generations.

Cieng begins at home with the family and follows the fiction
of the tribe as a family. This is evident from such expressions as
cieng baai, denoting people living together in the family, home,
tribe, or nation. In fact, the focus of all the various meanings of
cieng is a manner of 'living together'.

It will be seen in the songs that *cieng* has both sacred and historical support, being represented at its highest and most embracing as
conformity with the will of God as the universal father, and
further with the great ancestors and divinities. God, the ancestors,
and the divinities correspondingly have their value to society acknowledged and revered by fitting conduct.[2]

[1] The importance attached to unity and harmony has been observed in many
traditional African societies. For example, Professor Gluckman writes, 'Many
writers have discussed the process of law in tribal societies in such phrases as
restoring the social balance or equilibrium, securing the agreement of both
parties to a compromise judgement, and, above all, reconciling the parties. This
is the main aim of Barotse judges in all cases that arise between kin, for it is a
dominant value of the society that villages should not break up and that kin
should remain united.' (Gluckman, *The Ideas in Barotse Jurisprudence* (1965), 9.)
Elias draws a distinction between Western and African traditional law. Quoting
from Lambert's *Kiambu Guide*, he says, 'The native method would tend to adjust
. . . disturbances of the social equilibrium, to restore peace and good will, and to
bind or rebind the two disputing groups together in a give-and-take. The
European method would tend to widen the gulf between the two groups by granting all the rights to one of them to the exclusion of the other, because it would in
general concern itself with facts and legal principles, and take no cognizance of
social implications.' (Elias, op. cit. 269.)

[2] According to an educated Dinka, '*Cieng* becomes that which God would

To maintain a good name is important for preserving the honour of the ancestors and continuing one's own good influence into posterity. A good name requires honour, dignity, and pride. A person's honour and dignity partake of the honour and the dignity of his lineage, both as a group and as individuals.

Honour, dignity, and inner pride as well as their outward appearance and bearing are part of what the Dinka call *dheeng*, which has many meanings. Singing, as an expression of one's personality, is *dheeng*. Initiation ceremonies, celebration of marriages, the decoration of 'personality oxen', dancing, indeed any personal demonstration of an aesthetic or sensuous quality is considered *dheeng*. The way a man walks, runs, talks, eats, or dresses expresses his *dheeng*. As a noun, *dheeng* means such things as dignity, beauty, nobility, handsomeness, elegance, charm, grace, gentleness, richness, hospitality, generosity, and kindness. The adjectival form of the word is *adheng*, which may also be used as a noun, and is often used to mean a 'gentleman'. Among the Ngok, *adheng* also means an initiated man as opposed to a boy. This usage is very closely linked with the meaning of 'gentleman'.

The value given to honour and dignity among the Dinka has been stressed by observers. Major Titherington, for instance, wrote of

... the higher moral sense which is so striking in the [Dinka]. Deliberate murder—as distinct from killing in fair fight—is extremely rare; pure theft—as opposed to the lifting of cattle by force or stealth after a dispute about their rightful ownership—is unknown; a man's word is his bond, and on rare occasions when a man is asked to swear, his oath is accepted as a matter of course.[1]

The Dinka idea of honour, dignity, and pride involves, more particularly, courage. As an example, it is said that during initiation, which is an extremely painful and sometimes lethal operation, the relatives of the initiate-to-be would in the past stand ready to kill a relative who caused dishonour by cowardice. No instance of such a killing has ever been reported, the implication being that such cowardice has never in fact been displayed. In the words of Major Court Treatt, 'The Dinka . . . is a gentleman. He possesses a high sense of honour, rarely telling a lie',[2] and, 'I must add, a rare

approve of, and God's will would not come in the form of hell or heaven. It will mean physical health and prosperity.'

[1] Titherington, op. cit. 159.
[2] Treatt, *Out of the Beaten Track* (1930), 115.

dignity of bearing and outlook.'¹ Linked with this is a striking sensitivity to insult or anything touching on one's honour or dignity. Many a man, if he survives, bears scars of club and spear fights provoked by incidents not always significant though sometimes causing death. This is a factor behind their resistance to imposed authority and in particular outside control. Audrey Butt, summarizing much literature on the Nilotics and particularly the Dinka and the Nuer, said:

They consider their country the best in the world and everyone inferior to themselves. For this reason they . . . scorn European and Arab culture . . . Their attitude toward any authority that would coerce them is one of touchiness, pride, and reckless hatred of submission, and [a Dinka] is ready to defend himself and his property from the inroads of others. They are self-reliant, brave fighters, turbulent and aggressive, and are extremely conservative in their aversion to innovation and interference.²

The Dinka sense of pride, which makes them see themselves as the standard of what is dignified and honourable and therefore the best, may be illustrated by the fact that, to emphasize the value of a human being, a Dinka will speak of *raan macar* or *raan col*, 'black man'. It is not uncommon to hear a protest against an outrageous treatment expressed in the words, 'How can a black man be treated like this?' and needless to say, they are thinking not of all the black races but of themselves.

Treatt also observed of the Dinka, that 'in common with many other charming people they are highly temperamental, alternating almost hysterical joy with . . . depression and gentleness with violent temper'.³ But the Dinka reinforces his high sense of honour 'with a golden gift of humour; indeed, he often works these two virtues in double harness'.⁴ Many a time one sees men and women, young and old, exchanging insults and badinage, talking and singing, to the amusement of their hilarious audience with the one provoking the more laughter as the winner.

These values and characteristics must be kept vividly in the reader's mind, for they emerge strongly in the words of the songs and in the total social situations in which they are presented.

¹ Ibid. 116.   ² Op. cit. 41.
³ Op. cit. 116.   ⁴ Ibid. 115.

IV

MARRIAGE, KINSHIP, AND FAMILY

DINKA family loyalty involves much more than the sentimental attachments common to all peoples. Members of a kin-group 'help one another against outsiders, and . . . act together with little or no submission to any external control . . . and the freedom from domination which every Nilote expects as his birthright is largely assured by the strength of such bonds of common descent'.[1] Yet, family loyalties often dominate the individual as they protect him, and the image of the plaintive dependant emerges in songs even as they exalt the family or the group on which he depends.

The balance between individual and group interests is best exemplified in marriage, which is not an exclusive affair of the couple, but a union of both themselves and their families. While the preliminary 'seeing' of the girl—the choice, that is (*ting de nya*)—may be initiated by the bridegroom or by any other relative,[2] no marriage can be concluded without the consent of the bride-groom's elders, especially the father, unless totally unreasonably withheld. The father in this situation need not be the real father; uncles or other relatives are sometimes designated for the role. The legal and the social formalities of marriage, including its celebration, negotiation of bride-wealth, collection and distribution of bride-wealth, and the performance of other rituals are all group activities. While the interests of the immediate couple are complementary to those of their groups, they are not always in harmony, as many songs show.

Formalities of marriage usually take not less than three years. 'Seeing' itself is not as momentary as it may sound. All the significant relatives should see the girl and, to start with, be satisfied with her physical appearance; there follows a careful investigation of her manners, and of her family background in terms of social standing,

---

[1] Lienhardt, 'The Dinka of the Nile Basin', *The Listener*, 69 (1963), 828.

[2] Except the mother or one's own sisters, whose influence in this respect is discouraged as part of the general tendency to minimize their prejudices and jealousies.

possible breach of exogamy, and reputation. Once she has been thus endorsed, messengers are sent to begin negotiations with her relatives, who usually show some reluctance however pleased they may in fact be. Unless she is uncompromisingly rejected, the bridegroom's relatives send cattle of betrothal (*amec*) shortly after.

The next stage, 'counting the marriage', follows much later, and involves discussing the amount to be paid by the bridegroom's kin. Since these discussions concern cattle and are often held in the byres, the occasion is sometimes spoken of as 'entering the byre', a frequently occurring phrase in songs about marriage. Although customs of respect and avoidance mark in-law relationships before and after the conclusion of marriage, this occasion is one of the most commercial aspects of Dinka life. Assuming that all goes well, which it does only with compromise on both sides, the next stage is payment, in full or in part, of the agreed amount. At this stage, or later, the bride's kin are also expected to pay, from their own cattle, what is called *arueth*, amounting perhaps to about one-third the total bride-wealth agreed upon. The final stage, 'giving the girl', may follow soon after the payment of the bride-wealth, but usually some little time elapses before the girl is given. The bride merely goes to her marital home accompanied by both her age-mates and senior women. The occasion is festive and sacrifices are made to bless the union.

These stages make the role of the group, and especially of the elders of both parties, an exceptionally important one, and however independently wealthy a young man may be, he must depend on them. Indeed, bride-wealth has a higher social value if contributed by the kin-group and not by the bridegroom's family alone. For that reason the bridegroom is expected to mobilize the help of his paternal and maternal kin. For both him and his relatives, this is a test of how much they mean to each other, since to be asked to help gives one the pride of being significant, and to be refused help indicates the unreliability of the relationship. Assistance of relatives is particularly needed for the first marriages; later ones may require less dependence, but even then, it is always more prestigious to be assisted in arranging the marriages and in paying the bride-wealth.

Legally, the consent of the immediate parties is unnecessary, and in most cases they conform to the wishes of their seniors.[1]

---

[1] O'Sullivan observes that, 'No girl is obliged to marry anyone unless she is herself willing . . . Fear of beating is used to influence a girl to consent, but such

However, their role is not merely one of following the wishes of the elders. It is they who conduct their courtship, *thuot*, which has also formal aspects and the participation of their friends and age-mates. Dinka boys and girls have many social occasions for meeting —dances, social celebrations connected with marriage ceremonies, and other festive occasions. It is perfectly acceptable and proper for men to approach girls walking along the road and accompany them with flirtatious motives. On any of these occasions, girls may be requested to select from among the men. Although the request is normally made by the men, the initiative can also come from the girls who will occasionally select a man out of courtesy, but are generally honest in their choice. In dances too, it is the women who select their partners. The principle of one man one girl is not necessarily observed, for consistently with polygyny several girls may choose the same man. The choice of a partner usually opens the door for a friendship which may end in marriage. In a process of courtship, with or without marriage in mind, girls may entertain young men and even share a hut without reprobation. While there are occasional breaches, certain norms of sexual restraint are expected and are generally observed.[1] To understand how much material investment there is in a girl quite apart from her own sense of honour and the honour of her family is to appreciate something of the principles behind such restraint. Although the family of a seduced or pregnant girl may be compensated with cattle, her marital value declines drastically and usually she is presented to someone for reduced or even nominal bride-wealth.[2]

Among the benefits of contact between boys and girls is that it creates opportunities for the right couple to meet and in most cases parents endorse the choice of their sons.

Once a man becomes seriously interested in a girl, even before plans for marriage are made public, there follows a steady courtship in which his relatives and friends play an important role, thus

coercion is against tribal law.' (O'Sullivan, 'Dinka Law', *JRAI* x (1910), 171, 180.) Farran, *Matrimonial Laws of the Sudan* (1963), 72, states that such torture is sometimes carried out 'under the authority of a Chief's Court'. It is somewhat paradoxical that a system of law which requires consent should not only permit but enforce undue influence and coercive measures to obtain it.

[1] Some of the possible consequences of violation may be seen in the songs included in this volume.

[2] But once she has children and especially daughters who will attract bride-wealth, the demands of her relatives rise and they may then demand an increase of the bride-wealth.

giving the girl the assurance of kinship security—a vital aspect of a Dinka marriage. For one thing, any of her fiancé's relatives may one day take her in levirate marriage. Furthermore, as a Dinka girl may be competed for, the effort of relatives and friends is needed to shelter her from the influence of possible adversaries. 'Gossip' (*lum*) or competition over girls is a recurrent theme in Dinka songs. Although girls will normally succumb to the wishes of their relatives, they are independent enough to frustrate arranged marriages by elopement with, or impregnation by, the men they love. While these do not necessarily obstruct the marriages desired by their relatives, they reduce their status and create serious legal and social complications.

Group courtship ends when the man and his age-mates assemble with the girl and her age-mates to discuss the matter formally. With some formal reluctance on her side and approval on the side of her group, the man is then accepted by the girl, *bi nya moc gam*. Of course this is not done if the girl is seriously hostile to the idea.

The two roles, those of the elders and of the youth, should not be seen as entirely separate. Associated with the formalities of the elders are social activities for young men and women representing the age-sets of the bridegroom and the bride. On most of these occasions, beer is brewed in large quantities, beasts are slaughtered for meat, and food is plentiful. Even though the bridegroom and certain members of his family must abstain from these, the occasions are flirtatious and more marriages result from them.

Some time after the 'counting of the marriage' a ceremony is carried out by which the consent of the parties, though not legally required, is symbolized. Public singing and dancing is interrupted and the couple sing in turn as though in a duet but with words that are mutually independent and have nothing to do with the marriage. The bride then anoints the groom while the 'maid of honour' and the 'best man' sing a duet.

Once the girl is given in marriage, the sharp contrast between all the flattery of courtship and the status of a married woman begins to emerge. As a 'guest wife' she begins by doing no work but ends up doing most of the work. From now on and for long to come, she must show particular respect to her husband, his children, particularly sons from other marriages, if any, other kinsmen, and the senior wives of her husband and of her husband's kinsmen. This status changes with age and birth of children—so much so that as a senior woman with grown children she becomes almost equal to her husband.

Throughout her marital life, her agnatic family maintains an interest in her affairs and comes to her aid according to need. If she wrongs her husband,[1] they usually appease him with cattle, a payment known as *awec*. If she is the complainant, they normally keep away and consider it a family affair, but in serious wrongs against her, they will intervene and may go to court. In extreme cases, conflicts between a husband and wife may end in divorce, whether initiated by the man, the woman, or her relatives. Divorce among the Dinka is, however, strongly abhorred and rare. Even from the economic point of view, divorce is undesirable as the conditions for the return of bride-wealth are complex. If the fault is that of the man, he is not supposed to claim the bride-wealth until the wife is remarried and the new husband can afford to compensate the ex-husband, which is very difficult since the cattle will have multiplied. If the fault is that of the wife or her relatives, they are expected to return promptly, if possible, the very cattle paid. If given in other marriages, which is often the case, or otherwise disposed of, they must be traced and returned. Sometimes, other marriages may break as cattle are withdrawn and no replacement is made. Only if the cattle have been taken to a foreign land, whether in marriage, sale, or otherwise, will substitution be accepted. Even within the tribe, the return of the original cattle or their substitutes is easier said than done. Divorce is therefore usually avoided. Even in cases of adultery, the husband of an adulterous woman will usually be content with the payment of compensation varying in number from area to area and according to whether or not pregnancy results. Where there are children, divorce is not allowed except in such extreme cases as when the wife has persisted in running away with another man.

Since children are the fruits for continuing the lineage, they are the central theme of family life. It is for children that a Dinka marries and just as divorce may be impossible because of them, a man may divorce his wife because of lack of children. Such is the case where a woman is barren, or childless because of such 'acts of God' as frequent death among her children. Sometimes she is suspected of being the cause, presumably for harbouring a sin with-

[1] Particularly sexual wrongs which women are supposed to confess or endanger their well-being or that of their children. Men are not required to confess.

out confession. Even independently of the husband's reaction, a childless woman, whether because of barrenness or death of children, cannot be socially and psychologically secure. A woman whose children were dying in infancy, and who attempted to leave her family against the wish of her understanding husband and relatives, sings:[1]

> What misfortune has befallen me
> O Abyor
> People of my father
> Do not blame me
> Is it not for a 'baby' born
> That a woman keeps her home?

So important are children that illegitimacy in the Western sense does not exist. A child is always somebody's, with all the rights of a legitimate child. This is sometimes short of enjoyment of biological and legal paternity in the same person. Dinkas look down on such a status and a usual theme of complaint, especially in songs, is 'Was I adopted?' or 'Did I come carried in a sling?' But everyone is strongly discouraged from doing anything that might hurt or defame a person of such status.

To maintain the affection of their husbands, women must treat both their own children and those of their co-wives, not only with love, affection, and care, but, in the case of male children, with respect and dignity. Because of polygyny, Dinka children are normally closer to their mothers than to their fathers and love and affection between them is more reciprocal than between a child and a father. Mothers nurse their children for as long as three years, during which there is a taboo against sexual relations, thus keeping the husband away from her and deepening her association with the child. While a child favoured by his father is very privileged, and a child falling out of his father's favour almost doomed, mothers hardly discriminate between their children and it is rare for a child to fall out of a mother's favour. Dinka mothers are said to incapacitate themselves, ritually, from inflicting a curse upon their children,

[1] Ke diit ci yɛn la lɔny
Wa Abyor eban
Mac de waa
Diet ki yɛn, e gɔk
Ce mɛnh thiin ci dhieth
Ku yen muk e baai?

while the fathers are said to be 'bitter' (*akec*), and may exercise their cursing power when wronged. A curse is believed to be effective even if the father is unaware of the wrong or its source. Furthermore, relations between a father and a child may be ritually severed in extreme conflicts, a practice which does not exist between a mother and her child. Because of polygyny, the principles of which extend into inter-familial relationships of the paternal kin (*waar*), jealousy (*tiel*), rooted in co-wives' or similar rivalries, is a well-recognized evil of kinship life. In their myths and other folklore, the Dinka often present the woman as the villain enemy of family solidarity and the breaker of kinship ties. In the interests of family unity and harmony, the influence of women must be restricted, while the influence of the father as the symbol of family solidarity must be maximized. From very early childhood, one grows up being frequently tested with the question 'whom do you love?' and such qualifications as 'the most' are rarely added to the question. The answer must be 'my father'; otherwise the child is ridiculed as his mother's son, a terrible image for a Dinka boy. The same goes for girls though to a lesser degree. While all Dinka children must refer to their father as 'father', they address their mothers by their first names. In songs the situation may be reversed and a child may refer to his father by his first name and his mother as 'mother'.

Women do not mind this appearance of subordination to their children. Their own image and dignity in society are very much associated with the children's, so that quite apart from the more intense love and affection between them, they also have an interest in promoting the reputation of their children. Indeed, no mother would want her child to answer the question above by saying that he loves her or to call *her* 'mother', at least not in front of others. Except among their maternal relatives who give prominence to the mother's name, the Dinka are normally identified by their first names followed by the father's first name and so on. Should anyone other than a maternal relative substitute the mother's name for the father's, the mother too would be offended by the insult, unless that were necessary for the purpose of precise identification, such as when a man has two sons of the same name so that reference to their mothers becomes necessary.

While the mother's influence is thus curtailed, the affection of her relatives for her child is recognized and encouraged, except where it threatens the unity of the family. A child is normally weaned by being sent to the maternal kin at about the age of three to five or six, during which time he is the centre of much love and affection and is thoroughly 'spoilt'. He visits and is visited by his paternal relatives: otherwise his contacts are largely with his maternal kin, who emphasize his maternal descent and play down the paternal side. So important are the maternal relatives that they are regarded as even more 'bitter' than the father and wronging them invites a particularly severe curse. Their share in the bride-wealth of their daughter's daughter must be promptly paid or evil follows. But there is less awe invoked by this than there is love and affection. Indeed, the relationship between a child and his male maternal kin involves the possibility of publicly expressing the intimacy between a child and a mother, thus combining the advantages of female closeness to children with male dominance. In a sense, there-fore, the maternal kin are closer than the paternal kin for whom demanded deference and piety somewhat formalize and impede parent–child relationships.

The deference and filial piety demanded from children do not imply a subservience which would inhibit a child and especially a son from making legitimate claims, even to the point of confronta-tion with the father privately or in front of other elders. This is part of the courage and independence of character required of a man.[1] But the balance between these qualities and aggressive, disrespectful conduct is a delicate one, well illustrated by these lines from a song critical of the reluctant attitude of the uncles to the singer's proposed marriage. The person asked to judge is the oldest member of the lineage:[2]

> Father, Great Majak,
> You are the man sitting on our head
> We the orphans of the clan
> If you see me in the wrong
> Lock me in jail
> If the wrong is my uncle's
> Tell him gently, gently
> The word of an elder should not be challenged

---

[1] In the words of Titherington, 'Independence begins at an amusingly early age. Any early sign of courage gives great delight to both mother and father and the child is petted and even kissed for it.' (Op. cit. 204.)

[2] See ll. 7–19 of 'The Wedding of Alai'.

Keep it soft
My father will think alone at night
If he rejects the word of his son
I will cry inside myself.

As was the case in this instance, such words often receive a prompt and favourable response.

Children are taught such things as recitation of the father's genealogy, identification of various clan-divinities and their emblems, cattle life, and the code of Dinka behaviour according to status and relationship. Apart from direct instructions, the children learn through songs, fairy tales, legends, and play. The special importance of songs in the comprehensive sense—that is, words, rhythm, and occasion of presentation—is impressed upon a child very early. With its mother or nurse smiling and chanting, and the child beaming with smiles, he is bounced up and down in a dancing fashion. Any chanting of praise may be used, but usually every child has his own little chanted praises (literally, 'songs of praising the head') which are used only for that purpose and not as lullabies. This example was about a girl born in the cattle-byre of the most senior wife and was therefore named *Nyanluak*, 'Girl of the Cattle Byre', a name she shared with the wife of her uncle, a chief:[1]

Cattle-byre, Cattle-byre, here she is
Our Cattle-byre
The Cattle-byre of the mother of Adau
The Cattle-byre is proud
The Byre of divinities
The Cattle-byre is proud
The wife of the Chief.

Nor do the words have to contain praise as such. The following concerned a child who was begotten as a result of the Prophet Cyerdit's blessing her mother after she had remained childless for long. Although she has a female name, the song praises her by

[1] Lua ke Lua kii
Luaŋ da
Luaŋ dhien de Man Adau wa
Lua ke guɔp alueeth
Luaŋ de Yeth
Lua ke guɔp alueeth
Tiŋ de beny.

calling her Cyerdit, the name of the male prophet. Her father lay sick during the period the praise-song was composed and used:[1]

> Cyerdit, daughter of Nyoong Magol
> Hold your heart tight daughter of Nyoong Magol
> If you are not lucky enough for your father to recover
> Will you not starve and be eaten by birds?

The idea was that, as her father was sick, there was no one to find food for her and among the Dinka dying by starvation is called 'being eaten by birds', presumably because when people died by starvation, it was such a universal calamity that no one was strong enough to dig the graves and bury the dead. This way of praising children is given at some length because it is one of the most affectionate ways the Dinka treat their babies and usually even if a child was crying before being thus praised and bounced, smiles and laughter are quickly substituted. Lullabies are also sung and when a child cries, the mother or anyone sings at the top of her voice, even in the middle of the night, with the music of a gourd containing grain accompanying her. Such songs are by no means lullabies in the Western sense. Any song is a lullaby to the Dinka. Since words do not provide the whole meaning of a Dinka song, it is not too important that a child is below the age of cognition, but the educational significance of Dinka songs goes beyond the child's being sent to sleep. While such a child may successfully be made to sleep, older children and adults sharing the hut and those in other village huts are almost inevitably awakened. They may enjoy the songs or at least listen to them. As Dinka songs cover a wide range of subjects, an intelligent child gets a deep insight into Dinka culture by listening to such songs in the quietness of rural nights.

Fairy tales have an even more direct impact on children. The traditional import of such tales is epitomized by their opening expression, *ke ghon ka* (literally, 'there is an ancient event'), which is comparable to the Western 'once upon a time'. In these stories, the world of beasts and inanimate beings is often fused with that of man. Fairy tales in Ngok Dinka dialect are known as *koor* (lion), because of the frequency with which lions are involved. In fairy

---

[1] Cyer dit, nyan Myɔɔŋ, Magɔl
Dut ye e piɔu nyan Myɔɔŋ Magɔl
Ci guɔp mit abi wuur rɔt jɔt
Ci yin bi ŋueet ee?

tales the Dinka include a truth which, though superficially unreal, has a deeper reality.

Fairy tales have a variety of themes in which virtue often prevails. Courage and strength form a recurrent theme of fairy tales, for Dinka boys are trained from childhood to be aggressive, violent, and physically courageous—qualities which are greatly admired even when superficially disapproved of and which, while at first restricted within the family, later express themselves in distinctive ways outside it. As might be expected, one of the most common themes of fairy tales is the need for affection and for curtailing co-wives' and step-kin jealousies.

There are also legends which tell of the achievement of ancestors, thus providing a basis for the status of their living representatives, as a class or as individuals. Many songs are about claims to status by virtue of such past achievements. Often, the younger generations, who have not yet fully assumed adult roles, brag the most about the achievements of their legendary heroes to satisfy their own egos and enhance their status. Nor need these heroes be men of distinction. Each young man praises his ancestors even if their deeds have no real importance to the society at large. Aggressiveness and physical courage are among the frequent themes of such praise.

There is no contradiction between the exaltation of aggressiveness in seniors by their juniors and the peacefulness of their role, since contemporary elders themselves were once youths who occupied the role now filled by their sons, whose success rests in part on living up to the vitality of their seniors when they were their age. It is customary for a Dinka father to appraise his son critically in such comparative terms as 'When I was your age, I used to . . .' or 'At your age, I would have . . .'.

Another means of education for children is games. Apart from the pleasure children derive from them, games give an insight into the Dinka way of life. In addition to acting out adult roles in cattle-camp life, family life, litigation, initiation, singing, dancing, and war, children play games which are less obviously informative but which are of great educational value. The words of the songs may not be very intelligible to the children, or to anyone else for that matter, but whatever interpretation children give to the words is not as important as the effect of the game, including the melody, the rhythm, and a mysticism which deeply affects them to the point that girls are sometimes 'possessed', and the game must then be stopped.

Conditioned by their education, children follow in the footsteps of their parents. It is from his father that a son acquires such knowledge as is necessary for a male of his age. While he is a child this is bound to emphasize aggressiveness. In addition to collective male characteristics, the Dinka attribute most good or evil traits to a man's father, or male ancestor, and many are the songs to this effect. The mother's influence over her daughter being greater than her influence over her son, a daughter tends to reflect her more than her son does.

The education of a child is not confined to his agnatic group. Since ties with the maternal kin are highly regarded, it is important that a child should know the people in those circles; he must revere their divinities and their ancestral heritage. This knowledge is especially acquired during the years of weaning, when a child is sent to live with the maternal kin.

Perhaps a crucial point to keep in mind in appreciating the paradoxes of Dinka songs combining dignity, pride, and satisfaction with bitterness, helplessness, aggressiveness, and complaint is that a Dinka individual is a vitally important element in the life of the group, but less free and more dependent than among more individualistic peoples in the modern world, who, however, just because they are so free, often also feel alienated and unneeded, and therefore insignificant. Dinka ties with kin and other groups enable them to take their personal significance for granted, even when in the songs they are lamenting their lonely sufferings and frustrations.

V

PROPERTY AND ECONOMY

ALTHOUGH the Dinka spend more time in their villages than is often assumed, animal husbandry and a transhumant pastoral life are primary features of their economy and they are rich in livestock. Among their possessions are cattle, sheep, goats, fowl, and pets such as dogs and cats, but by far the most important are cattle. It is difficult for anyone to explain fully, and even more difficult for an outsider to understand completely, what cattle mean to the Dinka. Their preoccupation with cattle is an obsession which limits their utilization of land resources, and although they grow various kinds of crops, and fish as well as collect honey and other wild products, they see the value of land largely in terms of cattle. The application of such terms as *wut* (cattle-camp), and *dhien* or *gol* (cattle-hearth) to territorial and descent units respectively gives a rough idea of the dominant role of cattle, not only in the economic life of the people, but also in shaping their group spirit and their political institutions.

Cattle provide an essential part of their food supply, and materials for manufacturing objects suitable to their environment and needs. For instance, their hides are used for sleeping on, their horns carved as trumpets and spoons, and their dung is used as fuel and fertilizer. Cattle provide the most important medium of exchange and are the subject-matter of constant litigation in customary courts.

Cattle have a significance beyond their economic value. The fact that they are used as bride-wealth means that they are linked with the maintenance of the lineage and the race. The cattle collected by the bridegroom's relatives are shared among the bride's family, including very distant relatives, and the reverse payment made by the bride's family is similarly shared by the bridegroom's relatives. Cattle thus strengthen the ties between husband and wife, and between their respective relations. As the Dinka honour this network of human ties very highly, the cattle are not just 'bride-price' but are regarded as symbols of these valued ties so that they acquire something of the sentiments involved. Cattle are also paid as compensation for homicide, to be used in ghost-marriage. Most male names are ox names and most women's names are cow names, based on their colour pattern.

Important also is the religious significance of cattle, not only as God's special gift to man, but also as the medium of reconciliation between man confronting God and ancestral spirits through sacrifice and dedication. The term *aciek* (literally 'creator') is often applied to cattle. Apart from these considerations, cattle are seen as having sensuous value, giving the Dinka intense aesthetic pleasure. The sight of his herd, the sound of their bellows, the smoke from their camps, and all that is symbolic of cattle have a special place in a Dinka's heart. The physical comfort they slave to give every beast approximates to their own. They share with them almost suffocating smoky byres, and sleep among them in the ashes of cow-dung. Dinkas will, and do, die to acquire or to protect cattle. In the words of Godfrey Lienhardt, 'Their value is that of something to which men have assimilated themselves, dwelling upon them in reflection, imitating them in stylized action, and regarding them as interchangeable with human life in many social situations.'[1] The aesthetic value of cattle is especially striking in oxen, which have the least utilitarian value.[2]

Although sheep and goats do not occupy the same position as cattle, some of the same reverence is extended to them. In addition to their economic significance, they are used in sacrifice to represent cattle in minor crises when sometimes goats and sheep may be referred to as 'cattle'.

Cattle are acquired in various ways. In the old days they could be captured in tribal wars, but recent attempts to capture the cattle of neighbouring tribes, and their subsequent return by the government, have made the practice obsolete, although it is still associated with tribal warfare. Bride-wealth is another means of acquisition. Akin to that is blood-wealth. Cattle are also exchanged as reciprocal gifts through a form of contractual friendship and are acquired by trade, for example exchange of cattle for grain, or loans on interest (the loan of a ram might be repaid by a small bull). They are also received as compensation for wrongs, including sexual violation

[1] Op. cit. (1961), 25–6.
[2] The Dinka speak of the owner of an ox as its 'father' and not 'master'.

of rights in wives or daughters. Thus, except for such modern
means as working for cash and buying cattle, the normal channel of
acquisition is kinship.

Cattle are in constant circulation. A man receives them as bride-
wealth only to dispose of them in marriage; he gets help from a
relative or a friend only to return the favour some day. It is because
of this circulation that two Dinka proverbs are significant: *ke ci
gaam ke cath, ku ke ci liek ke riar* (what is given circulates, and what
is consumed is wasted) and *weng eken jang eben* (cattle belong to all
people). Even more precisely, a Dinka will refer to his own cattle as
ghok ke kukuar or *ghok ke wa* (cattle of my grandfather, or cattle
of my father). For this reason, the right to control and use cattle is
geared towards social objectives, and is determined by one's
position in the lineage order. If a man must pay bride-wealth in
order to start and maintain a family, the society must afford him
the necessary control over wealth. Herein lies the foundation of
male dominance, although it is a chicken-and-egg riddle whether
the male is dominant because he pays or whether he pays because
he is dominant. Male dominance is exemplified by the pivotal
position of the head of the family in whom ownership of cattle is
vested for the use of its members. Cattle are allocated by him
according to houses and according to the seniority of the houses.
Those allocated to a house are redivided among the individual
wives constituting the house, but needs of individuals are provided
for by whoever can afford to do so. Any cattle that are not allocated
are the collective property of the family. The sons of each house
inherit from their father the cattle under their control, but if the
father has treated any one of them unfairly, other brothers may be
compelled to make good the father's injustice. While he is alive,
neither the wives nor the children can dispose of cattle without his
consent.

A man cannot dispose of cattle dedicated to God and ancestral
spirits except for a certain authorized purpose like special marriages.
To do otherwise is believed to provoke a religious sanction thought
to cause death.

While ownership and use of cattle is familial, herding is generally
more collective and is by section or sub-section. In this collective
herding, each family has to care for its own cattle except during
grazing, when they may be accompanied by members of the wider
group in turn. A person may hire a herdsman to look after his

cattle, either paying him with cattle or pledging to pay his bride-wealth when the time comes for him to marry.

There is a marked division of roles in cattle husbandry, with the general principle that the older a person the less involved with cattle. For children and young men and women there is always much to be done. During the rainy season, when cattle are kept in cattle-byres at night, children take them out in the early morning, clean the cattle-byre by removing their urine and dung, spread the dung to dry and to be ready for making smoky fires to chase away flies, help the women milk the cows, release the cattle to go grazing, take care of them while grazing unless there is fear of wild animals, in which case the older men go instead, and in the late afternoon, when the cattle return, make the fires, tether the cattle each by its special rope and to its special peg, help again with the evening milking of the cows, and, when all is over, take them back into the cattle-byre for the night, each again tied to its special peg. They sleep lightly so that they can respond readily to any disturbance at night as when a cow breaks a rope or a peg. These are only examples of the boys' labour. Girls sometimes assist with these tasks, but otherwise their function is largely dairy work such as milking cows and making cheese and butter. It is part of the pride of 'gentlemen', that is, initiated men, not to milk cows and drink the milk. If circumstances make their milking inevitable, they milk for one another. Because of the wild and dangerous conditions of herding in far-off grazing areas, adults and not the children take the cattle for grazing away from the camp.

When moving the camp, a decision which is made by the leader of the camp (*majong de wut*),[1] also known as 'chief of the camp' (*beny de wut*), people wake up very early in the morning, milk the cows, tie the ropes to the necks of the cattle to provide for easy carriage, and, in the case of personality-oxen, tie the collars and the bells to their necks, both for carriage and for accompanying music. During the journey, children and women carry the gourds of milk and other dairy products, while some men help in driving the herds, and others precede the group to select the new sites and to cut pegs if the distance is too far to carry the used pegs. Small calves, like children, are carried on men's shoulders, while babies

---

[1] Mijok, the colour-pattern on which this title is based, is the most senior in the hierarchy of the colour-patterns distributable according to the custom of *kit* (for which see introduction to ox songs).

are carried by their mothers in leather-slings hanging on their backs.

These activities are sometimes carried on under hard conditions. It sometimes happens that young men go to far-off areas leaving most of the milch-cows at home to provide food during the lean season when most milch-cows go dry anyway. The hardships of far-off herding sometimes form the subject-matter of ox songs in which named persons are praised for their excellence, anonymous persons condemned for their weakness, and the singers boast though not without lamentation. Whatever its difficulties, being in the cattle-camp is seen as a source of dignity and pride. When visiting a cattle-camp, usually in the evening, a Dinka cannot fail to feel its superior atmosphere even from a distance, as he sees the illuminating smoke of cow-dung fires reaching into the sky and marking the location of the camp. As one draws nearer, the singing of the men, the dancing of the children, the bellowing of the herds, the chiming of the bells, the jokes and the laughter all indicate the profound difference between the atmosphere of cattle-camps and that of home. As the visitors from home enter the camp, it is indeed not uncommon for the children, when they first notice their arrival, to shout such slogans as 'bringing flies into the camp', echoed by children throughout the entire camp. On the other hand, when people come from the camp, they are guests with a sense of superiority—well-fed, wholesome, and proud.

'But if the Dinka has been mainly known to the outside world as a devoted owner of cattle, he . . . deserves also to be known as a cultivator.'[1] The usual assertion that they lead a semi-nomadic life is true only if 'semi-nomadic' means that a proportion of the population accompanies the cattle in temporary camps in search of better grazing areas; otherwise, 'The villages are in every sense of the word permanent, and are always inhabited by the older men and women who remain there even when the younger people are away with the bulk of the cattle on the far-off grazings.'[2]

Land has intrinsic value to the Dinka. They build their settlements on it, cultivate it, hunt on it, use its water in diverse ways, gather and eat its fruits and other foodstuffs, make medicines from its herbs, and use its wood and clay. The land is also associated with the ancestors. A Dinka will swear on land to establish his

---

[1] Stubbs and Morrison, 'Land and Agriculture of the Western Dinka', *SNR* 21 (1938), 251.   [2] Ibid. 253.

truthfulness, thus symbolizing his submission to the judgement of the ancestors, a connotation which has a bearing on the rules favouring perpetuity in traditional land tenure. Connected with their love for cattle is also the special value of land for grazing live-stock.

Dinka land was originally occupied either by peaceful settlement where there were no prior inhabitants, or by conquest. In their migrations the Dinka were led by members of dominant clans whose lineages founded and still hold tribal or sectional chieftain-ships. Mythologically, if not actually, the leader of the tribe dis-tributed land among his original followers, and thereby formed the sub-tribes or sections. The heads of these sections re-divided the land among their internal groups, and so on, according to the segmentation mentioned earlier. It follows that various rights in land are held by the descendants of the original occupiers of the area. Later accretions only acquire such rights by association with those lineages. This is not of much practical significance today. Every Dinka now has the right, within his section, to settle and cultivate a piece of land, provided that such land has not been cleared by any other person and is not so close to any residential or arable area as to form part of that area.

Rights and claims in land are complex. Although the individual member of the community is relatively free to acquire land subject to territorial division, theoretical control, at least, is vested in the Chief. It is he who can allocate land to newcomers; it is he who will protect the land; it is he who has the over-all power by virtue of his divine prerogative to control elements destructive of produc-tion; for example, rain, birds, and locusts. He cannot eat of the new crops, the maize for instance, unless he has made thanks to God and the ancestral spirits through a ceremony called *mioc piny* (literally 'offering to the land'). The control of the Chief over land is largely minimal in so far as members of his tribe are concerned. He does not allocate land to them, since there is land for everyone to occupy without friction. Disputes about boundaries do, of course, arise, but they are often solved by local headmen, except for those on the tribal level concerning sections' grazing areas.

In Dinka law, nobody can sell land, but the individual can make a gift of his land, residential or arable, to a member of his group. Any change of residence, from one section to another, requires the assent of the chiefs of the sections concerned.

Rights over land are inherited by children from their parents. Generally, any child who comes of age and marries ceases to be a dependant, and acquires independent residential and arable land for his new family. But as a rule the oldest son, *wendit*, of the first wife is the heir to the father's land, residential and arable. This land is usually what the father held for the family in common; it is called *panom*, literally 'of the head'.

With respect to land use and cultivation, an elementary family usually works its own land and also builds its huts and cattle-byres. They can, however, hire other people to help in cutting the grass for thatching, or the poles for rafters, or even to carry out the actual work of building. Such hire may be settled by payment, or by inviting friends to a feast of beer and food. The exception in this respect is work for the chief whose huts are built by the age-sets of the different sub-tribes. Even then, he gives them beasts to slaughter for meat.

Dinka land and particularly Ngokland (which falls into the central clay plains considered the most fertile in the country) is difficult for agriculture, not so much because of non-fertility of the land as because of the climate. The land is frequently flooded; too much and sometimes too little rain may destroy the crops. Yet the Dinka work and produce what would be sufficient but for their pattern of consumption. Among the crops produced are durra (sorghum), maize, groundnuts (peanuts), sesame, beans, okra, and tobacco. The main food crop is durra and among the Ngok it is cultivated twice a year. The first crop, *rwath*, is sown in the early rains and cut in September, while the second crop, *anguol*, arises from the stubs cut in the first harvest, and is harvested in November or shortly after. Agricultural work comprises clearing the fields during the dry season, sowing the seeds at the beginning of the rainy season, weeding at least twice a year, guarding the crops against birds and animals, and harvesting and threshing them. Most of the work is shared by all, with some division of labour on the grounds of sex and age. Thus in sowing, men make the holes while women and children plant the seeds. Weeding is primarily men's work, while women do most of the harvesting and the whole of the threshing. In the work done by both sexes, allowance is made for women's task of housekeeping. In a polygynous family the head of the household often has a field which he cultivates separately from those of his wives, although he usually assists them

as well. Sons are also expected to assist and in the interest of family
solidarity and minimization of jealousies they help their father's
other wives rather than their own mothers. Anyone can always get
help by giving a feast of beer, meat, and other food, and inviting
friends and neighbours. To this may be added gratuitous help by
blood relations or relations-in-law. Apart from asking any age-set
to work his field, the chief is also assisted by some men attending
his court, during the cultivation period.

Cattle may be grazed outside the home territory provided that
permission is taken from the authorities of the host territory. Without this, such intrusion would, in the past, have led almost inevitably
to tribal war. Even today, when such trespass is supposed to be
settled by special courts, the traditional disposition of youth to take
the law into their own hands continues. The activities of junior age-
sets is particularly striking in this regard. There are still frequent
attempts at tribal wars and, while they are usually prevented by
the intervention of the police, some succeed.

Land is also used for hunting and fishing, which are done
collectively. Meat from hunting is distributed among the hunters.
Ivory is subject to more definite rules since it is a valuable com-
modity which can be exchanged for cattle. The Dinka use ivory for
bracelets and bangles, which are highly regarded. The first person
to spear an elephant is usually entitled to the right tusk, and the
second person to the left tusk, even if the wounds they inflicted did
not lead to the death of the animal. When fishing, there is a custom
among the Ngok known as *dom* (seizure) by which the first man to
seize the fisherman's spear after the fish is speared gets the fish. He
need not physically seize the spear as long as he shouts his claim.
Theoretically, the claim is subject to the acceptance of the spearer
who has the right to refuse, but practically no one refuses as it is
not considered gentlemanly to do so.

Other activities connected with land are collection of wild fruits
and honey. A person may make a bee-hive or mark any trees where
bees are likely to swarm, thereby ensuring that any honey produced
is his private property.

Perhaps the various economic activities of the Dinka may best
be summarized with reference to the four main seasons which
they recognize, and which are frequently mentioned in the songs.
Of these seasons, two are wet, two dry. *Ker*, the season from
May to early July, and *Ruel*, from July to October, form the wet

season, while *Rut*, extending from November to February, and *Mai*, from January to May, form the dry season. During *Ker* (spring), the early rains fall, the fields which had been cleared earlier are planted, and the cattle gradually come back to their permanent camps near the villages, while some cows are kept in the villages to provide food for those working in agriculture. In July, mosquitoes increase and it becomes necessary to bring the cattle home so that they can be kept in the cattle-byres at night.

Ruel, somewhat corresponding to summer, is the period of heavy rains and permanent residence in the villages. Agricultural work, including harvest, falls into this season. The end of the rains is referred to as *anyoic*, the period when crops are ripe and the cattle begin to graze further away from the villages, but are brought back during the harvest of the second crop. This is a period when the fields have to be properly protected from the cattle, which love the flavour of this second crop, *anguol*. Conflicts often occur between owners of cattle and fields over crop destruction by herds. *Ruel* is also the season for select young men to go to their rest or cathartic period, leaving cultivation to be done by women and older men.

Rut, winter, is the coldest season marked by the north wind blowing in November. While younger men start to gather wood and wattle for the repair of homes and cut thatching materials before the grass is burnt off, older people remain in the villages to complete the harvest. Road-construction by younger age-sets, introduced by the Government, is also done during this season. As the pasture soon gets exhausted, the cattle get driven out in small herds to grazing areas in the forest and along the upper reaches of the watercourses.

Dinkas, though active fishermen, are not keen ones; and they look down on people who engage in fishing as a main occupation, but they consider fish important for supplementing their diet, and fishing takes place at most times of the year. In November the fish follow the flood-water into the main river and they are trapped and speared from dams built across the streams. As the Ngok move northwards to *gok*, a higher land with even less flood than the mainland, the Tuic and the Malual Dinkas, whose land, *toc*, is flooded, move into Ngokland, and afterwards, as the Tuic and the Malual return southwards into the *toc*, followed by the Ngok, the Baggara Arabs, whose land becomes too dry, move into Ngokland. Ngok territory is therefore of special value to both the Southern Dinkas and the Arabs, and is often a ground for tribal conflicts which make the task of administration particularly trying for the Ngok Chief.

During *Mai*, autumn, the main cattle camps in the *toc*, which had been started during the *Rut*, begin to concentrate as there is little green grass left near the permanent villages. This is the hottest time of the year; water supplies are scanty and wells are dug near the permanent settlements. Since the rivers and water-courses are drying up into pools and shallow lakes, February and March are the months for intensive and collective fishing.

Since the songs reflect a great deal of status- (almost class-) consciousness to a degree not normally exhibited by the Dinka, it is worth saying something about economic stratification and status in Dinka society. A Dinka's social and political prestige is largely determined by his wealth. The married status is of paramount importance and is achieved through the payment of cattle as bride-wealth. A man's prestige is largely determined by the size of his family. The more wealth a man has the larger the family he can afford.

Words of social prestige are associated with wealth. *Bany* ('chiefs') is a term collectively applied to all those members of chiefly clans, but the word *bany* is also used as an adjective and means 'rich', although there is another word, *ajak*, which means the same thing. It does not necessarily follow that the owners of the land are also the richest in cattle, although this is generally true, as has been observed by Stubbs and Morrison: 'All clans of the Western Dinkas own cattle, and in each are found the wealthy cattle-owning families who form the aristocracy of this area. It is they also who have the biggest and best cultivations while the poorer classes rely largely on fishing to supplement their smaller harvests.'[1]

A poor person is usually referred to as *raan abur*[2] or *raan ayur*, while a rich person is said to be *raan ajak* or *raan bany*. While there are social classes determined generally by wealth there are no social barriers between the classes. There is a respect for the wealthy, but the spirit of equality does not permit the rich to look down on the poor or the poor to look up to the rich. The Dinka form an egalitarian society in which the privileged have sympathy

[1] Stubbs and Morrison, op. cit. 251.
[2] This term is applied to poverty concerning cattle, sheep, and goats. It does not apply to any other form of property.

and regard for the less privileged, who in their turn bear no grudge against the rich.

Wealth with consequent social prestige carries with it commensurate social responsibilities. The Dinka words *adheng* and *ajak*, which mean rich, may also be translated as kind, generous, gentle, or, in a word, noble, while *ayur*, one of the words used for poverty, connotes the opposite of these virtues. To call a man 'rich' is therefore to describe what is expected of his relations to other people. A rich man who is not responsive to these expectations is in a sense 'poor'. For every use a man has for his property, he has a corresponding obligation to provide for the same need in his relatives, friends, and other fellow men. Thus the need for the individual to maintain himself and his family corresponds to his obligation to assist hungry kinsmen, neighbours, friends, and even strangers; his need to secure for himself a wife corresponds to his obligation to assist others in paying their bride-wealth; his need to protect himself from evil by sacrificing a beast corresponds to his obligation to help other relatives do the same. In consequence of the above, society provides for the needy through the bounty of friends, relatives, or chiefs. Because of the personal aspect of the system, even situations involving the chiefs and strangers, the relations of man to man and man to community, are such that the individual is by and large naturally responsive to the needs of others in his community. In dealing with individuals conditioned by these values, political authority, tribal, sub-tribal, or familial, cannot but put emphasis on persuasion rather than on coercion.

VI

THE AGE-SET SYSTEM

IN a society as concerned with continuity as that of the Dinka, age enhances status as it brings men close to the ancestors and increases the wisdom of experience. Furthermore, the older one becomes, the more the need for immortalization through posterity. Dinka respect for age is institutionalized through a system of age-setting whose main purpose is military, but whose dimensions and implications cover almost all aspects and stages of Dinka life.

Children are introduced to age stratification through both informal and organized activities. While herding, boys provoke fights to determine age-sets not so much on the basis of age as of courage and strength, largely determined by wrestling and fighting. A boy may be sent on an errand and, on his return, be given false information that while away another boy had insulted him; a fight follows in which wrestling, beating with branches of trees, and hitting with bare hands are used. Such fights are provoked not only as a training but to foster family solidarity. For instance, the insult may be said to be against a brother or a relative. The ox of an absent or younger half-brother may deliberately be removed to the kraal of another boy as though captured by him, and a fight ensues.

Age-grading may be through more systematized fighting. In a neighbourhood or a cattle-camp, children of various age-groups may get together to grade themselves into formal sets. The crowd is asked to fall into any of several sets led by the most representative, most courageous, and strongest leaders. Those who claim a set for which their qualification is in question are made to select and fight any one of those qualified. Crying in the fight, or being too easily thrown in wrestling or otherwise subdued, is among the criteria used to determine the outcome.

As children grow older, the system becomes more formalized and the characteristics of adult age-sets begin to emerge. Thus a form of initiation is used in which the formalities of adult initiation are followed. The initiation marks arranged on the forehead are scratches that hurt and bleed but do not leave permanent scars as do those of adult initiation. This operation is accompanied with social activities and festivities, imitating adult celebrations and ending with the 'release' of the initiates to what they consider adults (*adheeng*), or 'gentlemen'. The children then play young warriors and the fights between age-sets (*biok*), with clubs and protective weapons, follow in imitation. Using the stalks of durra (sorghum) or long, thin, sharpened branches of trees to represent spears, they imitate tribal or sub-tribal wars.

Apart from mock initiation, there are other customs which classify children on the basis of age. Thus, at about the age of five to seven, boys but not girls are circumcised among the Ngok. Unless one is an imbecile or chronically ill with some illness which makes aesthetic concerns unnecessary, every boy must be circumcised and not to be circumcised is a reason for being shunned and ridiculed in a very obnoxious manner by both age-mates and adults. Some even refuse to share food with an uncircumcised boy. It is noteworthy that the tribes which do not circumcise are just as prejudiced against those who do.

After the second teeth have grown fully, children undergo another operation by which the lower four front teeth are extracted. Whereas circumcision is said to be not only aesthetically desirable but also clean and healthy, the Dinkas give only aesthetic reasons for the extraction of teeth. They say that unextracted teeth fill the mouth, press the lower lip outward, and, all in all, make the mouth and therefore the person look ugly. Whatever the rationale, extraction of teeth is a custom all Dinkas observe, and to be seen with unextracted teeth is to lack the dignity of a Dinka gentleman or lady.

Formal initiation, traditionally around the ages of sixteen to eighteen (though the age is steadily being lowered), is one of the most significant experiences in the life of a Dinka. Until formally initiated, a man is a 'boy' and must do all the things boys do. We have said, for instance, that an initiated man does not normally milk cows except in compelling circumstances, in which case he cannot drink the milk. Apart from milking, uninitiated men do most of the day-to-day work of cattle husbandry, and only in exceptional circumstances such as being in an area where ferocious animals might be are initiated men expected to herd. An uninitiated man may be sent at any time by any initiated man even though the latter may be younger (which sometimes happens since initiates known as *anyat* are young boys ahead of their time). Uninitiated men are not permitted to parade oxen with songs, even though their titles to oxen accrue on birth and they may have children's ox-songs for children's competitions. Instead, they are required to lead the ox for the initiated as the latter sing. Formal dating, dancing, or flirting with girls is not permitted before initiation. If it occurs, the girl is shunned and ridiculed, and the uninitiated man may find himself physically assaulted by the initiated age-mates of a possible competitor. All they can do is act as agents of the initiated men in the processes of courtship. Because of such subordination, initiation is one of the greatest ambitions of Dinka youth.

The formalities of initiation cover a period of years, beginning with the designation of the father of the next age-set, usually a member of one of the leading lineages of the sub-tribe,[1] the father's naming of the age-set,[2] and the formation of the corporate spirit of the age-set through various social activities and consultations with their father. Months before the desired time of initiation, the age-set ask their father, the Chief of their sub-tribe, and the Head Chief, to permit their initiation. Permission may be denied on such grounds as the presence of an epidemic disease, a poor harvest, or the unavailability of fish (a particularly important ingredient of the initiates' diet since they may not drink milk or eat any dairy food). Permission granted, they then invite experts on the cutting of initiation marks, of which there are only a few and sometimes none in a sub-tribe. Not infrequently, they are invited from other tribes, particularly if, as sometimes happens, a number of sub-tribes initiate at the same time.

A period of festivities and dancing follows. The intending initiates are then unarmed except for whips and a bundle of durra (sorghum) stalks symbolizing spears. The Dinka consider it unnatural for a man to go bare-handed, but unwise for the unruly youth to be armed with dangerous weapons. The few days preceding initiation are marked with all-night dancing which continues into the morning

[1] Since age-sets are sub-tribal.
[2] In some Dinka tribes, the age-set acquires its name from a bull sacrificed for their blessing prior to the performance of the operation. Among the Ngok, however, their names are based on animals, birds, and the like. Examples are *Kiec*, 'Honey-bee', *Cour*, 'Great Vultures', *Anyaar*, 'Buffalo', and *Nyang*, 'Crocodile'.

of the operation day. The operation itself entails making seven to ten deep, well-ordered cuts across the forehead—the most painful and bloody customary operation in Dinka society. Initiation is conceived of as a war of emancipation, a recurrent theme in initiation songs. Rarely, it may cause death. To have endured the pain of initiation is to give joy to relatives and friends, including girl-friends, with whom association is otherwise not permitted. In the name of joy, a great deal of damage is done; houses of others may be burned with the intention of compensating them; other people's livestock may be killed with the same intention; women wrapped up in clothes and unable to swim throw themselves into deep rivers; and not least, their cries of joy are almost deafening.

The excitement implies fear as well as joy, but no specific incidents of cowardice or of the killing of the coward which is supposed to follow are reported.

The recovery period that follows, and continues for several months, is very colourful. Initiates reside collectively by lineages in special villages. Considered somewhat impure still, they are not permitted to go near cattle and as already pointed out they must abstain from milk and other dairy products and confine themselves to porridge, meat, and fish, on which they gorge themselves. Though confined, they are free and have no responsibility, and indeed are exceptionally indulged. From palm fronds, they make long, beautifully designed and dyed head-dresses and decorative accoutrements with which they cover their otherwise naked bodies. With their remarkable dignity and pride of bearing, their initiation songs of bravery and their initiation dances, they impress everyone, especially the girls. In settlements, known as 'houses', they compete in dances which often lead to fights and destruction of property— with good reason, therefore, spears and clubs are kept away from them—so they are armed with whips and stalks of durra.

Termination of their status as initiates, *luny*, literally, 'release', is marked by all-night dancing and singing. At dawn, completely unarmed, they are mockingly, but painfully, beaten by the older age-set into a deep river across which they must swim and from which they emerge as adults.

The conduct of a young man, once released as a fully fledged adult, radically changes from that of a boy to that of a respected, honourable, and responsible gentleman. Having now disposed of their initiation dresses, they decorate themselves with such objects as beads and shells worn on the waist, neck, and forehead; the skin of the serval cat with its leopard-like colours, from which outfits for dancing are made; ivory bangles worn on the upper arm or the wrist; and long coiled wire bracelets wound on the arm. Both the bangles and the coils are sometimes a source of discomfort and pain, also reasons for a proud display of the arm as one walks. Bleaching the hair to a reddish gold colour, which begins at childhood, becomes even more marked, and it is considered indicative of mourning for a young man or a girl to leave his or her hair black. All these and more show the tremendous significance the Dinka place on physical appearance and bearing. To be deformed, disabled, or otherwise made less wholesome is to be left with a sadly deprived life.

Not long after release a period of violent competition with the older sub-age-set follows and expresses itself in institutionalized fights known as *biok*. Fights between them are restricted to the use of clubs, against which heads are protected with helmets. These fights are considered a practical way of training the younger warriors eventually to assume the role of the dominant warriors. It is also an institutionalized expression of competition and opposition between generations, especially over girls, and it is in this context that the songs insulting other age-sets which provoke fights are to be understood. Fighting between sub-age-sets is only a partial expression of their unruly, aggressive, and violent disposition. Ideally, this quality is developed to protect the tribe.

After the initiates are 'released' they retire with their 'father' and are instructed in both war skills and ethics. They must fight only in a righteous cause, and should receive the blessing of members of the chiefly clans so that God and ancestors may be on their side to ensure victory. In practice, they provoke and fight wars even in opposition to the chiefs and elders. Therefore, many war songs openly show pride in disobedience to the orders of the chiefs and elders against war, though always with the allegation of provocation and the plea of self-defence. Instead of resorting to established decision-makers, that is, the chiefs and the elders, for peaceful settlement, they take the law into their own hands. Where, for instance, members of an age-set compose songs defaming other sub-tribes, or where they violate territorial boundaries in grazing, there are peaceful means of correcting the wrong. However, the age-sets consider it cowardice to wait for any peaceful settlement. Once provoked, the wars are fought by the young and the old alike, for not to fight in war is one of the most shameful things a Dinka can do.

The violence of the warrior age-sets is not confined to *biok* and wars. They take physical measures against a member who has disgraced the group by committing a serious moral offence. A typical example is theft. Even if the object of theft be of little or no value, the wrong is considered grave and calls for age-set punitive action. Other wrongs may be rape, refusal to participate in collective work of the age-set, and any wrong which the set would consider injurious to the reputation or the integrity of the member and therefore of the age-set. Usually, the members of the age-set seize the wrongdoer's personality-ox and ceremonially skewer it with spears, thus killing it in a disgraceful manner to symbolize their attitude towards the owner.

But not all the activities of age-sets are violent. We have seen that they participate as a group in the marriage, the ceremonies, and the courtship of their age-set. In a modest way they share as a group in the bride-wealth and the reverse payments of such marriages. From the member's family, they receive a beast for meat known as *biol*, 'the beast for feasting', and another from the bride's family, known as *akuath thiek*, 'the beast for driving the cattle of marriage'. What is important in these is not so much the meat as the symbolic significance of their shares and the occasion they create for social intercourse with corresponding female age-sets.

Since many of the activities of age-sets revolve around girls, a word about the age-set system among women is appropriate. As already pointed out, Dinka women have age-sets which cover a longer period of time than those of men because they are not divided into sub-age-sets. While some tribes initiate girls, others, including the Ngok, do not, although corresponding women-age-sets participate side by side with men in most of their activities. Even in war, they follow the men to assist the injured, collect spears for the fighting, and otherwise encourage them. It is part of Dinka war etiquette not to injure women, and although Dinkas are supposed to skewer a fallen enemy to death (lest his ghost follow one as having been his friend among enemies), a person embraced by a woman must not be killed or hurt. Female age-sets identify themselves with their corresponding male age-sets who are in theory their spouses and in their collective songs they say 'I' when they mean the corresponding male age-set—a practice similar to that of wives when referring in song to their husbands.

Although the activities of age-sets begin to diminish when the initiates settle down as family men, and almost disappear when they become elders, age-sets are permanent and throughout one's life they widen one's circle of associates by providing additions or alternatives to kinship ties. Indeed, age-mateship among the Dinka is a term which is almost synonymous with friendship. It is in this context that courtable or otherwise potentially befriendable people are sometimes referred to as age-mates.

Age-set system among the Dinka is thus an important institution which, while it satisfies people, puts individuals in circles of intimacy and equality. In these circles preoccupation with military and aesthetic values together with a degree of non-dependency on the family blurs the significance of family stratification, thus reducing the chances of reaction against the stratification and helping to sustain the system.

VII

RELIGION AND SPIRITUAL WELL-BEING

RELIGION is at the heart of Dinka values, especially that of immortality through posterity, and unity and harmony, on which well-being largely depends. The Seligmans observed that 'the Dinka and their kindred the Nuer are intensely religious, in our experience by far the most religious peoples in the Sudan'.[1] Dinka religion is, however, not an affair of the soul in a world yet to come; it is rooted in Dinka demands for a secure life in this world and guaranteed immortality through living descendants.

In the religious hierarchy, God is farthest removed; other supernatural spirits are nearer to man and are symbolized by emblems which are more commonly encountered. Nearest to man are the dead, whose spiritual existence, proximity, and physical presence are evidenced by their progeny. Their belief in this complex system of supra-natural divinities tends to blur the monotheistic picture of Dinka religion. None the less, the Dinka 'assert with a uniformity which makes the assertion almost a dogma that "God is one". They cannot conceive of more than one god and, did they know what is meant, would deeply resent being described as polytheistic.'[2]

In their practical life, the Dinka are more concerned with ancestral spirits and 'clan-divinities' and 'free divinities' than with God.[3] These divinities and ancestral spirits may protect or injure people, as their whims may dictate. A clan divinity, 'that of the Father', may also be called upon to mediate between man and another divinity. Divinities usually have particular characteristics which manifest themselves through human experience. Some of them are known to inflict specific types of pain or illness. Some are known to have certain likes and dislikes. When they 'fall upon' a man and possess him, they can be identified by the peculiar aberrational behaviour they induce in him. The relationship between a clan and a particular clan-divinity may be traced to a mytho-

---

[1] Seligman, op. cit. 178.   [2] Lienhardt, op. cit. (1961), 156.
[3] Ibid., chaps. II and III.

logized incident in the history of the clan. In this sense, divinities represent specific aspects of human experience.[1] First, we shall consider how a single experience may give birth to a divinity, and how experience may reveal the power of divinities. Then we will consider the unity of Divinity itself.

The following story illustrates the origination of a clan-divinity. As we have already pointed out, the Ngok trace their leadership under the clan Pajok whose name derives from its founder, Jok. According to a historical myth, the Ngok, on their way westward, were confronted with waters they could not cross. Jok, in self-sacrifice, decorated his own daughter, Acai, and offered her to the powers of the waters in order that the tribe might cross. She was taken by those powers, which in return caused the waters to part, allowing the people to cross dry-shod.[2] The memory of Acai has remained to this day and is celebrated at least annually when offerings are made to her in the waters. Not only is she believed to protect the clan from evil, but in her turn she makes demands from the clan which must be satisfied.[3]

[1] This concept of human experience in religion, which is the outcome of Dinka emphasis on the myth of permanent identity and influence with all its pro-creational and social underpinnings, has been very ably demonstrated by Lienhardt. Briefly stated, the memory of an experience is projected from the mind or interior of the remembering person to form an image which acts upon him, as he sees it, exteriorly from outside himself. Divine power is attributed to this externalized image, which is understood by the remembering person to be capable of making demands or of conferring benefits. Although the image takes an exterior appearance, the fact that it originates within the experiencing person and exerts influence on him shows a unity between him as the object and the image as the subject. Dr. Taylor expresses this unity of experience thus: 'Not only is there less separation between subject and object, between self and not-self, but fundamentally all things share the same nature and the same interaction one upon another—rocks and forest trees, beasts and serpents, the power of wind and waves upon a ship, the power of a drum over a dancer's body, the dead and the first ancestors, from the stone to the divinities a hierarchy of power but not of being, for all are one, all are here, all are now', *The Primal Vision* (1963), 72. Thus not only is there unity between self and image, but there is a unification of diverse experiences within the self. Not only is the experiencing self, to a certain degree every human being and to a greater degree the ancestors, part of the divination of the experience and therefore divine, but the objects with which one interacts assume a particular value of divination as well. Animals, trees, snakes, birds, and so on, may thus be consecrated as symbolizing divinities. In so far as mystic experience images the power of a spirit, the sum total of human experiences forming a unity symbolizes the unity of God within which there is the diversity of spirits.

[2] See Howell, op. cit. 242.

[3] For another example in which a bird became a divinity see songs 9 and 157.

The same notion can also be seen on the levels of the individual and the family. To mention a few examples: a man who has suffered a serious disease may become recognized after the disease has passed as possessing a spiritual power to cure similar diseases. This is especially true where a man has suffered a disability or a deformation as a result of the disease. Once established, the power becomes hereditary. A man whose herds have been wiped out by a disease, rendering him poor, may similarly acquire a power of purifying cattle of like diseases. Not everyone of similar experience achieves the same results; it depends on the severity of the impact made upon the person and his community by the memory of his experience. In all cases the memory must be honoured by appropriate rites, sacrifices, or dedications of animals or objects. Failure to do this may result in harm inflicted by the neglected power.

Whenever a man suffers illness or injury he is likely to attribute it to the powers of divinities. A woman who has committed adultery feels her guilt as physical pain which can be alleviated only if she confesses. A man who swears falsely sees his illness or that of a close relative as punishment for his unlawful deed, and the threat of death can be removed only by his confession followed by rites of purification. Ill-treatment of an elder or a kinsman may be understood as the immediate cause of bodily suffering. A man who has committed a secret murder bears the heavy responsibility for whatever deaths occur in his family. He also fears for his own life unless he confesses and the evil is removed by compensation of the deceased's kinsmen followed by ritual purification.

These individual experiences reflect the power of lesser divinities. Divinity in the sense of God is not limited to any particular feature of human experience, but embraces all aspects of life. God is therefore a unification of infinite diversities. Within this manifold and yet unified mythical system, the Dinka sometimes refer to individual divinities as *Nhialic*, the Creator, thus appearing to equate individual divinity, a part of the whole, with *Nhialic*, the whole itself, an anomaly which recalls the Christian concept of the Trinity.[1]

[1] Lienhardt has drawn a distinction between Dinka religion and Christianity by pointing out that the Trinity is a revealed truth: 'Divinity as a unity, and Divinity as a multiplicity, are not the products of logical or mystical elaboration of a revealed truth as are our own theological considerations of similar apprehensions', op. cit. (1961), 156. While the Dinka do not claim revelation in the Christian sense, it could be argued that revelation is implicit in the totality of

In keeping with their conception of Divinity as unity in diversity. as the Father of all and the fathers of many, the Dinka believe that mankind as a totality is subject to the one supreme power of God, for it is God who creates and destroys all men. But at the same time the Dinka recognize that different men have different gods and, consequently, sometimes different religions. It is thus said that the Arab has his God, and the European his God; and in fact, each individual human being may have his God, though nearly always as a member of a family. The relationship between Divinity as a totality and any individual man is sometimes expressed in such personal terms as 'God of my father', or 'God of my forefathers', or simply 'My Grandfather', or 'My Ancestor' (less frequently as 'God, My Father'). When the relationship is qualified by 'of my . . .', it implies the pivotal role of ancestry and the need for at least one forebear above the father. As a corollary to this segmentation of lesser divinities, it is understood that the exclusive Dinka divinities do not have much power over Arabs, Europeans, or educated Dinkas. Likewise, exclusively European and Arab gods do not have much power over the Dinka. The over-all God, however, has an all-encompassing power.

Since in the order of their proximity on the basis of human experience this over-all God is farther removed from man than the smaller divinities and ancestors, also visualized as small creators, he is less conceivable by man, less possible to be symbolized by natural phenomena, and less understood by man. An explanation of this ignorance in terms consistent with the experiential nature of religion becomes imperative. The Dinka conceive of God as having once been physically connected with the world and of life as having then been perfect. According to various myths the connection with God was severed owing to the fault of a woman; offended, God withdrew from man and willed that the world be immersed in suffering and misery—as it is today. He remained linked to the earth by a rope which the finch was eventually sent to cut, leaving no link with God. A recurrent theme in Dinka religion is the imploring of God to restore the harmony which once existed. The need for this becomes especially manifest when man suffers

their experience which, as we have seen in the concept of *cieng*, the Dinka consider God-given and divine. It might be added that such explanations as the concept of revelation are prompted by the demands of an inquisitive culture. When it comes to the nature of God, the Dinka ask few if any questions.

the misfortunes of sickness and death consequential to the separation.

The above myth addresses itself to the question, 'Where is God?' which the Dinka sometimes wonder about, and not to the question Does God exist?' Among the Dinka, the latter is never posed. Should it be posed, as is now possible with the introduction of inquisitive Western culture, the immediate answer would be a counter-question, 'Who created you?' If the sceptic says that it is not enough to call the Creator 'God' (for who and where is He?) the Dinka might give the myth of the disrupted world and God's severance from man as an explanation.

Though separate from man, God is not entirely removed from his cognizance. He is still very much involved in the universe, and man sees evidence of Him in all the unexplained facts of nature. Among the variety of unexplained phenomena which the Dinka often associate with Divinity are thunder and lightning and the rain, all of which are associated with divinity Deng, the closest divinity to God. Thunder is the angry voice of God, and lightning the glittering club with which He strikes the evils of this world. The solar system is known to them only in that it guides them in measuring time and following seasonal changes. The sun is understood to travel from the east to the west, returning to the east in the darkness of night. Man may not see it while it is returning. The vision of that return, which some occasionally claim to see, is an ominous revelation, demanding sacrifice to avert death. Since God supplements the parents with the creation of every child, begetting of children is considered a gift of God; He may choose to have a woman barren, but might change His mind when appeased through appropriate rites.

The Dinka call upon God to give *wei* (life) in its full value—spiritual and physical, individual and social. The dead are important because their world is a projection of and into the present world. *Wei* is sometimes translated as 'soul' or 'spirit' by Christian theologians, mainly because it leaves the body after death, but '*wei* in Dinka is not, as "soul" or "spirit" tend to be in popular English, a kind of dematerialized replica of the personality. Consequently, we cannot speak in Dinka of the "souls of the dead", but only of their "ghosts", or of the "life" which has left them.'[1] When 'life' leaves a person or an animal, it is believed to be trans-

[1] Lienhardt, op, cit. (1961), 207.

missible to others. In sacrifices, for instance, the vitality of the sacrificial beast is symbolically transferred to the sick person. This symbolic action is important as an analogy to the myth of immortality. The lives of the dead are not lost. If their line is maintained, their *wei* is transmitted through posterity so that the dead are rendered immortal. Because of this link with the dead and other mythical participants, well-being is basically magico-religious.

On the negative side, there are evil practices against life which may be individually acquired or inherited. Typical of these are the evil-eye (*peeth*), and evil-medicine (*wal*), the power of which is contained in fetish bundles, distinguished from the herbs ordinarily used for curative purposes by spiritually authorized people. *Wiel* is a more inclusive practice of symbolic action desired to bring death or some misfortune to whomever it is directed against. These various practices may be utilized by a genuine victim to punish a wrongdoer, but they are loathed and deplored. This is because they are believed to victimize innocent people and to counteract righteousness. Many of these evil practices, especially the use of fetishes, are considered originally non-Dinka, and the Ngok consider them particularly non-Ngok, being attributed to the peoples farther South.

Legitimate power to bless or curse a deserving person is believed to be in every man's 'flesh' (*ring*), by virtue of his being a human being, but differing in degree according to status and the nature of the relationship involved, particularly in terms of descent and age.

Divinity is held ultimately to reveal truth and falsehood, and in doing so provides a sanction for justice between men. Cruelty, lying, cheating, and all other forms of injustice are hated by Divinity, and the Dinka suppose that in some way, if concealed by men, they will be revealed by him ... Divinity is made the final judge of right and wrong, even when men feel sure that they are in the right. Divinity is thus the guardian of truth—and sometimes signifies to men what really is the case, behind or beyond their errors and falsehood ...

The Dinka have no problem of the prospering sinner, for they are sure that Divinity will ultimately bring justice. Since among them every man at some time must meet with suffering or misfortune, death or disease among his family or his cattle, there is always evidence, for those who wish to refer to it, of divine justice. It is a serious matter when a man calls on Divinity to judge between him and another, so serious that only a fool would take the risks involved if he knew he were in the wrong, and to call upon Divinity as witness gives the man who does so an initial presumption of being in the right.[1]

A Dinka therefore strives to maintain unity and harmony between himself and the world outside and reads cosmological discord into the mishaps of life. Harmony is best achieved by attuning one's demands and desires to the spirits, ancestors, and other fellow men;[2] it often fails, and when it does, the cause is immediately or eventually divined and harmony must be restored through such rites and ceremonies as a diviner recommends.

The Dinka who is visited by illness or disaster explores the depths of his inner self or that of a close relative in the hope of finding the sin which has brought on the discord. Even when the physical 'cause' of an injury is clear, as when a man falls from a tree and breaks his arm, the Dinka often looks beyond the evasive notion of 'accident' and attributes the mishap to a supernatural force. In searching for a sin which might have angered the Gods, the chances are that he will find some fault on his side or on that of a relative.[3] It is postulated that Divinity has the transcendent right to expect man to yield to his will; but, when his legitimate expectations are satisfied, he is supposed to rid man of evil.

But Divinity is not always predictable. Consequently, it is not always possible to explain his harshness; nor is it always possible to appease him. Since the notion of a morally anthropomorphic God is revealed through the realities of Dinka experience, He may display a nature which is both harsh and gentle, both cruel and kind. The Dinka are occasionally forced to say 'Divinity has no heart', or 'Divinity's eyes have no tears', meaning that He lacks sympathy and understanding. Such extreme judgements are passed only where a disaster occurs for which man cannot find justifica-

[1] Lienhardt, op. cit. (1961), 46–7.

[2] As Dr. Taylor says, 'A man's well-being consists in keeping in harmony with the cosmic totality. When things go well with him he knows that he is at peace, and of a piece, with the scheme of things, and there can be no greater good than that. If things go wrong then somewhere he has fallen out of step. He feels lost. The totality has become hostile and, if he has a run of bad luck he falls a prey to acute insecurity and anxiety. The whole system of divination exists to discover the point at which the harmony has been broken and how it may be restored', op. cit. 74.

[3] 'It is your right, Grandfather (or ancestor)' is frequently uttered even when God has been harsh with man, but in some cases this is more a concealment of felt criticism in fear of worse consequences than it is a sincere and full appreciation of God's invariable goodness.

tion, or when divinities capriciously refuse to be reconciled by propitiation or to help in any situation where they are implored to do so. The Dinka are thus a submissive people, living in a world they cannot control, and subject to the will of a God they do not fully understand.

The Dinka have very little concern for physical cures without mysticism. As Titherington put it, 'Ignorance of cause and effect, and a credulity which never ceases to astonish the observer, cloud his life with the constant dread that he has neglected some precaution against the malevolence of man, spirit, or nature, and he hardly distinguishes the last two.'[1]

A man's well-being is the concern of the whole family and the kinship-group. 'Illness, catch me that I may see my people' is a popular saying. When a person is sick, relatives and friends all cluster around him in prayer or in silent watch. When an animal is to be sacrificed, a group of people form a circle, invoking spirits, with one person speaking at a time, and the rest repeating after him in chorus.[2]

The concern of the community for the patient is symbolized by the division of the sacrificial beast among a wide range of families, and in accordance with strict rules descended in perpetuity. In Dinka metaphor, people are thus put together as the different parts of the bull are put together.[3]

Divinities or ancestors may be the cause of illness whether justifiably or unjustifiably, in which case they are called upon to correct the situation. The cause of illness may be a spirit, in which case other spirits are called upon to help. If the infliction of harm is a just retribution by a wronged person, the matter is settled with that person, but if it is an unjustified evil deed, then the divinities are called upon to cure the sick man and punish the evil-doer. If it be discovered that a wrong committed by the sick person or his kinsman is the cause of the malady, confession is made as a step towards readjustment. A diviner is called to diagnose the grounds for sickness or diabolical possession only when the patient has not been able to do so. Sometimes, the power behind the illness may

[1] Op. cit. 170.
[2] See Lienhardt, op. cit. (1961), 220–31 for examples of such prayers.
[3] 'Since every bull or ox is destined for sacrifice, each one demonstrates, potentially, the ordered social relationships of the sacrificing group, the members of which are indeed "put together" in each beast and represented in their precise relations to each other in the meat which it provides', ibid. 23.

make itself manifest through the patient's mouth. The diviner may discover the grounds either by going into a trance-like condition or by inducing such a condition in the sufferer or his kin, or both.

Although we have presented the Dinka as dependent on superstition for physical and mental well-being, this should not imply that their approach to well-being has no practical aspects. In addition to the use of herbs for medication, some experts are skilled in surgery and bone-setting and are capable of performing very delicate operations. Even where the approach is clearly religious, the interconnections of the psychic well-being with the physical well-being are secularly significant. Diseases or other evils are not always corrected successfully. In such a case, the Dinka find an easy answer in the refusal of divinities to be appeased, or perhaps in the failure of the diviner to have discovered the real cause. It would seem that where the organic disease is one which psychological cure cannot effect, or where the patient's condition is too serious, the diviner's psychological cure is likely to be ineffective. In such cases, some diviners are honest enough to tell the relatives that they can do nothing.

The attribution to inheritance or lineage of the evils of the lineage members means that when a person dies, the relatives of the deceased avoid and are avoided by outsiders. There is a taboo against their drinking or eating in the homes of outsiders or mixing with others on social occasions. Appearance tells if a person is in mourning. Women cut their leather skirts short, leave them un-oiled, dry, and untrimmed with beads, and leave their bodies white with dust and ashes. Neither men nor women wear beads or any ornamental decorations, and they must leave their hair black, not bleached as is usual among young men and women. The mourning period lasts for months and sometimes a whole year, at the end of which they are ceremonially cleansed and may then resume normal life.

Despite the continued association between the dead and the living, they are paradoxically separated by a ritual known as *cuol* performed three days after death for a male, or four for a female. By this ritual, a ram and a chicken are sacrificed in the middle of the night some distance away from the homesteads. The chicken is waved over the relatives and thrown away, and the ram is also left uneaten by the relatives, though it may be picked up and eaten by non-relatives. The idea is to combat the disease symbolically, and send it away from the living.

Thus the Dinka dread death as a going into nothingness which is only mitigated by the immortality of procreation. When a person dies, it is often said that 'God brought him and God has taken him', and dying is sometimes described as 'leaving in the lurch' (*wer wei*), but in no way is it felt that a dead man may be gone to a better life. It is therefore life in this world which really matters to the Dinka; it is for it that they pray to God and other spirits and it is in it that the dead continue even as they exist somewhere else.

VIII

POWER AND THE LAW

DINKA conceptions, institutions, and practices of power and their legal expression have changed a great deal as a result of the nineteenth-century upheavals when, to the Dinka, 'the world was spoilt', and then of the Turco-Egyptian and Anglo-Egyptian colonial administrations. No easy distinction can therefore be drawn between what is normal change and what resulted from the breakdown of order under the chaotic conditions of the nineteenth century, or between what was indigenous and what has been implanted by alien powers. The trends have not been uniform throughout Dinkaland—some lineages emerged in leadership as a result of the war conditions of the nineteenth century, others disappeared under the purge of colonialism, while yet others have consistently held their combined religious and secular leadership, through war and peace, in tradition and in modernity. This is particularly true of the Ngok, among whom traditional leadership has not only been maintained and confirmed by successive administrations, but has also been highly enhanced in status by Arab influence.[1] This is noticeable in the terms now used to identify chiefs, for while *beny* (chief) is a general term, the position of a chief is qualified not only by the Dinka words *dit* (great or big), and *kor* (small), but also by Arabic titles.[2] Since this volume focuses on the Ngok, the application to other tribes of what is said about Ngok power-process must be particularly qualified.

Traditionally, Dinka power-structure was both family-oriented and segmented in such a way that each descent and territorial unit, as discussed earlier, was autonomous, but the whole system centred around the 'Great Chief' (*Benydit*), now designated by the Arabic word *Nazir*, his subordinate chiefs in the territorial hierarchy, now referred to as *Nazir* or *wakil* (singular), and other elders. While the discussion of tribal power must focus on the Head Chief, it is important to envisage him in a Council of chiefs and elders, for

---

[1] Howell, op. cit. 264.   [2] Such as *Nazir, Wakil, Omda,* and *Sheikh.*

although such a Council now tends to follow the Head Chief un-
questioningly, it is significant to the Dinka that the Chief acts in
Council and not arbitrarily or singly.

The most powerful lineages among the Ngok are the Pajok and
the Dhiendior. Pajok provides the Head Chief and now one of his
two deputies,[1] and Dhiendior provides the other deputy. In addition to these three positions, their leadership is reflected in the
many subordinate chiefs who head the sub-tribes and who are now
called by the Arabic word *omda* (singular), the sections, and the
sub-sections referred to as *sheikh* (singular). On the descent level,
the public authority is the clan-head (*nhomgol*), whose position has
been so radically altered and used for tax collection that it has been
reduced in status.

Since the religious and the secular are fused in Dinka thought
and practice, political leadership is considered divine and is traced
through legends which are continually repeated in order to reinforce the *status quo*. The emphasis placed on such legends,
especially in songs, is often exaggerated and the religious beliefs
embodied in them appear archaic, but to the Dinka, they explain
why things are the way they are. They give the social system
stability and promote continuity.

The Dinka practise a qualified form of primogeniture and in
the stories of authority stress is placed on its importance and the
attributes of the chief as the father uniting not only the living
members of his community, but also the community and its
ancestors. In the ceremonies of his installation, the chief is ritually
lifted up toward the sky by certain representatives of the community and the participation of the commoners is vital. Thus the
unity of the tribe behind him, and the divine acceptance of the
designated man, are symbolized in the ritual. Nor is the matter a
pure formality; although primogeniture means that the eldest son
of the most senior wife succeeds, circumstances for the application of the rules can be so complicated as to permit deviation and
choice. In the case of succession to the late Chief Kwol Arob, for
instance, complexities arose as to which son was in fact the senior
son of the senior wife, Deng Majok or Deng Makuei (also known
as Deng Abot). Deng Majok's mother had been betrothed first,
but because she had refused her consent, her betrothal had been
suspended, though some of the sacred cows of betrothal had not

[1] As a result of a compromise to the succession conflict reported below.

been withdrawn. Later, an illness believed to have resulted from
the curse of refusing the chief in marriage forced her and her family
to change their minds; they apologized to the chief, her marriage
was performed, and she was given to him after he had in the mean-
time married Deng Makuei's mother and brought her home.
Although the first to come had been treated as the first wife, traditional uncertainties over the seniority of her son, Deng Makuei,
combined with modern considerations of administrative competence, permitted Deng Majok to succeed through elections.[1]

In the genealogies of leading families, there are cases dating even
further back in which sons other than the most senior, or those of
the most senior wives, have prevailed over otherwise entitled senior
sons for even less complicated reasons.[2] Not too infrequently,
leadership even gets out of the immediate family; a chief dies,
leaving children too young to succeed; his brother, cousin, or uncle
succeeds, establishes himself too firmly to give room to the deceased's children when they grow up, and begins to pave the way
for the succession of his own son. After his death, competition
ensues between his children and those of his predecessor. These
complications and changes in circumstances, by introducing
competition into the political process, give the people a choice,
so that primogeniture neither creates too much security to
guarantee good leadership, nor imposes leadership on the people.
It merely limits the circle of choice—a circle duly disposed to
leadership, trained for it, and believed worthy of it.

Notwithstanding and because of their advantages, these variables
create serious conflicts over power. With respect to the chief *vis-à-
vis* the community, conflict was traditionally narrowed by the recognition of only a few lineages as the wielders of power. The fact
that, generally speaking, identical powers were wielded on the
descent level and on the territorial level minimized the motivation
for power among the commoners, although in rare cases dissatisfied
commoners might disaffiliate themselves and join the jurisdiction
of another chief. Between and within the Pajok and Dhiendior
lineages among the Ngok, conflicts are more serious. The subordination of the Dhiendior to Pajok was traditionally expressed
in a form of division of powers which tended to minimize tension

[1] For a detailed account of the case see Howell, op. cit. 266.
[2] This was said by a member of the Kiro family of the Rek tribe to be particularly true of them.

between them. Since settlement of feuds was the most important function of the chief, the division of power was over jurisdiction where wounds were inflicted by clubs or spears. The Pajok assumed power where spears were used. This is significant because clubs are used on the sectional level and spears on the sub-tribal level, and the seriousness of conflicts on the latter level necessitates the intervention of the Head Chief—the Pajok, in other words. Political opposition is further reduced by continuous intermarriage between the Pajok and the Dhiendior so that the chief and his deputies are always related by blood or by marriage.[1] None the less, conflicts do occur. In the past, such conflicts might lead to disaffiliation, with the Deputy Chief terminating his allegiance to the Head Chief and setting up a new group, though the whole of his own lineage would not necessarily follow him, since among themselves there would also exist jealousies and competition.

The struggle for power within the ruling families is not essentially different from the familiar jealousies and frictions within polygynous families, but it is intensified by the importance of the disputed positions. Conflicts may be between father and son, between brothers, or between other members of the lineage. The areas of conflict are innumerable, but one can single out competition over succession as an outstanding point of confrontation.

It is worth emphasizing that the disuniting and conflict-generating competition for power between and within the chiefly clans did not normally place in question the fundamental acceptance of the chief as the uniting leader. Rarely did people break away from his authority, though there might be opposed factions both within and outside his descent-group. This opposition was often subtle, so that half-brothers or chiefs known to be in opposition none the less appeared united. The advantages of competition's bringing into power an able and worthy leader thus outweigh the disadvantages of conflict and disunity over power.

This brings us to Dinka conceptions of what makes a worthy leader. Traditionally at least a Dinka chief is not a ruler in the Western sense, but a spiritual leader whose words express divine enlightenment and wisdom and form the point of consensus and

[1] It is said that a daughter of late Chief Kwol Arob was married to a nephew of late Chief Jipur Allor with over a hundred cows and a girl-slave.

reconciliation. In order to mediate between men, the chief himself must be a model of purity, righteousness, and, in Dinka terms, a man with a cool heart.

A cool mouth and a cool heart . . . are associated with peacefulness, order, harmony, and truth. A man whose tongue and heart are cool is a fit person to adjust the differences between those who quarrel, to see the rights and wrongs of both parties, and to reconcile them. This is the character of the ideal master of the fishing spear.[1]

It is because of their divine enlightenment that a Dinka said to Dr. Lienhardt:

See our masters of the fishing spear are like that [hurricane] lamp. Look now it gives a bright light, and we see each other and we see what is on the table. If the lamp goes dim we shall not see each other so well, and we shall not see what is on the table . . . [God] made our masters of the fishing spear thus to be the lamps of the Dinka.[2]

The principal task of the chief, his subordinates, and his elders is to adjust human relations. Owing to the family orientation of the system, most problems of social relations are either familial or inter-familial. Within the family they concern individuals; outside the family they often concern groups, although such groups are usually represented by individuals. When there is a disaster such as crop failure or epidemic, the chief's task is seen as one of mediating between the empirical and the spiritual worlds to correct the loss of harmony and unity believed to have caused the problem. Even in these cases, however, the ancestors or divinities are invoked as members of one family group or another. The ancestors of the chiefly descent-groups are invoked as protectors of the whole tribe. This is revealed in a hymn, now sung on the inauguration of every Ngok Head Chief, which was first sung on the installation of Kwoldit, an ancestor of the present Chief, by his age-set, *kiec* (lit. Honey-Bee):[3]

[1] Lienhardt, op. cit. (1961), 139.
[2] Ibid. 140.
[3] 'Kiec bir ka wayaa'
Dɔngbɛk aye Kwɔl tooc ee
'Lek Kwɔl na yik we wei wa Bulabek.'
Ka cen bɛny, bɛny e cɛɛth ku
Bɛny e looŋ dɔk
Tony de Bulabek
Kiec bir ka wayaa.

Honey-Bee this is a flash of light to light your way
Dongbek honoured us with Kwol
May Kwol give you the life of my father, Bulabek.
We had no chief to guide our way
No chief to untie our words
In the land of Bulabek
Honey-Bee, this is a flash of light to brighten your way.

But the role of the chief goes even further than that. As the spiritual father of the tribe, he is the keeper of the people, both as a collectivity and as individuals. The continuous theme of self-sacrifice in the stories of chiefly families is a testimony to the responsibility his position bestows upon him. A needy person, whatever his need, looks to the chief for personal remedy. In order to meet these responsibilities, the chief must be endowed with all the values essential for his duty and hence he should be the tribe's most indulged and most indulging person, with no favouritism to his immediate descent-groups or to any who may wish to bribe him. Logically, then, the chief should be most receptive to new ideas and practices which will continually improve his value-position and therefore increase the benefits he can bestow on the community. The Ngok Chief has in fact been the leader of Ngok social change. This has consistently been a selective innovation, weaving the new with the old, while preserving the Chief's distinctively Dinka character. This is part of Ngok expectation, as reflected in these lines from a song in praise of the late Chief Kwol Arob:[1]

O Kwol, keep the people of your father
And lead them to the people of the world.

This is not inconsistent with Ngok Dinka conservatism. Innovation is so restrained and selective that it reinforces rather than threatens tradition. It is this linkage of the old and the new which gives the chief the experience essential to his unique position, thus equipping him to continue the heritage. When a significant stranger comes into the tribe, it is for the chief to meet him first. What follows from an extraordinary meeting may be a matter of exaggeration and fantasy. Small incidents may become miracles, to be recounted as manifestations of the divine powers which have descended through the divine ancestry of the chief.

[1] See lines 6 and 7 in 'Kwol,' song 140.

In carrying out his duties, and in accordance with the values of the Dinka, the chief is supposed to emphasize persuasion rather than coercion. Indeed, when one recalls that *luk* (to persuade) also means 'court' or 'trial', it can be understood that litigation among the Dinka is not a fight in court. The chief and elders are mediators whose aim is to reconcile the adversaries. Unless they succeed in this, the conflict is not adequately resolved. Every detail is examined, every chief and elder who wishes to be heard is heard, and a general dialogue of persuasion continues until the alleged wrong is revealed to the party at fault and the parties concur. In many cases, when a final settlement is reached, a ceremony of reconciliation usually follows either before the chief or privately. Only then is the case fully resolved and harmony restored.

To the chief are attributed the divine association of power for life and death, and other forms of benefits and deprivations. We have already said that such divine and secular powers, though concentrated in the chiefs, are shared by members of chiefly lineages. Because commoners do not wield equivalent powers they are sometimes somewhat comically referred to as *micar ageer* (the black bulls with low-lying horns); a bull with such horns has a hard time fighting bulls with upward and pointed horns.

The spiritual power of the chief can be awesome, but the Dinka believe that should the chief err, and invoke the divine power unjustifiably, he will not be effective. The chief's religious sanction is therefore not absolute; and he must rely constantly on his powers of persuasion.

But further, the chiefly office is inconsistent with the use of force. A chief should not even see blood. If his people are attacked, when force is deemed necessary to stop force, the chief should bless the warriors and pray for victory far away from the battlefield. In a fight between his own sub-tribes, the chief, being the uniting element, should not take sides. He may draw a symbolic line, place his sacred spear on it, and pray that heavy casualties be inflicted on any group crossing the symbolic line in disobedience to his orders against fighting, which could include his own immediate group.

In view of the emphasis on the persuasiveness of the chief's power, it would seem paradoxical on a first impression that the symbols of his authority should be spears which, as we have said, are fishing- and fighting-spears among the Ngok. Since the spears are invoked to inflict a curse, the symbol is that of necessary but reserved coercion. Indeed, the power of the spear is linked with the power of the divinity Flesh from which the Ngok Head Chief derives his title and all Dinka chiefs derive both their persuasive and their coercive authority. Flesh 'is the principal inspiration of members of the fishing spear, . . . the grounds of their ability ideally to "light the way", to pronounce and define truth, to prevail in prayers, and to reconcile conflicting groups and interests'.[1] At night, when everyone is asleep, masters of the fishing spear are said to pray for divine enlightenment, and it is believed that Flesh sometimes reveals itself to them in the form of light.[2] The symbolic spears of the Ngok Head Chief are believed to shine brightly at night if they want to draw the Chief's attention to something. The information may accompany the illumination, or the truth may be subsequently divined. Yet, while a source of divine enlightenment and therefore of persuasive wisdom, the Flesh is a source of divine curse and death. Its revelation through the spears thus symbolizes righteousness, which embodies persuasion and the power to destroy evil and its human agents.

The chief's status as the head of the tribal family is reinforced by marriages with the various factions of his tribe and also other Dinka tribes with whom he has diplomatic relations—he is always the man with the most wives. Chief Deng Majok of the Ngok has carried the strategy much further, partly because of the additional problems confronting his administration as a result of today's waning belief in religious symbols. Since the rules of exogamy are very strict among the Dinka, these marriages link him with families unrelated to him by blood or previous marriage connection, thus augmenting his status and increasing his bases for a persuasive, family-like exercise of power.

It was to stress the importance of persuasion in Dinka society, and its divine and secular bases, that some scholars concluded that it functioned although it lacked the ingredient of coercion necessary for the Western conception of law. Law, a normative concept generally desired in the interest of order, should be seen contextually, for despite fundamental similarities between all legal systems, each system has its own social policies which it is supposed to serve. In doing so, it adopts ways and means that distinguish its characteristics from those of other systems

---

[1] Lienhardt, op. cit. (1961), 146.   [2] Ibid. 141–2.

though retaining the basic principles that are universally common to law.

A conspicuous feature of Dinka law before the advent of modern government was the minimum effectiveness of the chief and the prevalence of self-help through violence. During the early period of British rule, Major Titherington observed of the Rek Dinka what might be said of all Dinkas: 'Hardly a man but bears the marks of severe club and spear wounds, and fighting is still the most important part of a boy's education. The Raik [*sic*] life is still inclined to be violent, but the meaner crimes which elsewhere smirch the records of police courts are notably absent.'[1] On the other hand, the disruptive conditions of the nineteenth century may have contributed to a breakdown of order. It is common in Dinka literature to speak of the days 'when people lived by the force of the arm', and this may have been an attendant evil of a 'spoilt world' rather than a natural aspect of the legal system. This view has been expressed by some observers. Titherington, for example, writes:

There is no doubt that the [Dinka] social system and personal outlook, as we so lately found it, was in a state of deterioration directly resulting from the continued harrying they received from the Northern slavers, and the demoralizing effects of half a century of subjection to crime at the hands of every stranger before the coming of the present [British] Government. That they did not succumb altogether, like so many Southern tribes, speaks highly of their stout-heartedness; nor did they take to the vile, but common practice of selling their fellow tribesmen into slavery. They lost hundreds of thousands of cattle; men, women, and children in thousands were slaughtered, carried off into slavery, or died of famine; but the survivors kept alive in the deepest swamps, bravely attacked the raiders when they could, and nursed that loathing and contempt for the stranger and all his ways that even now they are only just losing.[2]

It is evidently hard to live by one's ideals under such conditions. The colonial regime, in order to remedy the ineffectiveness of the traditional system without abolishing it, reinforced the Chief-in-Council with coercive powers of modern government.

[1] Op. cit. 169.   [2] Ibid. 159.

IX

THE IMPACT OF ALIEN CULTURES

THE Dinka have not been uniformly affected by the social change of modern times; a few have been almost transformed culturally, others have barely been touched, and the society has fallen into a sharp division between tradition and modernity. The Dinka were in contact with the Arabs during the pre-colonial period, but slave raids militated against cultural assimilation. As between the Ngok and the Baggara, the leading families were in diplomatic contact as friendly neighbours and a certain amount of cross-cultural influence, especially in the political field, took place. The Turco-Egyptian administration was more interested in collecting taxes and in other forms of exploitation than in the people, and was therefore not taken as a model for change, but it activated the assimilation of Arab political ideas and practices. Outside the political sphere, each culture assimilated whatever it adopted and remained distinct and apart from the culture of the other. A typical example has already been given in the adoption and adaptation, by the Dinka, of the concept of the Mahdi, while the Dinkas successfully resisted Northern rule under the leadership of the Mahdi.

With British rule, these peoples and cultures were brought into unity in a modern state, but kept separate or mutually independent. This facilitated cross-cultural contact, but assimilation was kept at a minimum by the Southern policy of separate development. When this policy was abandoned in 1947, contact with the North intensified, but still under British supervision, so that neither felt dominated by the other. On the contrary, the educated of both the South and the North saw a common enemy in the British. The atmosphere therefore was ripe for a genuine contact towards a more integrated Sudan. It was then that the average Dinka could go into the cities and become even more exposed to Arab influence. Before that, going into Arabland brought shame on a Dinka and invited insult songs.

After independence it became an official policy not only to permit but to encourage such cross-cultural contact, but because of political conflicts, something of a cycle had been completed and to the Southerner the civil war recalled the days of slave-raids. Rejection of Arab culture is never quite possible in the mixed conditions of modern Sudan, especially since the goal of cultural uniformity is officially pursued as a means to national integration. As the situation is confused and confusing, it is a matter of conjecture what the outcome will be. Many Southerners have learned or are learning Arabic and some have become or are becoming Muslims; yet, even among the Ngok where this happens more naturally than in response to political pressure, many have abandoned or are abandoning Islam in political protest. Many who had acquired Arab-Muslim names now prefer their once-abandoned Dinka names. From the inception of Southern political movements against the North, Muslims have been among the prominent leaders of the South and there are Muslims among the extremists in the military wing of the Southern movement, the *anyanya*. While one cannot tell what the outcome of the Government's policies of Islamization and Arabization will mean to its political objectives, it is just possible that they could prove erroneous. After all, pioneering enemies of Western domination in Africa were the more Westernized Africans, educated mostly in the West.

The primary interest of the British in the Sudan was to establish order after years of disruption, corruption, and disintegration. This had to be done at minimum cost and with minimum personnel, and along traditional lines to reinforce the often-cited strategy of divide and rule. Where chiefs did not co-operate with the system or where the demand for competence required it, a Government chief was often appointed independently of the traditional leadership. Among the Ngok this was not the case, but segmental authority was replaced with a concentration of power in the chief. Sectional chiefs were left responsible only for administrative functions and became stripped of their judicial and executive functions. These are now vested in the Head Chief and his deputies, who, in various groupings with specially appointed court members, the *Makam* (derived from Arabic), constitute the Chiefs' Court in accordance with the Chiefs' Court Ordinance, 1931. The clan-heads, once elders in charge of their clans, were now to be appointed by the Chief to collect taxes: a change which reduced their status and necessitated the selection of people most able to discharge the new function. Clan-heads are now the target of many unrestrained insulting songs. Traditional authorities, including junior chiefs at all levels, continue to exercise a semblance of power, and most matters which reach the higher authorities will have passed through them. This is only time-consuming because in most cases the opinion of the Head Chief is sought.

The initial importance of chieftainship among the Ngok, the reception of Arab political practices with their emphasis on social stratification, and the introduction of further emphasis on the chiefly status by various regimes all combine to make Ngok power-structure more hierarchical than that of other Dinka tribes. The effect of a traditional and yet innovating leadership has made the Ngok political system adaptable to, and effective under, the new conditions. The Ngok have abandoned 'living by the arm' and have become more responsive than others to the authority of their chief. However, the chieftainship is losing its religious sanctity and reverence, for the chief as a secular–spiritual leader is now being replaced by fear of secular punishment even though the chief and elders continue to practise persuasion to a degree.

Where a chief is appointed whose ancestry has no tradition of leadership, which has happened in many Dinka tribes, the secular conception of modern authority and therefore the lack of traditional reverence due to a spiritual leader become even more conspicuous. A degree of divine authority usually evolves in consequence of such a governmental appointment, and relatives of the appointee may even claim some ancestral distinction through songs and the like to give traditional validity to their newly acquired authority. The alienation of the people from modern-day secular authority may be illustrated by the fact that the Dinka refer to the Government, even that represented by the Chief, as *jur* (foreigner).

With the waning of the sanctity of divine leadership among the Ngok, traditional conflicts between and within Pajok and Dhiendior lineages began to intensify. Because of restrictions on mass political disaffiliation (which have been unsuccessfully attempted) these conflicts manifest themselves in political opposition. By discrediting the Chief, his opponents hope to take over. Ambitious commoners who come into conflict with the Chief in one way or another begin to agitate, often with the backing of some members of the chiefly family whose expectations of taking over are greater. Complaints have been raised to national authorities which were calculated to discredit the chief in one way or another, although they have failed to do so.

In court, the chief and elders are often tempted to consider themselves as umpires applying the law, and may quickly resort to coercion. The Dinka reaction towards police, flogging, and imprisonment is one of indignation, and to have undergone these indignities is considered a cause for complaint. Until recently a policeman sent to seize a man's cow was likely to get hit on the head with a club. Today, governmental punishment has become accepted as one against which there is no retaliation—something to be feared and yet to be faced with courage and without the usual shame of a convict in Western society, unless the wrong is such as would be shameful by traditional criteria.

The situation is made more complex by the difficulty of determining what is part of the institution of chieftainship and what is prompted by the personality of an individual chief. Kwol Arob was the Chief who brought the Ngok under the British Government. On succeeding his father Arob Biong in 1905, he rode to El Obeid, the headquarters of Kordofan Province, and registered his allegiance. It was not until the thirties that many Dinka tribes of the South were brought fully under the new regime. Kwol was a very powerful Chief, and to this day most of the Dinka in other tribes still refer to the Ngok as the Ngok of Kwol Arob. In his later years, he had conflicts over power with his son Deng Majok, whom the Government not only recognized as his assistant with his half-brother Deng Makuei, but to whom they also gave judicial powers and eventually the main administrative and judicial authority, while his father was asked to retire and have only supervisory authority. Official records speak of Kwol during his later years as an autocratic and authoritarian chief whom people held in awe so much that it was felt wiser to qualify his power. The Ngok on the other hand remember him as a Chief who, though strong and made even more so by Governmental authority, governed by the ideals of a Dinka chief.

Deng Majok, who succeeded his father, being a man of extraordinary personality, has given the institution of chieftainship an unusual combination of tradition and modernity in which the Chief is still the persuasive traditional father he always has been in addition to being the coercive figure he now is. As such he is a highly revered and feared person whose word bears exceptional weight, so that once he gives an opinion it is nearly always the point of consensus even among those whose opinion had differed. But the threats and challenges to his authority prompted by change have added to the intensification of the Chief's autocracy. He now combines persuasive strategies in normal situations with ruthless coercion over those who dare challenge his administration. The result is a powerful but very controversial chief who combines the ideals of a Dinka chief with the tools of the modern state in intensified form.

Powerful and proud, Deng Majok has successfully maintained his own autonomy and that of his tribe against the ambitions of Arab chiefs with whom he now shares the Missiriya Rural Council and Missiriya District. Before the British left, the Ngok were given the option to join Bahr el Ghazal or Upper Nile where most Dinka are, but under his influence they opted for Kordofan. As a result of their closer unity in the Council and District, competition over leadership ensued between the ruling families of the Ngok and the Baggara, whose relations had long been cordial. The Paramount Chief of the Missiriya, Babo Nimr, whose jurisdiction extends over all the other tribes in the Council, Arabs and Nubas alike, cannot understand why the Ngok are excepted from his jurisdiction; Deng Majok is indignant that the issue is even contemplated. Though quite Arabized, he argues that the Ngok as a Dinka tribe should not be assimilated into the authority of an Arab chief. Both the colonial and the post-colonial administrations have consistently endorsed his position and he has remained responsible only to central authorities in judicial and administrative matters at a time when the chiefs of all the tribes in the Missiriya Rural Council are responsible to Babo Nimr, to whom appeals from their courts go. The crisis worsened when in 1961 some Arab chiefs entered into an alliance with the Ngok against the Nimr family, and elected Deng Majok as the President of the Missiriya Council. These developments have seriously strained the relations of the Ngok and Arab leaderships, with corresponding strain in the relations of their respective peoples—a strain which contributed to the Baggara–Dinka hostilities of 1965 in which hundreds (and some say thousands) lost their lives and in which Chief Deng Majok played a unique role in re-establishing and maintaining order.

Although he called in security forces, he saw to it that they did not usurp tribal power and turn their existence into a military occupation and a subordination of the chiefs as is now the case elsewhere in the South. These difficulties have left Deng Majok politically anxious but unscathed. Indeed, they have enhanced his already strong image and have made him a heroic leader even to his opponents. Furthermore, whereas in the South tribal chiefs are subordinate to specially constituted inter-tribal chiefs' Courts of Appeal as well as inter-tribal Councils, his independence from Arab chiefs without substitute subordination to any other Dinka chiefs makes him a uniquely powerful man. This is especially so since the central authorities, being ignorant of customary law and tribal administration, and desirous of maintaining obedience to him in order to be effective, usually confirm his decisions.

In the last century or so, there appears to have been an increase in litigation among the Ngok, who are in any case a litigious people. There are no available statistics to substantiate the observations of increased litigation and it may well be that the increase in the number of law-suits is only apparent and not real because, as a result of concentration of power in the Head Chief, litigation concentrates around him. His home is regarded as synonymous with his court, and he continually hears complaints from the time he wakes up until he goes to bed. It must be noted, of course, that while there are three divisions and an appellate division to the Ngok Chief's Court, there is only one Chief's Court under the presidency of the Head Chief; or, in the case of component divisions, under the presidency of his vice-presidents. Since the Court of the Head Chief is supposed to be reserved for serious cases of first instance and appeals, this concentration of activity in the Chief's home shows how different the human reality of Dinka litigation is from the abstract judicial system.

Despite the effectiveness of the new system there are still remnants of self-help which are usually undesirable even from the indigenous legal point of view, but are sometimes justifiable according to the circumstances, and are so much a part of Dinka practice as to be considered customary. For instance, in order to coerce a person into settlement, the plaintiff seizes his cow. Again, to hasten compensation in sexual violation of rights in women, the relatives of the women seize many of the best of the wrongdoer's cattle. After the settlement, they are given their due and the rest of the cattle are returned. These features of the traditional system, though still practised, are now discouraged.

Another area of Dinka life in which change has been most dramatic is the introduction of modern education. Initially, people disapproved of education. When the first school was opened in Abyei, the headquarters of the Ngok, in 1944, almost all the pupils were sons or relatives of the senior chiefs. Even in these circles there was much criticism, especially of the Head Chief, who took all his sons to school.[1] The idea of leaving no one to look after cattle was unimaginable. To encourage people to accept it, elementary education was more tied up with tribal life than it is today. Children were encouraged to influence their age-mates and elders to accept education. Social occasions were organized in which parents and tribal leaders gathered to see children display their new knowledge, and demonstrate their social responsibility and reverence for parents, chiefs, and elders. Singing was particularly popular as a means of reaching the people. But in time, for the Dinka, who see a linkage between knowledge and religious wisdom, writing and reading came to assume a respected place in their system of values as sources of wisdom.

The kind of knowledge education entailed did produce some conflicts. While schoolchildren were still disposed to respect parents, chiefs, and elders, the content of the very modernization which they often called upon their chiefs to introduce and accelerate undermined tradition. Because education was not oriented to the child's living conditions, modern knowledge and wisdom became acknowledged both by the traditionalists and by the educated to be well apart from traditional knowledge and wisdom. Education thus caused both participational and cultural disparity in that only a few people obtained it and what they obtained was little related to the pre-existing culture. Sometimes the educated and uneducated were seen as opponents, with the educated attempting to change tradition and the traditionalists to maintain it. The traditionalists consider the educated their 'eyes' because of their enlightenment in modern terms; but their radicalism is feared. It is not uncommon for the traditionalists to say, with reference to the educated, 'we have not given birth' (*wok kic dhieth*), meaning that the educated do not fully represent them.

Conflict with the Chief is particularly striking. The opposition

[1] Further evidence of the innovating role of the Ngok Chief.

against the chief already referred to is usually engineered and led by the educated who because they are considered by their relatives to be their 'eyes' are felt by the traditionalists to be the best equipped to confront the chief before national authorities. As already indicated, such attempts fail and leave the chief unscathed. This, together with other factors, often leads the educated to find life in the tribe intolerable. Almost all the educated of the Ngok who had held jobs in their own area, such as schoolteachers, executive officers, agricultural officers, and accountants, left because of conflict with the chiefs. Many of course leave simply because of alienation from tribal life and culture, and primarily because education does not prepare them for any occupation in the tribe. While it is geared towards white-collar jobs, it is often insufficient to obtain them. Those who go to higher levels of education get good jobs, but most of those who have only elementary education get lowly jobs, some of which are degrading, and yet others remain unemployed under humiliating urban conditions.

Conflict between tradition and modernity was particularly striking in the religious field since children were conditioned to regard traditional religion as primitive and irreligious. Snakes which symbolized divinities among the Dinka suddenly represented evil among the converts and were killed to the awe of the traditionalists, who expected evil in consequence. The cure of a medicine-man or the rituals of divination were refused and condemned. The meat of a sacrificial beast was regarded as evil and avoided. Family unity was in question in front of God, for the children were taught that on Judgement Day each person would stand alone. Consistent with the use of social occasions for announcing and producing change, these tensions between the old and the new were expressed not only in the family but in songs, plays, and other school activities. For a religious people like the Dinka, all these innovations, rather than casting doubt over their own religion, merely widened the gulf between the educated and the traditionalists. The former were dismissed in matters of religion as people who had been alienated and for whom their traditional elders were apologists in front of traditional powers.

These changes had their effect in the reception of modern health services, initially introduced by missionaries in most areas. At first, it was seen as repugnant to spiritual well-being, and any medication or treatment was feared and rejected. Even during epidemics from diseases like smallpox, adults would literally run away from vaccination, and sometimes had to be forced by law to accept it. The diviners themselves encouraged rejection of modern medicine, and saw any attempt to combine their efforts with those of missionaries or health officers as an aggravating provocation against the spirits and the ancestors. Despite these initial reactions, the usefulness of modern medicine was admitted once the results were obvious. This, combined with the Dinka's high regard for any genuinely religious man whatever his religion, won the Christian missionaries much respect as men of God and curers. None the less, it did not imply the acceptance of Christianity by the uneducated Dinka. To derive benefit from the spiritual powers of a person does not necessarily mean adopting his divinities or ancestral spirits— the powers which give real meaning to Dinka religion. Indeed in the course of time even the diviners began to profess that both they and the practitioners of modern medicine were interested in well-being and it is not uncommon for a diviner as a curer to administer his traditional cure and advise his patient to see a doctor as well so as to achieve maximum effectiveness.

Economic changes among the Dinka have been even more rapid. In the past, sale of cattle was considered shameful and going to work for cash in towns even more so. The colonial administration felt that the Dinka, being among the richest in cattle, and cattle being among the main resources of the country, were to be encouraged to sell their cattle. Taxes and fines were to be paid in cash, and since there was no paid labour in the tribe, sale of cattle was mandatory. Traditionally, when people were short of grain for food, they went after wild grain and other products. They fished, hunted, or just depended on milk and meat from their cows. With the modern market, grain became available in the shops of Arab traders and all one needed was cash, obtainable only by sale of cattle. Other things like clothes and salt were similarly available. As the prices of cattle were low and of consumer goods exorbitant, one family might sell several cows to pay the taxes, to survive a lean year, or to obtain other necessities. Soon after harvest, the Dinka, who never seem to plan for the future, would exchange grain for salt and other products, only to be sold the same grain when they ran short—and at excessive prices. So the Dinka tend to lose their cattle for little return.

With decrease in their wealth also came an increased need to migrate into the town or rural Arab areas for labour. Illiterate young men also saw in the modern market an opportunity to make independent wealth. Within the tribe, there was no paid labour, but more important, because of their intense pride, paid labour is seen as servility and is regarded as inappropriate for a gentleman; it must therefore be done far away from Dinka girls and in a country where it does not matter. As the saying goes, 'Honour, remain; indignity, let us go.' Which means in pursuit of something you pocket your pride in a foreign land. They do such jobs as cultivating Arab fields, drawing and distributing water, constructing roads, and building houses. They leave their fields at home to be cultivated by a few who produce just enough for subsistence and sometimes not even enough for that. The objective is always to make money fast and return. Consequently, they work hard, eat little to avoid spending money, but drink much to bring some pleasure to their otherwise miserable, unhealthy, and most degrading conditions. It is this group who, when they return, aim at buying cattle and controlling them independently of their families, but the marriages of their relatives or vicarious liability for such obligations, such as taxes or debts, often frustrate their plans. Some, after a few experiences, refuse to return.

The migration of youth is also abetted by the dwindling of the age-set system. As (among the Ngok at least) the Chief discourages initiation, the interval between one age-set and another increases, and, as the warring activities of youth become effectively curtailed, their vitality finds no outlet in the tribe. This is particularly so since the newly introduced operations on the roads, buildings, cultivations, and the like were abolished as forced labour. The warrior age-sets had come to regard them as part of their warrior activities in which age-sets competed.

Recently, migration has affected girls and families. Women are generally employed in homes under more comfortable and respectable conditions. Because of their intimacies with their employers, they are much more easily adapted to the new environment, and to the Dinka the result is often not as comfortable or respectable as it may seem. Dressed in Arab clothes and proficient in Arabic, not integrated into employing families, and therefore lacking supervision and cultural restraints, young girls grow up in an atmosphere of permissiveness and promiscuity. Whereas they came to acquire wealth to help their relatives subsist, and maybe buy cattle, they return worthless for marriage. Usually, there is their kind to marry them, but even then these are only 'limping' marriages.

All these changes have had, and continue to have, serious repercussions on the family. They undermine the family as the fundamental unit of society and the cohesiveness and the survival of the society itself is at stake. Children are going far away for education; education is suddenly questioning the validity of the old assumption of age stratification; there are no jobs to bring the children home after leaving school; traditional youths are also going into the cities for jobs; the modern and the traditional cultures are finding no encouragement for less painful integration; and the country is in a political upheaval which has also separated the educated from their backgrounds.

X

THE ROLE OF SONGS IN
DINKA SOCIETY

SONGS constitute an important and everyday aspect of life among the Dinka, and every Dinka sings both as an individual and as a member of a group. Songs are owned in the sense that every individual and every group has songs reflecting their particular situations and their ideas of what the social order is or ought to be. They may be composed by the owners themselves or for them by experts. Only the owner of a song may present it formally, but informally any person may sing any song almost any time and anywhere. A person may find entertainment in singing to himself while walking along the road, herding in the forest, or tethering the herds at home. During the season of cultivation, many people can be heard, each singing loudly in his own field. In the stillness of the night, a mother may be heard singing any song as a lullaby at the top of her voice.

To give some examples of the general significance of songs, the social structure, particularly territorial grouping, is reinforced by age-set group-spirit dramatized in initiation, warfare, and other age-set activities, which without songs would be barren. The concept of immortality through posterity receives a great deal of its support and implementation through songs. Singers not only give the genealogical accounts of their families, but also stress and dramatize those aspects which express their relevance to contemporary society. Young members of competitive families have been known to compose songs or have songs composed for them in reply to each other's allegations about incidents affecting the relative position of their families. In this process a young man may do a special investigation into the history of his family and of the tribe, to find additional evidence to sing about and bolster his family.

Unity and harmony as social ideals are frequently advocated in songs even as the singer boasts of his ability to use force against an opponent. In personal relationships among such a people, quarrels and disagreements are innumerable, inevitable, and often lasting. Songs are one way of modifying grievances by singing about them instead of brooding over them and making them worse. 'Fighting with songs', as one might put it, is, however, institutionalized, and goes beyond therapeutic singing. Apart from war songs which are presented in dancing, with mimed battle, there are age-set and other insult songs. Young men competing over girls fight with songs sung to others, but not face to face. The process may go on for months or years with new and more abusive songs being composed about the rival and his family. Such competitions usually end up in court, and the court may request that the songs be sung in court to determine the gravity of the insults, after which defamed elders may be appeased, conflict resolved, and reconciliation effected. The very idea of songs implies non-violent competition, whether such competition be merely in singing or combined with dancing, as these lines from a long ox song suggest:

> I, Mithiang, I may rush my songs
> But even if a man be a famous composer
> I can still defeat him;
> Those with whom our heads bang in competition.
> Even if a man be a famous composer
> I can still defeat him.

The idea of pacification through songs also applies to sub-age-sets and even to the warring territorial units which compete in war songs. War songs are more dramatic because they are presented in public dances in which the opposing groups may take part. It may be that a fight erupts once the existence of an insult song is known or during its presentation in a dance, but most dances are without incidents.

In the interest not only of social harmony, but also of each person's inner harmony, songs are used as a means of turning experiences which are painful, shameful, or otherwise undesirable into a subject of art which enhances one's inner pride and recognition by society. The indignities of prison life, traditionally unknown to the Dinka, the insult of rejection by a girl, or of divorce imposed on a loving partner, the misfortune of illness and maybe of disablement, and the misery of 'orphanage' (a condition which continues into adult life in the Dinka view) or of being without dependable relatives or friends are examples of themes which it is better to sing about than brood over.

Songs do more than that to achieve honour and dignity for the singers. The use of the word *dheeng* for singing and dancing indicates that these sensuous skills, both in their words of exaltation and in singing and dancing, are seen as essentially arts of grandeur in which a person does not have to excel to be exalted. In addition, they are established means towards winning recognition and enhancing one's social position.

Songs are also vital to Dinka family life as is evident in the continual reference to one's family as a group and as individuals. They uphold the ideals of the family even as they complain about their violation. Furthermore, they form part of the aesthetic skills which are often a basis for winning affection between young men and women, and for imploring elders to respond to the demands of the intending partners. They are also used by the partners themselves to influence each other in order to strengthen their hands against their opposing elders. Many are the cases in which marriages result from a song addressed to elders, the intended bride, or the groom.

The close relationship between singing and cattle and economy is evident throughout all types of Dinka songs. Disputes over cattle, suffering in the course of herding, contemplation and admiration of cattle, especially as symbolized by oxen, and pride in the cattle riches of one's family are some examples of the pervasive theme of cattle in Dinka songs. The age-set system is another institution which depends in a large measure on songs and related activities as exemplified especially by initiation songs, age-set insult songs, and war songs. In religion, songs and hymns are a means of communication with the spirits and the ancestors. By sublimating violent and otherwise destructive impulses, songs promote rectitude even though what is said in them would not be morally acceptable in a non-artistic context; they become accepted as art and are therefore not judged by the normal standards of decency and propriety.

Songs are also relevant to power and the legal process. Not only is the practical wielding of authority often justified or questioned in songs, but the ideals that govern the exercise of power are frequently invoked. Thus, in praising or criticizing certain trends, the ideals are upheld and reinforced.

Change can also be observed through songs. This is most conspicuous with respect to school songs, but it also exists in all types of song. In more traditional songs, or in songs by people who have not been particularly exposed to town life or other facets of modernity, reference to it is diffused and may not be obvious. But once a person has been exposed more intensely to foreign life, the impact on him becomes explicit in songs. Prisoners who have been sent to town and experienced modern instruments of power, men who have migrated to town for labour, or others in similar circumstances find it not only natural but also desirable to reflect their new circumstances in song.

To comprehend fully the functional significance of songs, it is necessary to go beyond their general reflection of the culture to know not only who sings what songs, but also what social position he holds. With the exception of songs which accompany religious rites, usually performed by elders or by specially inspired younger men, the singing group among the Dinka generally consists of young and middle-aged men and women. Older people who are particularly skilled may continue to compose, sing, and even dance, but the real meaning of song and dance would then be modified if not substantially altered. As the youths and women do not participate directly and to the same degree as senior men in the practical running of affairs, the aesthetic activities of singing and dancing, though primarily and normally engaged in by youth in any society, are also among the Dinka a means of making claims on the system and are a substitute for practical control.

Just as the elders are subordinate to God, other divinities, and ancestors, and must address themselves to them in hymns and religious songs, they are addressed by youths and women through 'secular' songs. This approach to superiors through songs explains something of the tone of criticism or complaint in hymns and other kinds of songs. Such criticism may be open and direct, or may be disguised and indirect. Because the overriding values of unity and harmony require deference to seniors, criticism of spiritual powers, as of the living elders, is always accompanied by praise for them. Even when criticism is directed against people other than the superiors or when the superiors are praised, the theme of discontent can still be found. A man glorifies the heritage of his family either because he feels that somehow it is not sufficiently recognized, or because his share in its advantages is insufficient.

Since young men are the most aggressive and disposed to violate the norms of society as defined by elders, they particularly use the peaceful outlet for dissatisfaction which I have already discussed as the function of songs. Furthermore, much of their vitality, which is potentially destructive to the system which subordinates them, is sublimated in their preoccupation with cattle, and the creativity centring around them. In particular, much of their potential aggressiveness and violence is satisfied through the bulls with which they identify. Young men sharpen the horns of their bulls and oxen, and while the castrated bulls, that is, oxen, are pivotal in the aesthetics of cattle and symbolize the opposite qualities of gentleness and submissiveness on the one hand and aggressiveness and physical courage on the other, all of which represent the personality traits of young men, they are praised mainly for their aggressiveness and physical courage even as men superficially criticize them. That oxen, though castrated, occupy such a highly important place among cattle sufficiently symbolizes the position of young men who, though subordinated to their elders, have a very high aesthetic value and gain satisfaction from the recognition of this in songs.

It may be judged from the following how songs, and such associated skills as dance, interact to give Dinka youth aesthetic pleasure and self-gratification, which minimize competition with their elders over power or wealth. The lines of the first two examples are *mioc*, that is, poetic chantings during dancing, and the last one is from an ox song:

> I am a brown gentleman wearing the beads of the chiefs,[1]
> I dance to drums and level my feet
> The girls of Abyor gather before me
> The wealth of Abyor gathers before me
>
> .   .   .   .   .
>
> When I dance to the drums[2]
> I do not dance with a girl who goes out of step
> The confused girl who disrupts harmony

[1] Ya Malual cieng bol e bany
Kac atoor aba cok ayit
Nyal Abyor thok ayan thok ayan
Giriic Abyor thok ayan thok ayan.
[2] Lines from song 28.

The bad [fisherman's] girl who lives on the river
I dance with a polished girl;
I am not simple at dancing to the drums
I am not simple
I am never challenged in our tribe
I cannot be pushed around at Akot [here at home]
I am respected as an officer.

In all its various forms Dinka dance is essentially a group activity
in which co-ordination of action is of the utmost importance. The
whole dancing group, and not the partners only, should be in full
harmony. The dancers jump up and down or stamp the ground at
exactly the same time, and, as the above song indicates, to be out
of step is to degrade one's self as a dancer. This co-ordination,
connected with the wider association of unity and harmony, is also
observable in group singing. Choral singing is one of the most
striking aspects of Dinka music. The power of a group song lies
largely in the chorus even though the role of the individual solo is a
pivotal one, showing that the significance of the individual is not
overshadowed by this group demonstration. The fact that there
are points in dancing when every individual chants his own *mioc*
shows the significance of songs and dance to the ego of each person. Even the group reference to 'I' indicates that group solidarity
is fundamentally a construction of individual egos.

Needless to say, singing and dancing are not the only substitutes
for practical action and practical power for Dinka youth. Such
sports as wrestling, racing, spearing, throwing the javelin, field
hockey, and other children's games like mock tribal wars are all
outlets for disruptive competition and aggression. In some tribes,
notably Bor, sports, and particularly wrestling, have a very formal
significance and involve the competition of settlements or segments.
Sports, like songs and dance, are indeed conceived by the Dinka as
elements of *dheeng*.

The Dinka are themselves aware of the 'compensational' function of these skills. A man is referred to as *alueeth* (liar), though in a
less derogatory sense than the word normally indicates, if he is not
particularly good at singing or dancing, or is not especially handsome or wealthy or objectively distinguished as an *adheng*, but puts
on an impressive show of being a good singer or dancer, bears
himself as though physically attractive, exaggerates his hospitality

as though wealthy, or acts in an excessive manner in any area where *dheeng* is involved. At the same time, a man who is distinguished in singing, dancing, or in any aesthetic field, and acts as though aware and proud of his distinction, is also referred to as *alueeth*. Every young man and woman is considered an *alueeth* by virtue of preoccupation with aesthetic values, and such an evaluation is not really a criticism to the Dinka. It is a critical praise which the Dinka regard as a compliment on the lines of the expression 'It's too good to be true.'

Composition of a song is seen in somewhat the same way. To compose a song is called 'to create' (*cak*); to tell a lie is to 'create words' (*cak wel*). *Cak* is also applied to creation by God. In all these meanings is a common denominator of making something which did not exist. In the case of songs, although there is an association with the usual exaggeration and distortion of incidents, the analogy is that they give young men and women positive values.

Dinka songs should therefore not be seen as abstract arrangements of words with a generalized meaning far removed from the particular circumstances of their origin. Songs everywhere constitute a form of communication which has its place in the social system, but among the Dinka their significance is more clearly marked in that they are based on actual, usually well-known events and are meant to influence people with regard to those events. This means that the owner whose interests are to be served by the songs, the facts giving rise to that song including the people involved, the objectives it seeks to attain whether overtly or subtly and whether directly or indirectly, all combine to give the song its functional force. This cannot be fully understood through the words alone whether spoken, sung, or, as is now possible, written. The words of the song, their metaphorical ingenuity, and their arrangement contribute to this force, but to appreciate the functional importance of the song, words must be combined with the melody, the rhythm, and the presentation of the song for a specific purpose.

Lienhardt writes:

When I used occasionally to read poetry and was asked what I was reading, I used to say I was reading songs; it was always asked then what *sort* of songs—prayers, war songs, courting songs, or songs for singing when accompanying a bull. Eventually I decided to call poems 'sitting songs' which at least suggested some sort of a purpose which they might serve ... I had great difficulty, even with people whom I had accustomed to the idea, to convey that words of a song could be separated from its music, for everyone is not thinking of the 'meaning' of what he sings, a meaning which could be paraphrased in some way.[1]

Even when a song is not written by the owner, it is shaped for his context. A man who desires the services of an expert provides him with detailed information about his situation and particularly the aspects he wants stressed. The glorious or glorified aspects of his lineal history, the relatives or friends he wants to praise and the reasons for doing so, the people he wants to criticize and the reasons for criticism are among the many details that are usually included in the background information. In the case of songs for groups such as war songs, the facts are often matters of general knowledge, but the age-set may wish to include certain incidents and personalities in previous wars, or ones which are connected with such wars but which may be unknown to the composer.

While an expert composes for others, people must be near him to memorize the song as it develops. The composer mumbles to himself, constructs a few lines, tells the people to 'hold this', and sings the lines. As he proceeds, they follow him. When a song is completed, the expert is likely to have forgotten it while they remember it in full. Assisting the composer by remembering a song in process is especially necessary when many songs must be composed in a short time, as is usually the case with initiation and 'cathartic' songs. It is unnecessary when composers create at leisure, as is generally true of ox songs. Only in 'cathartic' songs are the experts paid, and then very little. Several men may pay only a single cow to have an expert compose for each one of them. In a society which is the richest in cattle ownership in the country and in which bride-wealth sometimes goes beyond two hundred cows, such a fee is somewhat nominal. Dinka experts take pride and pleasure in their skill, and while it is by no means easy to compose, the mere fact that the songs they do compose play an effective part in the life of the people is almost sufficiently gratifying to them.

The total experience in a particular situation being what counts for the purpose of a song, logically unconnected ideas are fused together in a way difficult for an outsider to comprehend. In some cases, external logic is totally ignored; but to the Dinka, the

[1] 'Some African Poetry' (unpublished paper).

essential logic remains unaffected. An extreme example is in one of the initiation songs in which these lines appear:

> My right forehead with five
> My left forehead with five
> My head will carry twelve.

The composer and the singers must have been aware that five plus five equals ten and not twelve, but in Dinka twelve fits the rhythm better. Besides, among the Ngok, nobody has fewer than fourteen initiation marks, with seven on each side. Far from thinking it an error, no Ngok would take the song as even attempting to give a correct figure. The figures are chosen for rhythmical purposes.

Since most songs are retrospective, their influence is more likely to affect similar future situations than the ones about which they were composed. When people appraise judicial process in songs, and praise or condemn various judges according to their attitudes in particular cases, such songs, by honouring the allegedly good judge and embarrassing the bad one, could have an impact on future conduct of judges and could contribute to the judge's interest in reaching a consensus. The influence of songs may be more obvious, especially when a song is directed toward future events as when singing itself is a form of claim, or when a song is composed about a current event such as a marriage or a divorce which is taking place or has just taken place, but the final outcome of which the singer intends to effect. Whether as an unexpected consequence of composition and presentation, or as a result of a definite request by the singer, songs sometimes bring about immediate changes.

As part of the purposive quality of songs, there is a continuous reference to one's ancestors, relatives, and friends. Sometimes, these people are actually praised, but quite often they are simply mentioned. The singer's intention, though not expressed further, is to draw the attention of those mentioned or their interested relations and to dispose them towards him. This is considered an honour. Usually, and particularly among age-mates, a man whose name is mentioned in a singing performance responds with a *dip*, a short high-pitched song which, while saying nothing about happiness, is a demonstration of appreciation. In women's dances, a woman whose relatives are praised shows appreciation with a special cry of joy, known as *kieu*.

Similar to the mention of people is the insertion of ox names. This may be in the form of metaphoric ox names of people the singer wants to praise, but even more frequent is the insertion of the names of the singer's own oxen. It is to be remembered that oxen, or more appropriately 'personality oxen', of which a person may have more than one, represent the image of the owners, and the singer is of course very concerned with this image as the centre of his social relationships. Because of the multiplicity of the colours of the cattle among the Dinka and the possibility of one man's owning more than one personality ox, several names may thus be inserted at various places in a song. The reader is bound to be confused as to whether the singer is changing names for the same ox or praising different oxen. All this does not affect the central theme that it is he or other people he refers to through the ox names. A Dinka in the singer's social situation, the man towards whom communication is directed, would probably know which ox names refer to which of the people praised, which variations of colours refer to which oxen, and which oxen or metaphorical ox names belong to the singer. While a Dinka is capable of knowing all this, it is the total situation that counts the most.

In fulfilling their social functions, Dinka songs are remarkable in that they freely reveal things which are not normally spoken of. Such affairs as a man's sexual experience, or his observations of other people's sexual activities, are normally discussed only in the most intimate circles. The language of courtship is indirect, and rich with parables, sayings, and metaphors. Yet in songs one discusses a sexual experience with surprising candour and with no feeling of embarrassment. In everyday life, it is almost unheard of for a man to speak of his riches, praise himself, his father, or his lineage. Yet in songs it is often done and even exaggerated. Equivalent to this is the degree of freedom to complain without inviting conflict. Normally, a son very rarely criticizes his father, but in songs, even when a father has not neglected his paternal duties, a son will criticize him by alleging his father's failure to respond to his demands, and the father, far from being provoked, will attend to his son's request with enthusiasm. In their everyday life, a wife, especially when newly wed, is too shy even to mention her husband's name; in songs, she not only praises him in an exaggerated manner, but also identifies herself with him and refers to him as 'I'. The areas of candour are endless. By permitting such candour in songs, society provides a medium of 'freedom of speech' which is viewed as an artistic skill and minimizes the violation of the normal restrictions. It is also for the admiration of this artistic skill and the pride it gives the singer and his family that a father or any other relative who is praisingly criticized and implored to respond to the song ignores the criticism and enjoys the pride of praise and of the relative's skill.

Since the Dinka attempt in songs to reconstruct past situations they continually fuse past, present, and future tenses. In doing so, they vividly link the past with the present to dramatize them and increase their significance for the future. The fusion of tenses would also seem to be relevant to the Dinka conception of time in which the past is seen in continuous relationship with the present and as influencing the future, a phenomenon which makes the dead perpetually significant. This fusion of tenses does not apply to the use of tenses in normal speech.

Interestingly enough, the modern school system, while disregarding tradition and indeed working to eradicate it, utilized the purposive quality of Dinka songs to communicate its message or holy war against tradition, and in particular against Dinka religion. This figures very strongly in schoolchildren's songs, secular and religious.

The significance of songs not only as a mirror of Dinka social structure, but also of its dynamics, is obvious from the classification of songs, the social context in which songs are presented, and the wide range of activities connected with such presentation. Based largely but not exclusively on Ngok terminology the songs included here are classified into ox songs (*diet ke mior*); 'cathartic' songs (*diet ke waak*, literally songs of bathing); age-set insult songs (*diet ke ket*, literally songs of singing with 'singing' implying insulting); war songs (*diet ke tong* or *diet ke loor*, literally songs of spear— 'spear' also meaning war or songs of drum, 'drum' also meaning dance, that is, war dance); women's songs (*diet ke diar* or *diet ke tueeng*, literally songs of 'going to the front', that is women's dance in which the owner of a song or anyone goes to the centre, 'front', to lead the group in dancing to the song); songs from bed-time stories (*diet ke koor*, literally songs of the lion—because of the frequency of lions in these stories); children's play songs (*diet ke thueec*, literally songs of playing); hymns (*diet ke Nhialic*, or *diet ke yath*, literally songs of God or songs of spirits); and finally school songs (*diet ke gat*, literally songs of writing), or *diet k'agat wal* (songs of those who write), or *diet ke mith k'Abun* (songs of the children of the fathers, that is missionaries).

There is some logic in the order of presentation. Whereas ox songs and cathartic songs present a general picture of the social process, other categories are more specialized to certain cultural aspects. Women's songs are also somewhat general in nature, but as they represent the position of a distinct, largely subordinate, interest group, they have been presented separately after the presentation of the main features of the system. There is also another factor in the order of presentation. The ideals of the system, the glorification of oneself and one's lineage, pride, honour, and dignity, which justify such glorification, deference to one's fellow men which lays emphasis on restraint and persuasion rather than on aggressiveness and coercion, are represented to a certain extent by ox songs and cathartic songs. There is of course complaint in these songs, but such complaint invokes the ideals and alleged failure to conform. In the next three categories, initiation songs, age-set insult songs, and war songs, we see a spirit of physical courage, adventure, aggressiveness, and violence, which are measures for counteracting the negation of the ideals. Women's songs come next as a reflection of their subordinate position and their pursuit of happiness through identification with men. Hymns then follow to illustrate the conceptual link with the world of spirits. Children's songs are brought last not only to show the educational method of passing on the culture but as an introduction to the radical changes Dinka society has undergone and is undergoing through formal education. Under each category, songs which represent tradition are first presented, followed by those reflecting modern changes.

It was the intention to give a comprehensive picture of songs in Dinka society, but the field has not been exhausted. There may well be, and there probably are, other kinds of songs in other Dinka tribes which might not fall into any one of these categories. Even among the Ngok, there are miscellaneous types of songs or poetic expressions which have not been classified separately, mostly because they are often associated with other songs, or are sung in a context in which other songs are dominant. The few which have been included among them have been classified on the basis of content and the dominance of other types of songs. Thus songs of *dip* have been included as ox songs, and those of *door*, a short high-pitched war song used to arouse emotions in military or in peaceful group demonstrations, have been included under war songs, which they usually are, even when used in peaceful demonstrations. Those *door* songs which are initiation songs or women's age-set songs have been classified accordingly. There is also a special kind of song used for 'ox dance' (in which the arms are arched like ox's horns), which the Ngok received from the Rek and the Tuic, and which is known by the Ngok as *atoor*, *agaar*, or *dany* (note that the Rek and the Tuic call the women's dance *dany* and not *tueeng* as do the Ngok) and by the Tuic and the Rek as *loor* (the term used by the Ngok for war dances). These have not been included because in content they are identical with ox songs and among the Ngok the dance in which they are presented usually follows a war dance —so much so that it is considered one of its variants.

While groups of songs have names, Dinka identify songs not by title but by some descriptive or possessive terms. Thus an ox song is referred to by the ox about which it is composed. Cathartic songs, initiation songs, war songs, and women's songs are identified by reference to the individual or the group which owns them and their subject-matter, for example the war about which a war song was composed. In any particular context, a Dinka can identify a song whichever of the above or other methods he uses. Since relevant information on such methods of identification is lacking, and since they would be quite meaningless outside the specific context, it has been thought appropriate to invent titles for the individual songs. The titles are based largely on impressions about the songs, and are extracted or derived from the lines themselves. None the less, it is realized that they are not entirely representative. We have attempted to make the Dinka titles correspond to the English, but this has not always been possible.

Songs continue or cease to be significant, depending on the nature of their objective and the duration of the occasion of presentation. Generally speaking, individual songs, that is, ox songs, cathartic songs, initiation songs, and individual women's songs, as opposed to their age-set songs, are more limited in time than the collective songs. Ox songs and individual women's songs continue during the owner's life time, though the older one grows the less concerned with singing one becomes. When a man dies, strictly speaking, his songs die with him and should not be sung even informally. Cathartic songs, too, end once they have been formally presented to those for whom they are meant. The formal use of initiation songs by the initiated age-set ends with the termination of their status as 'initiates' upon their 'release' as fully-fledged adults. Age-set insult songs end once the older sub-age-set is fully replaced by the junior sub-age-set which then gets into competition with a new junior sub-age-set. War songs, hymns, and other kinds of songs on the other hand are unlimited and may be passed on from generation to generation in perpetuity.

The limitation in time illustrates the orientation of songs to people as members of a functioning society whose role must and does come to an end even as it continues immortally. However, there is a more classic dignity and significance in the older and longer-lasting songs. Thus, while there are famous singers whose songs are too difficult to learn or be remembered by the public, how popular a song is and how long it is remembered may in part indicate its quality. Even songs whose duration is otherwise limited, because the occasions for which they were composed have passed or because the owner is dead, can continue to be sung informally for a long time because of their classic quality. The emphasis given here to the functional significance of songs does not explain fully what it is that gives a song distinction. A person may have a very good cause to sing about, but his song may be bad. From the musical standpoint, the melody and the rhythm of the song, and the variation and the quality of the singer's voice, are important considerations. From the point of view of words, the intelligence of the song, its riches in symbolism, metaphor, and historical (often legendary) associations, are matters of great interest to a Dinka. That every song makes an attempt in this respect is obvious in the recurrent use of such terms of comparison as 'like' and 'as though'. Sometimes they are used as conjunctions into new themes or accounts, themselves indications of the singer's wide, often supportive, knowledge. A song lacking in imagery or associate literature is without depth or force. It is bad. Take this song for example:

> Our oxen are driven into the market
> Arob Allor has driven his curve-horned into the market
> His curve-horned Miyan
> And I will drive my Maper into the market:

My curve-horned Maper is bought by the Arabs
They paid in flying paper-money
Arob, what the Arabs have done
They have refused to give us coins
We took our oxen into the market
And the market became rich with oxen,
Then our cattle-camp remained without oxen
Abyor section has decided to sell oxen
Our section, Abyor,
If it spoils, it is ours
If it goes right, it is ours
Why is it not ours
Is it not our grandfather who carries the horns of the tribe?

These words have no inspiring effect on the reader, or for that
matter on the listener. The music and the singer's voice were
equally bad, and on this there was a consensus among all the Dinka
for whom I played the tape. Compare the words with the following
extracts from song 5, 'Rising Beauty':

Rising Beauty, Rising Beauty, born of the king of the wilds
If you reject man, you will be eaten
The Great Evil-Eyed coming from the wilds
The Black-Clouded One rises like a rain storm, brightens like a
    clearing sky
He is displaying his hump
My ox is displaying his narrow-waisted hump
The hump is twisting like a goitred neck
Staggering like a man who has gorged himself with liquor.
When he walks, the hump goes on twisting
Like a man travelling on a camel.

Or these lines from song 1, 'How Grow the Horns':

How grow the horns spreading!
How grow the horns sweeping the earth!
The horns of Mangar are straying
The horns of Mangar are straying like a lost man
The horns go to greet the things in the sky
The rafter-horned Jok, I call him 'the Breaker of Ropes'
The breaking ropes of the Flour-White One thunder-clap like
    shots on the rifle range

The trotting Curve-horned One has a voice like trumpets
And like the gourd of the wind . . .
On the back of my Mijok are four spots, close together
But they will never meet
They miss each other like the sun and the moon.

It is in the nature of songs describing oxen that they incite more ingenuity of imagery than may be true of songs which give accounts of events. But the blended tone of the bad song quoted above is far from representative of such songs. In these lines, for instance, the singer claims that he does not share in the indignities of gossip:

I have never gossiped with anyone
I have never been strangled by my words
May I die, I hate words that gentlemen say like the hiss of the
    spitting cobra
When the word of a gentleman is peeled like sugar cane
His honour is for ever gone.

A good song should move the audience toward its objectives. A war song must arouse a warlike spirit and a dance song must excite the dancers. If the objective of the song is to win sympathy in a sad situation, both the words and the music should be effectively sad. Compare these two songs by girls faced with a similar problem, breach of a promise to marry by their boy-friends:

Girls of the camp of Col
This man of mine is a man to whom I said my words;
We fused our words under a tree at Nyanmeer
My friend talked until he confessed
He spoke of the month when he would have cows;
Are the cows not yet found?
Why do you leave in silence
Why do you leave without telling me
Why don't you tell me thus:
'Ayan, Aciethyser, let yourself be married
Ayan, I am delaying your marriage'?
I have found the cowardice of a man who only talks
I shall walk but I shall look out in the road

I shall look out for the track of Guer
The track of light wood
And I shall hurry away.

My heart, do not remain perturbed
And twist your horns
It was you who pushed my head in the bush (of love)
If only I could pull you out to stand like a man
I would pound you with a pestle and burn you with fire
What about the beautiful thing which smelt like gee-oil at Mony-
      mau camp
Now I spend my nights vexing myself with a confounded heart
We have bestowed a curse on ourselves, O Kerieth of clan Pajok.

Another criterion is how amusing a song is. The ability to make
the audience laugh is particularly advantageous in setting competitions which are like joking competitions in which the person whose
insults receive the most laughter is the winner. Amusement in song
is derived from imagery and association which tend to ridicule
some person or thing. The singer may even make fun of himself
by relating accounts of his own experiences. Rarely, a song may
be such as will ridicule any person who happens to compete with
the singer. Since the song would have been composed long before
the competition, it is generally taken as funny and not particularly
insulting to the competitor. The following is an example of such
insulting lines:

How obstreperous the man is
The family of Mading are all galling
Including women and children
With a behaviour rough as a bad thatch
My ox beats the bell to make complaint
Like the ill-mannered women of the camp on the left
You with your shining [bald] head
A head as smooth as the tip of the tongue
Man, you will not defeat me [with your songs]
I have a few things to say [in my songs].

Of course, only a few songs combine the ingredients of a good
song. A song may be regarded as good because it is rich in metaphor,
knowledgeable in legends, touching in tone, hilarious in mirth, or

especially exciting for dance. What is lacking in words may be compensated for in music. The present volume presents only one aspect of the songs—words. Even words have lost much of their functional force from translation. While Part One of this volume has given a general sociological background, each class of songs is preceded with a brief discussion and analysis of its specific meaning and its social context in the hope of making more lucid the significance of songs as a mirror of society.

PART TWO · TRANSLATIONS

I

OX SONGS

Ox songs are usually about cattle in general and about oxen in particular; but the ox only provides a central theme for a variety of references. Among the Ngok, they ought to be composed by the owner, and if it is discovered that an ox song has been composed by somebody else it is considered very degrading. Exceptions to this rule are special types of ox songs adopted from the Tuic and the Rek Dinkas, composed by experts from these tribes and sung in their dialects. Though a man may continue to sing and even compose ox songs, the older he becomes the less involved he is in singing, so that only very distinguished composers and singers continue.

Each son in a household is allocated a colour-pattern (*kit*), according to the seniority of his mother and according to a known hierarchy of colour-patterns. For example, the eldest son of the first wife gets as one of his colour-patterns Majok or Mijok (Ngok), which is a black head and shoulders with a white flanking and either black or white hind quarters. When a bull-calf is born from a cow belonging to any member to the family, or when one comes to the family as bride-wealth, the son whose colour-pattern it is will lay claim to it. The colour-patterns are so intricate among the Dinka that frequent litigation centres on their determination. Although the allocation is determined by birth, it is officially effective only when a young man is initiated, when he really identifies and is identified with the ox of his colour. In addition to his personal name, he is known by the name of the colour-pattern of his ox, and also by the metaphorical names derived from it. The following are a few examples of metaphoric ox names: 'The

Victim of the Arabs' for a man whose ex-colour-pattern is that of the giraffe often hunted by Arabs; 'Pollen Grabber' for a man whose ox-colour is that of bees; 'The Dancing Head' after the colour-pattern of the crested crane which as the Dinka believe will dance and when sung to; 'Swimmer Over the Reeds' after the colour-pattern of the pelican; 'The Shining Stars' for a man whose ox-colour is a dark body spotted white; 'Ambusher of the Animals' after the colour-pattern of the lion; 'Respecter of the Cattle-byre' after the elephant which does not pursue its victims to the cattle-byre as does the lion or the hyena. There is no limit to such ox names, and, as the following collection of songs indicates, they are used in all kinds of songs to refer to men.[1] Thus the ox stands as a symbol for his owner and his social status. The shaping and the shading of his ox, the distinctive sound of its bellowing, the curve of its horns, which are trained from the animal's early age, are all qualities a Dinka extols, especially in songs.

The ox is usually decorated with tassels on its horns and a large bell hanging from a collar tied to the neck. A person may ask a girl to make tassels for his ox or to tan the collar-leather for the bell. These objects are delivered with ceremony. The girl is praised in subsequent songs. The piercing of the horns to make a hole for the tassels is also greatly celebrated and often described in the songs. How the ox sounds the bell and waves the tassels is a matter of pride. Sometimes, there are a detailed description and appraisal of natural phenomena resembling one's ox in colour and associations. For example, various birds may be described in praising oxen of their respective colours.

Ox songs are not about oxen only but include references to diverse social situations. For instance, a man may put his grievances in a song and seek the assistance of the chief, an elder, or even a possible sympathizer. Such appeal may take the form of 'begging', such as when the singer's personality ox has died and he needs a substitute. In ox songs, the family and the circle of friends are usually praised. In war songs young warriors present themselves as courageous aggressive bulls, buffaloes, lions, and the like; but

[1] As it has not been possible to translate all of them in the songs, many of them are left in the form of proper names. For more examples of metaphoric ox-names, see Evans-Pritchard, *Imagery in Ngok Dinka Cattle-Names*, B.S.O.S. (1934); also in Evans-Pritchard, *The Position of Women in Primitive Societies and Other Essays* (1965), 245.

in ox songs a man combines the courage and virility of a bull
with the gentleness and the submissiveness of an ox. He attacks
aggressiveness in his ox while expressing admiration for it and
will even sharpen the ox's horns for fighting with bulls and other
oxen.

Ox songs are formally presented in any one of several ways. They
are often sung in cattle-camps. In a cattle-camp there may be
thousands of cattle tethered in a large area within which are
hearths where men stay, and shelters or windbreaks for girls. In a
large camp several people may sing simultaneously but far enough
apart from each other for their voices not to conflict. The girls are
the ultimate judges of a singer's ability, though anyone can have
an influential opinion. A singer attracted to a particular girl may
stop his ox near her shelter until she 'releases' him, either by a
symbolic gift or by offering her friendship which may end in
marriage. Even if she is not herself the object of his immediate
interest, an admiring girl may also make such 'release'. In some
tribes 'release' is made by the girl's anointing the singer and the
uninitiated boy who leads the ox for him, and who is expected to
help out in singing should he lose his voice. We have already seen
that initiation entitles a man to compete in songs. Uninitiated
youths even though mature and good singers cannot participate
independently.

Ox songs may be sung in a sitting competition, at least among
the Ngok. Men gather with or without women on a social occasion
to compete either as individuals or as representatives of groups.
Where such competition is in front of women, they determine the
result: otherwise the male audience is the judge. Ox songs are also
sung while sitting to entertain, particularly the chief or the elders.
In the sitting performances, a man holds his hands up in imitation
of the horns of an ox, and moves his head and body in a way
suggesting the movements of an ox.

Ox songs are not accompanied with drums. When the singer is
accompanying his ox, the clanging of the bell and the bellowing of
the ox are taken as accompanying music. Where there is no ox, a
singer sometimes rings a bell and a companion will make sounds
to represent its bellowings, while sometimes high-pitched chanting
by the singer, his relatives, or friends adds to the accompaniment
of ox songs.

1. *How Grow the Horns* [Ngok]

This and the next two songs belong to one man, Maguith de Row. As my title for the first song indicates, they are about his oxen: the shape of their horns, the complexity of their colours, their bearing, their styles of bellowing, the chiming of their bells, and their aggressiveness. As is usual in ox songs, accounts of the singer's social position and his relationships are associated with the oxen.

How grow the horns spreading!   1
How grow the horns sweeping the earth!
The horns of Mangar are straying
The horns of Mangar are straying like a lost man
The horns go to greet the things in the sky.   5
The rafter-horned Jok, I call him 'The Breaker of Ropes',
The breaking ropes of the Flour-White one thunder-clap like
    shots on the rifle range.
The trotting Curve-Horned One has a voice like trumpets[1]
And like the gourd of the wind.[2]
Why my Mangar roars in the evening   10
Why my Mangar roars in the evening when the cattle are tethered
I do not know whether this will be a permanent way of bellowing
Or whether it is being gorged which rings the head of my father's
    Ngar
Like a man drunk with *aregi*.[3]
When the cattle return to the camp, his mouth is never quiet   15
He shouts like a man who is deaf
And in the evening when the cattle are tethered
He plays with a young cow, Mangar with a tight chest.
His voice thunders like Deng calling Abuk.[4]
Early in the morning when our cattle are freed in the *toc*   20
The fullness of the evening is over,
Mangar has not filled his skin with grass
And bellows faintly.

[1] Dinkas make trumpets with horns and gourds combined.
[2] As the wind blows into the opening of a gourd it plays a tune.
[3] A modern drink with very high alcoholic content, traditionally unknown to the Dinka.
[4] There is a correlation between the divinity Deng and the rain, also known as *deng*. Here thunder is metaphorically presented as Deng the divinity calling *Abuk*, a female divinity whom some Dinkas consider Deng's mother and others Deng's wife.

Our Pied ox is as light-footed as an ostrich
And as Mithiang de Pajok,   25
The man who overtakes the giraffe
And makes us smile with joy.[1]
Ahead of the cattle, my Spotted One in the lead,
Like a brave Nuer in front of a battle
He will never be overtaken,   30
Even if our cattle should mix with camels
Mangar will not be passed;
The Pied ox with legs as long as a man tires the oxen out
The oxen are worn out following Mangar;
He will not be reached   35
His feet clink as though wearing anklet bells
He tosses the tassels in front of the herds as though a wild beast.
On the back of my Mijok are four spots, close together,
But they will never meet,
They miss each other like the sun and the moon.   40
White and black
Skin worn by the Priests.[2]
Skin of the Men of Divinities
Skin of the Men of [Sacred] Spears,
I will pierce the tip of your horns,[3]   45
I am linking Makuac with the daughter of Bekrol[4]
The Egg-White Mijok is wearing the tassels of Nyanangeth;
I will pierce the horns of ten oxen
Porcupine,[5] Mangar, the feast for the piercing of your horns will
    be shared
Like the marriage feast[6] of a lean year,   50
It does not belong to one age-set,
I will not bore holes as our age-sets do nowadays,
Sneaking through the horns like raping a sleeping girl.
I will talk about it so that relatives will hear
And one day when I search my head[7]   55
The girls of the family of Aguen de Kur will bring yeast.

---

[1] As he thus makes meat available.
[2] Some religious functionaries wear leopard skins.
[3] To bore holes for tassels.
[4] From whom he requested tassels.
[5] His ox-colour-pattern is similar to that of porcupine quills.
[6] *Biol*, a special ox given to an age-set by the family of a bride-to-be, slaughtered in celebration of her marriage.   [7] Decide.

Mijok whose horns I will pierce one day
So that there be a flag of beer as in a drinking house.[1]
Some spectators will be with the flag
Others will watch my Makuac struggling with red-hot spears[2] 60
And my age-set will dance to the horns as in initiation.
Then, Mangar, side-striped, my name will be heard
As was my father's when he pierced horns with Matiok, striped
    on the neck.
Maker, a young man ceasing to milk[3] with nothing to give him
    fame,
Isn't it better for a man to steal and give him fame?[4]   65
Maker, a young man ceasing to milk with nothing to give him fame,
That is why I will hit the tip of his horns, daughter of Beekrol,
So that he may raise our names.
Angeth,[5] Angeth, daughter of Beng de Mading,
My Makuac shakes the tail of the buffalo as a monkey shakes
    sesame.   70
The Porcupine, when I praise him, I call him Jok Mangar;
Why I call him Jok Mangar,
There is one shade with which he supports the hump;
Here he is Maker and there he is Mangar,
Behind, he turns into Makuac,   75
And on the front he becomes Pied with a line across his shoulders,
Like the legendary cow the fox pulled out of the earth.
My Mijok breaks the ropes tied across his shoulders
Like a bull excited by cows.
It is because of Mangar that I walk in the bush;   80
My white Jok, I keep you with affection
Like a person breeding the hornless cow for another man.[6]
I hate a place where another man has hammered a peg
I hate it because he has used the grass
We like to settle in virgin lands.   85
Let us settle in Maker, let us settle.

---

[1] *Randai* (Arabic), a bar where beer is also brewed. The flag signals the avail-
ability of beer. Traditionally Dinkas freely shared any beer that they brewed.

[2] The horns are pierced with red-hot, unbarbed fishing spears.

[3] A Dinka symbol of maturity.

[4] Stealing is one of the worst and most shameful crimes to the Dinka. The
singer is of course being ironic and sarcastic.

[5] Shortened form of Nyanangeth, the girl who made tassels for his ox.

[6] Raising a girl to be married.

2. *Gathering Violence like a Rising Storm* [Ngok]

My Miyar has troubled us.   1
I say, 'Within three years
Even if your heart is as stout as mine
Miyar, you will abandon violence [and submit to me].'
Mangar is gathering violence like a gathering storm.   5
When I accepted the challenge [to subdue the ox]
I collected fibre¹ in the moonless part of March
And I soaked it into the river like a hyena hiding its prey.
I will not surrender, I will teach the Curve-Horned a lesson
I made the rope so that the skin peeled off my hands   10
Like the [skin on the] neck of the vulture.
I walked twisting myself like people carrying a tree-trunk for a drum
I accepted the challenge.
He is the ox for whom my father praised me
And said, 'It is not good for the ox of a gentleman to be unruly;
Now that he roams the cattle-camp   16
If he should become wild like a lioness
And like a rabid dog
He will make you hate the camp.'
And I said, 'Father, he is not unruly,   20
He is a gentle ox.'
My father said: 'Well, if you will smile
Call him not unruly, but he will make you hate the camp.'
The word of an elder is not futile
The word of my father has come true in one month   25
He has become exceedingly violent
So that I abandoned the camp as though it were that of strangers
I will not go to the camp
To struggle with the Shining One and the Rain
And when we struggle in the camp   30
White One, our grandfather, will hide life from us.²
The moon appears, the moon appears
Then the Flashing One of Deng,³ our grandfather, brightened the
    cows

¹ Dinka *tiam*, a plant from which Dinka make ropes.
² Rain (*deng*) is identified with the divinity, Deng, and referred to as 'grandfather'. Continuous rain and the problems of herding made them lean, hence
the metaphor of hiding life.
³ The moon, seen as a clan-divinity and as the son of the divinity Deng.

Mijok shines and the moon shines
Like ivory bangles, he attracts us. 35
The ox Ajok,[1] when the cattle are released
He walks in the bush, he does not walk in the open
He leads the cattle into the bush
Makuac is like a brave warrior
Who knows the weak spot that will break 40
And places himself close to the fight.
The Ngol of Kur Luak is ripe with grain
And our oxen grew fat
Like the fish of the fox fed with fruits.[2]
The great land of Kwot the Crested Crane 45
He cleared like the land for a shrine of sacrifice
So that his hump stood high [from feeding].
Mangar of my father, we have found the land for cattle
Mijok spent the winter at Pabur
Our oxen with millet 50
Our oxen love millet and millet has called our oxen.
In our camp, Mangar of Tong d'Ajing
I have never gossiped with anyone
I have never been strangled by my words.[3]
May I die, I hate words that gentlemen say like the hiss of the
    spitting Cobra[4] 55
When the word of a gentleman is peeled like sugar cane[5]
His honour is for ever gone.
With the appearance of the Morning Star
Miyom of Ngor of Aguek asks me
'Why haven't the cattle been milked?' 60
And I answer, 'They will be milked.'
The ropes are tied to the necks of our cattle[6]
And the oxen became quiet like sheep
Mijok, the ropes are tied to the necks of our cattle.
At dawn, O Mangar d'Ajak 65
That is when I tie the bell made by Ajuong.[7]

[1] Another word for *Mijok*, normally applied to cows.
[2] In a legend the fox feeds a fish in order to eat it later. The lion comes and takes the fish. Through some ingenious plan, the fox recovers the fish as it is cooking and puts in its place a baby lion.
[3] Lowering one's voice in gossip.
[4] Murmuring in gossip.   [5] When discovered to have lied.
[6] A practice by which cattle carry their ropes when the camp moves.
[7] The Malual, an iron-working tribe.

He is the great one who has smoothed the bell like clearing a field
He has never been out of harmony with the bell.
He attracts us like a new bride.
The voice of my White One is like that of a lion and the hummer-
    headed stork.
Gentlemen will stop milking[1]   71
Gentlemen will go to spend the winter at Bulei
Gentlemen will go to spend the winter at Ngol.
They say Mangar is not for a younger man
He is for an older man   75
But I will not leave him
Am I not the older man?
Did I not breed him myself?
Was not an older man once a younger man?
And will not a younger man one day become an older man?   80

3. *Bells sing to Mijok* [Ngok]

He sways the bell made by Jur Col[2]
My Mangar broke the bell and cut the collar
We are mourning over broken things;
The bell is broken
If Kwol[3] hears   5
Will he not be annoyed?
Akuei, Miyom, Kwol
Brothers born following one another are like twins;
What will he say?
Kwol heard me and fainted with laughter,   10
'Why, if your Akuac has broken the bell
And cut the collar
It is our common honour.'
He pierces the eyes of the bell like the spell of a medicine man[4]
The man who pierces the eyes of men.   15

    [1] Coming of age.
    [2] A non-Dinka tribe in Bahr El Ghazal Province that specializes in iron-work.
Here used to refer to a Dinka tribe in the same Province that also does iron-work.
They are called *jur* because Dinkas do not normally do iron-work.
    [3] His brother who lent him the bell.
    [4] Magicians make figures out of mud to represent their victims and then
symbolically pierce their eyes. This is then believed to affect the eyes of their
real victim.

He is Mabok on whom the bells will leave a curse
He is Mijok who will be cursed by the skills of the Jur of
    Abyem[1]
He tolls the bells of the Rek of Abyem as his father did
He beat it as his father did so that the iron cried,
Bells sing lullabies to Mijok as though he were a child.   20
In our camp, my father and I cluster the Decorated One[2]
My father had his side
And I had my side where I guard Makuac
At that time of the night when young men wander.[3]
Should anyone touch him   25
My father, Mangar of Jok, will rise like a storm
And like a rainbow reaching the sky from a dusty pool.
My father, Ngar de Jak, never leaves cows
He is like the cattle egret with cows
And I am also like the cattle egret with cows.   30
He is Mangar for whom my father has spoilt me
Has not my father spoilt me?
My father Mangar de Deng d'Ajak Teem
My father Row has surrounded his hearth with shining blade and
    white cattle[4]
My Mijok looks as though he were dressed in paper.   35
Mijok gazes at the winter grass
The Curve-Horned wakes up in doubt
Like gentlemen herding cattle in the *toc*[5]
Where the man with a greedy heart remains in doubt
Believing he has not received his share.   40
The Decorated One despises the *toc* where people behave like wild
    dogs
The *toc* where words are cheap.
He shakes his horse-tail tassels
And freely kicks his limbs

[1] The iron-working tribe who make bells.
[2] It is unclear whether he means that he and his father have oxen of similar colour-pattern with which they surround themselves or whether they surrounded the ox with cows. The latter is probable.
[3] To seize cattle by stealth, usually by way of self-help in execution of a debt.
[4] Dinka, *rial*.
[5] Young men and women go to grazing areas too distant for grain to be carried in sufficient quantities. Hunger for food made from grain is therefore a usual characteristic of this period. Milk may also be short as cows tend to dry up at the same time and some are needed for children and older people at home.

With a head heavy as that of durra[1]   45
And as the hair of a woman of Ruweng[2]
Dancing with a make-up of red ashes.
People are amazed by the growth of the horns of Atuot.[3]
I have bred Mangar to accept old age.
In the land of Deng d'Aguer   50
Mangar has accepted old age.
Tassels are tassels, but each man shows his skills
Tassels are tassels, but mine is the skill of the son of Minyiel.
I run after happiness like the legendary Kur Luak[4]
The man who wanted our girl in marriage   55
The girl was married in the big camp of the Nuer
When a hundred cows were released, but Kwot[5] refused
When a hundred cows were brought, Kwot refused;
Kwot refused, but said: 'If you insist
Let a cow with two tails be brought to me.'   60
When a gentleman courts a radiant girl
He does not tire, he returns,
He came with a cow whose tails were two
But Kwot refused: 'I will take them both
The one hundred cows and my daughter.'   65
Kwot was pleaded with like the ancient chiefs.
My grandfather's courage nearly killed him.[6]
My grandfather crossed a river with an unhollowed boat
He reached the other side on an unhollowed boat
My grandfather, Malual the chief, crossed at Nyideng   70
He reached the other side of Nyideng.
The bull, Mading d'Aguer, Kur
Has now borne me a grandfather, Mijak who swims across the rivers.[7]
My grandfather left my father
And my father has borne us   75

---

[1] Sorghum.

[2] A Dinka tribe in Upper Nile Province who wear their hair long.

[3] A bull or a cow with long horns; named after the Dinka tribe, Atuot, from which long-horned cattle presumably originated.

[4] From this line, the singer does what Dinkas often do, namely, cites incidents in their lineage's history even though their relevance may not be direct.

[5] The singer's hero ancestor in the story.

[6] A new story is introduced here.

[7] The singer's ox has a colour-pattern resembling that of the pelican. Here, the ox is referred to as 'grandfather' because the pelican swims as did the singer's ancestor in the story.

My father, Mangar Jak de Paweny, has borne us.
During the old days when words flowed one way,
Like words heard by fish[1]
A man who had disputed a cow with my father
Slept wondering how Row would respond the next day. 80
Mangar de Jang d'Aguer
My father, Row, attacks with two horns
Like Maleng de Lual Amiek[2]
It is like my father, the son of Gitbong
The man who owns Mijok with three colours 85
Mijok whose shades are cut off from one another like the isolated
  home of a greedy man.
Mangar grazes with a collar and rings on his neck
And with tassels which I made.
When our cattle come to the camp
My Mangar comes in the lead 90
Like a cow going with a bull.
Mangar has captured the camp from the bull
He has captured the camp from the sacred bull of the sons of
  Pabong clan
The bull of the sons of 'the Pied Pattern'.
Because of the Egg-White Jok, my father praises me 95
Like the son of a woman whom she calls 'darling'.[3]
Mijok attracts us like the birds of the town.[4]

4. *The Pool blew with the Wind* [Ngok]

The singer's ox-colour-patterns are Mijok, which resembles the colour
of the goose, and Mijak, which resembles that of the pelican. The song
is mostly about these birds and particularly the pelican, whose life is
described in detail.

The pool blows with the wind
The camp of Malual slept away.
He[5] drank salt water at Mithiang Noon.[6]

[1] Fish follow in one direction, and are thus symbolic of harmonious relations,
but the singer believes that harmony among young warriors traditionally depended on fear of retaliation.
[2] A small insect believed both to bite with its mouth and to sting with its tail.
[3] *Aguen*, an affectionate word used by women to call little children.
[4] Pets.   [5] The singer's ox.   [6] A grazing area.

Mijok roared in the camp of Lual.[1]
'Shaker of the chiefs',[2] of Minyiel of clan Payaath,   5
The dust-storm you see rising far
It's the goose on the move.
Agurbiong,[3] throw your spears into the war[4]
The pelican is piercing the eyes of the fish
The fry of the Nile perch are bubbling;   10
The pelican is piercing the eyes of the fish
And the fry of the perch are bubbling.
The grey pelican has glasses on his eyes.[5]
The teeth of the balloon-fish are exposed
The pelican has stuffed him with grass.   15
Hopelessly rolling on the ground
He is the ball of the schoolboys[6]
The schoolboys of the pelicans.
He begins the attack heading for the reeds
Begins the attack heading for the river Lol   20
And proudly displays his sharpened sword.[7]
During the winter breeze, he lies on the shore holding his sword
Frightening the people[8] with his sword.
A mighty one who when he swims
The river Lol bubbles with racing minnows   25
And *adhidhob*[9] also bubbles in the race.
And when the sun reappears
They descend at Manluel.[10]
Beware people, there comes an attack
With wings heavy and wide-spread   30
The spears of the wings pointed and spreading
With spears like the horns of the cows of the Falata[11]

[1] The Chief.
[2] The horse. The Dinka consider brown with a white spot on the head (*Miyom*) as the usual colour of horses, and horses are often owned by chiefs. The term 'Shaker of the chiefs' is the metaphoric ox name of a man whose ox is *Miyom*.   [3] The pelican.
[4] The fishing of the pelican is presented as a war between the pelican and the fishes.
[5] Probably referring to the protective mechanism of the pelican's eyes in the water.
[6] Ball is associated with football (soccer) introduced to the Dinka through schools.   [7] The beak of the pelican.
[8] The fish.   [9] A type of fish.   [10] Another area.
[11] A nomadic cattle-owning tribe who migrate from Nigeria into the Sudan in search of grazings. Their herds have long horns.

And the cows of the Nuer
Brought by my grandfather of the River Clan.[1]
The Great One whose horns have grown exceedingly high   35
Like the poles on which the Government hangs people
The poles of the judge
With which he is finishing the people in the South.[2]
My Mijok, I have trapped you with a rope of wire from a ship
Ghaau,[3] he splintered his peg.   40
Hit the bulls of Malual Noon
Throw the peg in their eyes
Like the ancient war between Abyor and Mannyuar[4]
When you pulled the roots of a tree from the ground.[5]
He pulled the roots of a tree from the ground.   45
Mijok with curved horns has a face black like a hip.[6]
My white ox is dying of valour
With eyes glowing like the building of burnt bricks
And like the day the army rose
With eyes like the fire with which the army rose.   50
The Hoe-mouthed has moved to the bank of the river
Carrying an axe sharpened by the green pelican
He has cut the tail of a fish
He cut the tail like a slaughtered beast disputed by age-sets[7]
The older ones are fighting over young girls with shining breasts
The bigger ones are fighting over the young girls [of the fish]   55
Songs of war are booming in the river Pathieu
The river Pathieu is attacked
And dust covered the sun.
He is daring as the white lion which pulled the cows   60
When the world was spoilt at the camp of Rakayan

[1] Some clans were founded by people who performed miracles or heroic deeds in some way connected with the river. These call themselves River clans.

[2] Here the singer is alluding to the South–North problem even though presumably uninformed about it.

[3] The sound of a breaking peg.

[4] The dominant sub-tribes of the Ngok, one, Abyor, providing the Head Chief, and the other providing a rival assistant. The two are among the major warring units.

[5] The link with the war is unclear except to symbolize the haste of moving the cattle to protect them from being captured by the enemy.

[6] As Dinkas sleep on hard surfaces, the point of the hip is usually rougher and darker than the rest of the body.

[7] In which people cut off parts of the slaughtered beast even before it is skinned.

He broke the fence at the camp of Rakayan
The camp of Dinbil
The camp has remained with Nyok, the Carrier of the Crest.[1]
Carrier of the Crest, our chief Timbek Miyar   65
We were pushed back on the brink of the meadows.
I remained, wandering in the forest like the chick of a bustard.
Friend, Magak of Amacbeek,
A war in which shields pierce is coming in the morning.
My black-faced one whose horns are curved into a circle   70
Mijok has twisted his horns
With horns tilted on the river Lol of Jekeny[2]
The great one is like the fishing Jur[3] with their canoes
The people who race with the mother of the hippo
The land of Juk[4] has fattened Ajak[5] to be smooth.   75
Burnt grass runs with Yom[6] in the wilderness of Mithiang Noon
Until he ends the chase in the land of Kondok.
Tomorrow we shall proceed to the *toc*
And the Tuic said they would stop our herds.
Orders are strict   80
The men with feather hats[7] are displaying their guns.
We are stopped
Great Wek, Great Wek[8]
Great Wek Agoth has forbidden us the *toc*.
The horses of the brown ones[9] have reached Alal   85
The herds of Ali Nimr[10] flock like sheep together
The herds of the Arabs rampage like sheep together
They have reached Alal.
I told Marial of Dhiendior
Son of the clan of Col   90
Our move is prolonged
We hammered our pegs under a mahogany tree
The camp of Deng, Pelicans—Gather, has moved,
Mijok rises in a heap like a hill
I hammer pegs in areas of good grass   95

---

[1] The crested crane. Nyok's ox has a colour-pattern resembling that of the crested crane.   [2] A Nuer tribe.
[3] A riverine people who hunt the hippopotamus and other river creatures.
[4] Chief of a tribe of the Tuic.
[5] The singer's ox.   [6] Another name for his ox.
[7] The soldiers in their uniform.   [8] A Rek chief.
[9] The Arabs.   [10] Baggara Arab chief.

Miyom Akiec says that the calves are tired
My Mijok has made the pace
And covered the sun with dust
Like the horses of the Baggaras.
I, Mithiang, I may rush my songs   100
But even if a man be a famous composer,
I can defeat him;
Those with whom our heads bang in competition
Even if a man be a famous composer,
I can defeat him.   105
The Ngok have tied the Tuic with a rope they will never break
A rope that has disappeared from sight[1]
A rope covered like a trap for doves.
His head[2] is white like the animal which grows horns in the place
      of teeth
The elephant grows his horns in his mouth   110
My Mijok has grown his horns in his mouth.
His bell chimed in the river of the Nuer.
The ancient greed of the cows of the North
They have mixed with the cows of the South
And the cries of war arose.   115
The sun was covered with black dust
And when it reappeared
It shone again, and spears rattled.
The soldiers of the Tuic ran to the scene
The Nuer have waged a war   120
Nowhere for a flank to pass
The land was covered with clubs.
Unpeg our herds
Don't you hear war-songs have reached Malual
Have they not reached Malual Adenydou?   125
The camp of Nyuol Gitbong moved in the heat of the sun
The attack has appeared like a lion
War is bad
Many are pulling out of the battle.

[1] The idea is that the Ngok leadership has dominated the Tuic in a clever way the Tuic do not notice.

[2] His ox's.

5. *Rising Beauty* [Ngok]

Rising Beauty, Rising Beauty, born by the king of the wilds[1]
If you reject men, you will be eaten[2]
The Great Evil-Eyed coming from the wilds
His eyes glow as he eats a man.[3]
The Back-clouded One rises like a rain storm, brightens like a clear-
　ing sky.
He is displaying his hump   6
My ox is displaying his narrow-waisted hump
The hump is twisting like a goitred neck
Staggering like a man who has gorged himself with liquor.
When he walks, the hump goes on twisting   10
Like a man travelling on a camel
His hump shakes like a man on a camel,
Grey One of my grandfather, Arob d'Ajuong
Your hump has fallen.
Deng de Kwol d'Arob de Biong,   15
Is like the Creator at the head of the tribe
While I sing over my antelope, Malith.
He roars in the evening with a greedy heart
The curve-horned ox roars while the cattle are tethered.
In the camp of my grandfather, Ajong de Col   20
I sing over an ox with a dark-brown body,
His horns have grown as long as the thorn of *peth*.[4]
Malith has a heart like a buffalo
When he sees a cow mounted, rattles with a breaking peg
Maleng de Yak and I are age-mates   25
Tuong Awith, Malek of the clan of Jador
When cattle move to the *toc*
Malith grazes on grass as delicate as a ripening girl
Whose sight attracts people and gives them joy.
When he bellows, his voice descends on the ground   30
Like the thundering of a morning rain.
My Athieng is as black as the darkness of the night
Gingerly he places his feet like a girl wearing coils on her legs,

---

[1] His ox-colour resembles that of the lion.
[2] The ox is here conceived as an ox and is warned against lions if he is unruly
and uncontainable.
[3] Back to the metaphor of the ox seen as a lion.
[4] A large tree with long thorns.

Malith lifts bulls from the ground
He hides behind the cows of the camp of Cuor   35
He falls on a bull
And the bulls roar as though a lion has jumped on a cow.
The girl named after my grandmother, mother of Deng de Bong,
Her conduct[1] is as good as that of the ancient Dinka
She brought me great Malith[2] with an expanded body   40
Like the great animal
Elephant, beware
You are at war with the brown Arab.
Is it true, have I seen what it is to be an orphan?
Is maturity a bad thing   45
That I have found the sadness of an orphan?
My father left me with the daughters of my mother
And there was a girl who ill-treated[3] me.
For the sake of Malith, I have given up the words of the land[4]
He will not be lost for ever   50
Like the ancient camp for which spears were fixed
And which was sought with fire at night.[5]
The sister who is the oldest of us
Will not go away[6]
Without a brown ox like the brown hippo in the river;[7]   55
I am keeping animals
I am keeping a buffalo and an animal of the river
The brown one with a shimmering back.
He has cleared the *toc*
He cuts the grass and swallows it   60
As a python swallows its prey,
He munches the crisp re-growth making his mouth stink
Like a man chewing onions
A clan head without hope.[8]

---

[1] Manners, conduct, behaviour; Dinka, *cieng*.
[2] Through marriage. Conduct of the girl is important not only for the marriage as such but in determining which individual cattle should be given to her relatives as bride-wealth.   [3] *Kuoc Cieng*
[4] He quarrelled with others who wanted Malith.
[5] So determined were the people to capture or regain the camp that they attacked at night carrying fire with which to see. Dinka wars are normally fought during the day. The singer is as determined to regain his ox as those warriors were to get the camp.   [6] In marriage.   [7] In her bride-wealth.
[8] A clan-head who is alleged to have nothing in town but onions to eat, part of the deprivations of their limited power.

Mother of Wor, Mother of Wor, Mijok   65
Never have I found so daring a woman
She ventured to sell the ox of a gentleman,
What evils the market has brought into the land
That a man breeds the ox of his pride
Then comes a woman and wants him for sale;   70
For Malith, I have refused
I redeemed him from the mother of Dau with a black ox
That year[1]
Then I redeemed him from a wrong I had done[2]
That year   75
And I stopped him from being slaughtered for Nyannuer's wrong[3]
That year
I clear [away problems concerning] the ox like separating the shell
    from the kernel
He will remain in our sacred camp
Relatives who hate me will say   80
'Lual has become a wild lion.'

6. *Mithiang roars like a Lion* [Ngok]

The singer's ox was illegally seized in self-help and taken away to Arabland. Pleading with the chief to help him get his ox back, he wonders how
such a thing could happen in a country under the rule of law. The chief
sent a court order to the Arab authorities for the arrest of the wrongdoer and his return with the ox. The singer himself, also carrying a court
order, went to Arabland in search of the culprit. As is usual in ox songs,
the theme wanders into other areas with the ox as the focal point.

I have a great tawny yellowish ox which bellows like an ostrich
I have a great dark brown ox which roars like a lion
I will ask the Great Chief
'Chief,[4] governor of the land,

    [1] The focus on 'That year' here and later is significant. The year was a year of
famine in which people against whom wrongs were committed or people who
had legitimate kinship claims were particularly adamant. The stress on the year
is a polite way of insulting them.
    [2] The tone implies that he had impregnated a girl, an offence for which re-
dress was claimed.
    [3] When a member of an age-set, male or female, commits a wrong judged
disgraceful to the set, the set slaughters his favourite personality ox or, in the case
of a girl, the ox of her closest agnate as a punitive measure.
    [4] Arabic *Nazir* used in the Dinka text.

Should a man be robbed in a land which is not spoilt?'[1]   5
A man has robbed the gentleman of Marial of Ker.
I rose in the early morning like an invading army
I will ride in the car of Ali[2]
I shall depend on God
I slept on the way   10
Next morning, we met in the court.
He is my old one, my ancient one,
'Your ancient one?
Then what do you call him?'
'Is he not Mithiang and Miyan?'   15
I have Malou and Miyan and Malou[3]
My Malou which my father gave me
The ox of pride, brought by good-hearted Awut of my father[4]
He beats the bell with an iron rod from a steamer
Mithiang, if you do not ring it well, we shall be mocked.   20
Visitors standing on the way ask me
'From where did you get your Malou?'
I got him from the house of Awut of my father
Even if his eyes are rheumy[5]
I got him from the house of Awut of my father.   25
I have sent a message like the telephone after Mabeek[6]
It has gone as far as Arab land
My ox, if you should meet with the writing of the government[7]
The writing of the girls of the government[8]
Then hurry in returning home.[9]   30
How can I miss
When I have acquired a curve-horned ox
The mighty ox who roars?
The camp of the Tuic is moving
The camp of Bol Col[10]   35
The camp of Bol Aturjok[11] is moving to Ameth.

[1] Standard usage for the nineteenth-century upheavals caused by wars of slavery and the Mahdist revolution.   [2] An Arab merchant, al-Abyei.
[3] Presumably several oxen rather than several patterns.
[4] Being well-mannered, Awut attracted high-quality bride-wealth.
[5] Even if he should look unattractive to other people.
[6] Reference here is to the chief's written order tracing the wrongdoer.
[7] Should the culprit be found with the ox.
[8] The Ngok apply the term *gat* both to the design of gourds and calabashes by girls and to writing.   [9] He would then be returned.
[10] Chief of a sub-tribe of the Tuic.   [11] Bol's praise-name.

Spending the summer without shelter does not hurt him.
He becomes huge as a *tebeldi* tree[1]
The ox gazed at me with penetrating eyes
And when I rose and took my spears,   40
He began[2] leading the way.
The Great One walked swaying his haunches
Like the girls who live on the river Alal.
I do not listen to the words of gossipers
I hold my head above gossipers   45
Like a rooster denied the news of a moving camp.

7. *Bellow, my Ayaau* [Ngok]

Pagol of my father,[3] give me the tassels to honour Ayaau[4]
Give me the tassels to honour Ayaau
My age-mate, give me the tassels to present to Ayaau.
Beek[5] is now perfect
Rol[6] looks as though created with the ornaments he wears.   5
Marol de Deng, please carry the bell
He pulls it to his chest when he sees the bull, Mijok.
When the cattle are released in the camp of Thoor
Beek returns to the camp harassing a cow
Marol is preventing the cows from being served.   10
Even if grazing is as far as Mading,
I will go, I will not remain
I will sharpen your horns.
You confronted the bull of Deng Col
So I woke Mangar of my father,   15
'Deng, get up, we have to move again.'
He threw himself into the river of the son of the Crested Crane
And Beek groaned like a man with a hurting hand
Agany, son of my father, Marol anxiously twists his neck.
What I say is the same as what Malou says   20
And what Malou says is the same as what I say
We arranged to move without consulting the Roaring Leopard;[7]
Moving to the spring camps does not attract many men.

---

[1] A tree so large that the Arabs store water for the dry season in it.
[2] To graze.   [3] His half-brother.   [4] His ox.
[5] The same ox.   [6] The same ox.
[7] Presumably an elder who would have objected.

The camp is segregated like the age-sets of children[1]
Awet and Mannyuar will take the *toc* of Anyiel   25
And Beek will keep his ancient *toc*.
And why run flashing between things
With a bulging stomach
Like the gentleman frog chased by a snake?
In search of grass we went to the *toc* during the moonless part of
  June   30
Why is it so far as our Father Madhol above?[2]
He made me say the name of the divinity of Bol
I nearly felt like spearing him with a spear made by Amath
To be speared the second time by Mithiang, the Helper of the
  Calves
The season would be as short as a forest of food[3]   35
And the world would be clear like dawn.[4]
I exclaimed, 'Brown One with which my father has made me a
  bull'[5]
And when we go to dance, I shall chant[6]
'Wa Yee Ye Wa Yee
Beek is wearing the tassels   40
Yee
The hippo has lost the tassels
Yee
The hippo has broken the tassels
Go, tassels of Mijok of the Father of Kon';   45
The Great One runs like an ox driven to Nuerland.
What evils can come from herding far!
It has closed my throat like mumps
My eyes shut as though I were losing breath,
I relied on the daughter of Deng de Maker on the way;[7] 50
I filled the spoon the way the Arabs do
Even if a man should insult me
'Why does he fill the spoon
As though he had never had enough to fill a spoon?'

  [1] Children's age-sets are determined by courage and fighting skills. Distant
cattle-camps are known for their hardships.
  [2] God symbolized by the sky.
  [3] An irony. If he had killed his ox, there would be plenty of food in the *toc*.
Ṭ̣e journey through a forest seems short when there is plenty of food.
T [4] The Dinka liken the ending of famine to dawn.
    His *mioc*.   [6] Dinka, *mioc*.   [7] To provide him with food.
5

I will brush it aside like a fly;   55
What evils one meets in the *toc*
The age-set split like the river of Acueng[1]
My curve-horned nearly provoked a fight.[2]
We cut through the *toc* like Ayaau
And Beek groaned like a man with a hurting hand   60
We found the burnt grass sprouting.[3]
My Marol trots
Like a Tuic going to buy grain
Whom the Arab insults, '*Naal abuk*'
And he says, 'O Mijong Akuur   65
The Arab knows Abung e Mawien.'[4]
The Ox with a curved mouth
Like the teeth of a buck-toothed man
With which he bites his food.
In the future, when I grow old   70
So that only my heart will dance with my age-mates
I will chant, 'Bellow my Ayaau, bellow my Ayaau!
The great ox who tosses the tassels!'
The black foreigner[5] groans like a cooking pot.
The daughter of Kiec has a determined heart   75
She let the leather of the hippo boil all day
Like the stone of the son of Angau.[6]
She put it to the left side of the house
Where the rats remain hiding,
When a rat bit the leather, its teeth broke   80
When he attempted it with his feet, his feet broke
Then he lay like Miyom with a diseased leg.

[1] People became divided and selfish because there was insufficient food available.
[2] His ox took him to the camp where a fight almost occurred.
[3] The Dinka burn off dead grass to make it grow again.
[4] *Naal abuk* is Arabic for 'cursed be your father'. The Ngok say that the Tuic know no Arabic and are continually abused by Arab traders. This is part of the Ngok myth. The Tuic is delighted to hear the Arab speaking of his mother, Abuk.
[5] The bell is called *jur col* because it was made by Jur Col tribe.
[6] Ngor d'Angau owned the ritual pot and stone for trial by ordeal. According to the trial, now prohibited, the stone was put into a pot of butter which was then boiled all day to make it very hot indeed. In an elaborate ceremony of invocation and hymn-singing, the disputants were asked to take the stone from the boiling butter in the belief that only the guilty one would be burnt. Here, the girl praised boiled the leather in order to make a bell-collar for the singer's ox.

Ageeng, sharpen the knife
Left-handed girl, sharpen the knife
Sharpen the knife then cut the collar's tail,   85
When the collar meets with the Grey of the Bush
The sound of the bell will cover the land.
In our camp, *Beek*[1] has known me
Even if born by a dog, *Beek* has known me
Even if born by a goat, *Beek* has known me   90
Even if brought by a girl,[2] *Beek* has known me.
I threw stones at the Big Bellied of Mijong de Bong[3]
And said, 'Gentleman with tassels on the legs, move away.'
The tassel was oiled and hung by the daughter of Kiec, the Crested
    Crane
The vulture looked around and licked it   95
I threw stones at him and said,
'You with your goitered neck,
In ancient times, did you not eat your Yom[4] with your maternal
    uncle, the Hyena?
Or do you want other people to make butter for you?'
Species with hearts as greedy as the pigsty.   100
The fox, the fox, is their hawk.[5]

8. 'O Kur, Help' [Ngok]

(Extract)

My Mijok is sweet to me
Like tobacco to a pipe
When there is no tobacco
The pipe goes out;
His speed and mine are the same.   5
He leads the herds wearing the bell
The bell of the son of Malek

---

[1] Ox-colour-pattern; white cutting across black.
[2] With bride-wealth.
[3] Vultures.
[4] The legend is that the vulture and the hyena had a cow, *Yom*.
[5] In legends, the fox outwits the vulture and the hyena. The hawk being
a ferocious bird, the Dinka metaphorically refer to a person who overcomes
another, be it by force or otherwise, as that other's hawk.

Mijok smooths the bell like a tobacco plot[1]
He chiselled it like a gourd carved for guests
And the bell cried: 'O Kur, help.'   10
Because the journey was long, Majok, bartered with a cow-calf,
The bell asked Kur: 'Is the destination near?'
In the grazing area of Mading Gaatawan
Mijok grazed and covered his ribs.
I have a white Mijok   15
Mijok as white as the foaming flood
Grass tickles Mijok like guinea-worm
He is struggling with the bell
Like a man carrying twin buckets of water.[2]
My Mijok is white like tin.   20

9. *A Leopard's Will* [Ngok]

(Extract)

The singer's ox is spotted like the leopard.

The old man of the leopard world,
Gives his will the day he dies,
'My children, the forest of Ameth
Never leave it
It is your home.   5
That is where to hunt.
That is where to steal the goats.'
The big leopard of the son of Mijok,
When he finds a goat of the Falata,[3]
He eats it;   10
When he finds a goat of divinity,
He eats it.
The leopard has many things against him
Like Monywir Rian[4]
The man who was impossible for the Tuic.   15

[1] Although it is grown in very small quantities, the Dinka attend to tobacco very carefully.
[2] Dinka do not carry water this way in their home. When they go to town for labour, their primary occupation is carrying water.
[3] A nomadic Nigerian tribe.
[4] A Tuic chief who was deposed.

10. *Beer* [Ngok]

(Extract)

The effect of beer is related to the power of his ox by the singer because the colour of his ox, like the colour of Dinka beer, is *Malou*,
dark grey.

A woman sent a child,
'Akenyai, fetch me a beer-filter from that house.'
A greedy man heard it and directed his ears
He pulled his spears and moved around
Tracing where the filter came from   5
Drank a calabash of beer and exclaimed,[1]
'O my Great One, I speared an animal!'
The pride of beer has no colours[2]
Beer strikes a man's head with a club
Like the flashing of lightning   10
The intestines groan with sourness
Yeast and grain mix
And porridge ferments
Like a place where monkeys fought.

11. *Lack of a Cow* [Ngok]

(Extract)

'It is the lack of a cow', says the monkey.
'We would sacrifice for our sick.'
It is the same for me
It is the lack of an ox
I would pierce his horns.   5
If cattle are scarce for those with two legs
You monkey-folk with four legs
How can you expect to find cattle?
Should I find him in the future
I shall breed him to grow his horns long   10
Like the shafts with which the Tuic fish in the reeds.

[1] Text, *mioc*.
[2] Normally a *mioc* concerns oxen and metaphors about their colour-patterns.

The people called the Tuic
Even when they come to Ngokland
Do not leave their greed,
The Tuic have hearts like weasels   15
A debased people fond of begging
Never forgetting the things of the past.
They said to us
'Had you come the year the ox Malou was slaughtered
You would have eaten.'   20
We grazed our herds in the *toc* of Bol,[1]
And the herds returned full like sacks of grain,
A *toc* forbidden for us to enter
We shall liken it to Mithiang of the Nuer
Of which people speak   25
People with long foreskins[2]
Owning such wonderful land.

12. *Friendship has Many Insides* [Ngok]

(Extract)

A song about the adventures of two friends who seized a calf in self-help
and took it to Nuerland in order to barter it for a personality ox.

Friendship has many insides:
There is friendship with girls
There is friendship for food
And friendship in which men walk together at night,
I told Dupeer, 'Take that way   5
We will meet
There is something we will take at night.'
We pulled our cow at night
Like people eloping with a girl,
We will swim, Pied One, Majok son of Diing Ajok   10
Even if Lol be flooded to Akortong
We shall go.
A Nuer jumped out of his byre,
Dinkas, are you the owners of that *yang*?[3]

[1] A Tuic chief.
[2] Nuer do not circumcise, unlike most Dinka tribes.   [3] Nuer for cow.

We looked around expecting to see Nyang e Yang¹   15
But it was the cow they called *yang*
Then he asked, 'Are you [Ngok] Dinkas of Kwol
  [that you may go]
Or Dinkas of Ruweng
That we may fight?'
As though fighting were like the fighting of animals   20
To begin when people have not quarrelled.

13. *After a Cow* [Ngok]

Acuil Athuai tells of the hardships of litigation as he pursued the case
of a cow.

That of the Arabs² confounded me
If you were that of our land you would not have confounded
  me
And here I am starved,
That day in the house of the chief
I ate so much that my back bent like the stealer of shields   5
I continued to eat the food in vain
And remained lean like a basket full of wild grain,
My fields were given over to the weeds.
I kept the paper in my left hand
And took it as far as Amiet   10
I held it like that [the penis] of an imbecile
Which remains in until after daybreak³
I held it tight, held it tight until my hand got stuck
Like a penis whose mouth is grabbed by a black ant
I have never been accused of saying a word with a trimmed head⁴
I cut my words like drops of urine⁵   15
And make it sweet to the ears of the chiefs.
I told Miyom, 'O Miyom, O Miyom

¹ Name of a person whom they knew and who they feared might have followed.
² Northern Sudanese food in the chief's home.
³ It is improper for the Dinka to have sexual intercourse in the daytime.
⁴ A lie.
⁵ In Dinka, *ajuolac*, a urinal infection which makes urine pass in drops and
painfully.

Are you not clansmen with Deng Kuei?
Ajang de Deng, born by Deng Kuei   20
Is he not your clansman?
Miyom, let go of the rope,
Ajak is your man.
Why? What about Kucmuk, Kucmuk
Is she not truly the daughter of Biong Jaclek?'   25
O my cow
The cow for whom I used to leave early in the morning
With my eyes splashing
Like flood-water filled with little fish rising
And an uncircumcised penis which does not stop dripping.   30
A man who met me on the way said to me
'Why do you go to court when you are so starved?'
'You pity me without even taking me to your home?'
Agok, the White One, advises me
'Acuil, son of my mother, go ahead   35
A man without a sister must speak well[1]
I cannot go, the guinea-worm has swollen my knee.'
At Kolcum, I smelt fried flour[2] like spring sesame,
And nearly turned off my way like a village dog,
My nose filled up with the smell of fried flour
And when I placed my feet on the ground   40
My ears rang like those of a frightened man
Then I stood and groaned.
O my cow
The cow whose case was settled by the father of Nyaantiwit[3]   45
Who even scattered her with ashes[4]
That is the cow whose flesh the lion devoured
With hind-quarters narrow as a spearhead.

---

[1] A man without a sister to attract bride-wealth must largely depend on himself to acquire cattle.

[2] Dinka, *akop*, a typical Ngok food in which durra is ground without being sieved, turned into a paste from which tiny rice-like balls are made, and fried. It may then be eaten with all sorts of dressing like sesame butter, ghee, milk, or meat-sauce.

[3] Chief Jipur Allor, then the deputy of Chief Kwol Arob.

[4] One way of blessing or dedicating a cow.

14. *A Rat near a Peg* [Ngok]

(Extract)

The singer portrays his ox as speaking.

A rat has made a hole near my peg
And when I lie, he meets me with a bite
This is why I push Mijok, the ox of Deng, with my horns,
'Mijok, please move a little.'

15. *Nights without Sleep* [Ngok]

(Extract)

Mading de Deng d'Awan
I have a friend with clear eyes.
I do not know what itches the bottom of a gossiper
Why he never accepts a seat.
O Ajith   5
Aren't you Ajinh de Tong
And is not part of you that of my grandmother?
And you being also the son of my sister
Our relationship is complex as the hippo's stomach
Are you not Ajith for whom I used to run to the court tree of
    Abyei?   10
And now you slip from the mouth of a maternal uncle
Like a tortoise falling from a marabou stork
So that I spend my nights without sleep.
My father loved me
And when the day of disaster came   15
I was by his side
My father bequeathed me the Crested Crane [an ox]
My father bade me not to leave my bird, the Crested Crane
I have taken over the colour-pattern of my father
An old man is replaced like an old rope.   20

16. *O Creator* [Ngok]

(Extract)

O Creator
Creator who created me in my mother's womb
Do not confront me with a bad thing
Show me the place of cattle,
So that I may grow my crops   5
And keep my herd.

17. *God Withdrew* [Ngok]

The singer whose ox is grey, which is why he later mentions the camel,
refers to various legends which are not fully explained, but which have
a bearing on the colour-pattern of his ox. Among these is the myth of
God's withdrawal from the world as a result of a wrong committed by
a woman. God then sent the finch (which is blue-grey) to cut the rope
which still linked Heaven and Earth, thus ending the complete happiness
which had prevailed and turning man into a suffering and mortal being.
Guuk, a species of the dove (also blue-grey) who was then betrothed to
God's daughter and had already paid one hundred cows, lost both his
bride and his wealth. Another legend is that of the glossy-starling which
borrowed the eyes of the moth (also greyish) and never returned them,
leaving the moth half blind. Yet another legend is that of monkeys who
are believed to have descended from boys and girls who were gathering
roots of water lilies, which stained their hands black. The girls refused
to return to the camp with unclean hands and so they, together with the
boys, went into the forest to form a separate race. There is also a mention
of the fox (also grey) which is presented in many legends as the cleverest
animal, which outwits all other animals. Apart from these several explanations, there are details we are unable to explain.

Feud, the ancient feud for which hundreds died
He will find a bird and seize its mandibles
The feud of the storm
The ancient feud when the finch cut the rope
And turned your mother into a mortal being,   5
Then the glossy-starling did it again
And disappeared without your vengeance
O moth, you are a nothing-man
If you were really a man

You would have continued chasing after your eyes   10
Even if you had been defeated by the glossy-starling.
In the past when disaster nearly killed women
If it were not for the wit of man
Things would have burnt to ashes
It was a fire which could not be extinguished   15
A fire which could not be seen
A fire without smoke.
Monkeys are debased
The great debased monkeys who cry oi oi
Monkeys are debased   20
Their girls are courted on one side of a tree
While parents sit next to them,
The girls of the monkeys have tousled hair
Have you seen, they are like dogs[1]
The ancient girls who refused the people's camp,   25
'We cannot return without clean hands'?
Monkeys, what great things you have left behind.
There are girls who decorate themselves with red ashes
And dance the dance of your race.
When asked, 'How is the dance of your race danced?'   30
Monkeys say: 'We cannot dance
But the fox cannot climb.'
The girls who dance with many ornaments
Your girls are reputed to wear pied and beautiful beads.
Animals say that the fox is the lord of the land   35
My head is stuffed full of problems
The case of my ox heard by the tribe
Clan-heads
The judges have gathered in the court;
My Malith like the ancient Malith of the dove above.   40
The beauty of your original world
A home in which you were all bound one to another, even the
    dove
How even the dove dared to marry the daughter of the Chief;
The finch is the person who hates other people's prosperity
He cut the rope   45
And a man who was married was left then with nothing

[1] The text combines *ber*, the Dinka word for calling dogs, with the Arabic
word *kulab*, derived from *kilab*, Arabic for dogs.

The hundred cows of the dove remained in the sky
And in the evening when the sun goes down
God tethers the herds of the dove
And the dove cries: 'Has it dawned   50
So that I may go to divorce
World, bring the morning soon
So that I may go to divorce?'
The fox calls, 'Gwak'[1]
My Malinh-Jok   55
The curve-horned is like a lion.
People see the buttocks of the Arab
Here he is
He is an animal[2] which has spoiled the buttocks of the Arabs
The great one with disordered teeth.   60

18. *A Strange Bird* (Rek)

(Extract)

A strange bird which became a divinity of the singer's clan.

The feathers were plucked, and yet the bird said,
'O people of Bol Wiel, I am a messenger.'
They broke his bones, and yet the bird said,
'O people of Bol Wiel, I am a messenger.'
They drank his broth, and yet the bird said,   5
'O people of Bol Wiel, I am a messenger,
Our home is above; I am a creator.'
When Bol Wiel heard it, he was bewildered
Bol Wiel doubted and said, 'Let the bird go'
But Akok insisted;   10
'Let the bird go',
But Akok Maker insisted
Akok Maker went on eating the bird
He was not an ordinary bird like the pied crow
He was not an elephant-grey bird   15
He was not a pigeon or a guinea fowl
He was not an ordinary bird like a partridge
No, a partridge is different and known to men.

[1] Dinka interpretation of the sound the fox makes when it cries.
[2] The camel, which is mostly grey.

19. *I Must Say It* [Tuic]

The singer, engaged to Akuol, one of the two girls critically appraised in the song, went to sleep in a hut with the girls according to Dinka custom. Such sharing of the room, and perhaps the bed, is not neces-sarily an acceptance of sexual intercourse. While thus in the hut, the singer attempted to force sexual intercourse with Akuol, who cried out to her friend, Ajok, for help. Ajok squeezed the testicles of the man to subdue him, hurting him seriously. This and the next two songs are about this.

One thing I have found
And I must say it
All our chiefs, I must say it
Cyer Rian,¹ I must say it
Lang Juk, I must say it   5
Nyol Bol, I must say it
I must say it to our chiefs:
Is there no compensation in sex-fight
Or what is done about it?
O our chiefs   10
I understand that it has always been compensated with cows.
When I went courting in the home of Great Ajok Arob
I found Ajok in the house
She does not sleep
She stays awake with open ears   15
All things to the front and the back of the house
She knows them
Ajok knows them all.
Why does Ajok fight over another girl's vagina?
And you Akuol too   20
Why did you wake Ajok?
In affairs of this kind
Each person handles his own
Another person is not awakened;
You both have done wrong in Aguot   25
People will point at you for that.
Her hands felt their way
O daughter of Arob
You have pulled my testicles

¹ Cyer Rian, Lang Juk, and Nyol Bol are all important Tuic chiefs.

A woman plays only with those of her husband   30
She does not touch those of a visiting man.
When we go to talk in court at Turalei
Your eyes will be like giraffes hunted by horses[1]
Like giraffes chased by horses.
We were three in the hut   35
Ajok, Akuol, and myself
They had accepted me into the hut,
I had my spears
And I had my club,
I went and lay still   40
I lay still
And when the evil heart came
It said to me: 'Why are you sleeping near food?
From ancient times, Dinka men who share huts
Sleep, but they move   45
Ring, move!'
But when I began to move
Akuol cried,
'O Ajok of my mother, help!
Ajok of my mother, help me.'   50
Ajok Arob e[2] Deng
Caught me in a way I hate to this day
She caught my testicles
Then she pulled me like a coconut
And squeezed me like a fruit juice   55
As though I was a lactating goat,
O Ajok milked me like a cow.

20. *She Held the Club where it Hurts* [Tuic]

Paguek, our clan,
I have withdrawn
The marriage of Akuol Aduot
It has turned itself away
I am a man who has remained in the cattle-camp.[3]   5

[1] The text uses *ajuath*, derived from Baggara Arab word *juad*, for horse.
[2] The Tuic use *e* as the Ngok use *de* or *d'* to show parentage.
[3] Usually it is unmarried men and women who go to the cattle-camp and remaining in the cattle-camp is used to mean being too old to be still an unmarried person. It is more often applied to women than to men.

Ajok has killed me out of scorn
Akuol has killed me out of scorn.
O Dau Kuacnyiel, it is the weakness of the heart[1]
Which made me reach the river Lol
To go and find experienced girls;   10
Ajok Arob is an experienced girl
Akuol Aduot is an experienced girl
Ajok who has remained unmarried
Akuol who has remained unmarried
They have remained gazing on men   15
They have known the areas of pain
Ajok has known the areas of pain.
When she woke
She held the club where it hurts
And my [future] children became perturbed.   20
She bent my limbs[2]
And I went out of breath,
Ajok Arob
Halt
Akuol, daughter of Aduot Dau   25
Halt, halt.
Camp of Ater, let us gossip
I do not blame you all,
You, clan Parum
It is not you all   30
Even you Awek e Ring
It is not you;
In clan Paguet, I have a word,
But it is not with all the people of Aguet
It is with the two girls   35
They gang up against me in a war of sex.
War of sex is like magic
It is left to a person alone
And people keep away.
Deng Kuac Nyiel,   40
I only think of what will become of me
In Nyang Agher

[1] Literally, 'It is the heart.'
[2] Immediately after death, the Dinkas bend the dead person's arms and legs
to prepare him for burial.

Shall I be sterile because of Ajok,
Ajok who knows the area that kills?
What if I should be sterile in this land   45
And Akuol stands
And Ajok stands?
The world of today
Is not the world of yesterday.
A man hopes for two children   50
Or for three children;
Three, I no longer can
Two, I am no longer sure.
Ajok of my mother[1]
You refused to hold us apart   55
And you refused to be a witness;
You made me impotent.
My children will flow away in the grass
My people will flow away on the plains.
The daughter of Arob has pulled me apart   60
I do not know whether I will give birth[2]
Nyang e Col
The daughter of Maper Adiel has castrated me.

21. *Castrated Me* [Tuic]

The land remains with jealousies
People stay not knowing each other
The land remains with jealousies.
Even Ring e Dau
I will blame,   5
Madut e Ring
I will blame,
Riin e Ring
I will blame for ever.
Dan e Ring did not bring me close to him   10
If he had brought me close to him
I would not have left Nyang Kuac

---

  [1] Any mother of a girl who is eligible to be his wife may be called 'mother'
by a Dinka.
  [2] In Dinka the same verb is used to express the roles of both father and mother.

And Nyang Agher
To look for Akuol in the *toc*.
Akuol Aduot has remained[1]   15
The girl is with Ajok who pulls out the inside of men.
Dan e Ring will let Noon[2] hear the word
Did I not say I would marry near the road
In the Ngok of my father Marialdit,
In the Ngok of my father Deng 'Crested Crane' and in Maper?
Akuol Aduot has pushed me aside   21
I will marry in the centre of the tribe[3]
In Adiang of Maper
Dan e Ring pointed at her,
'Madut e Ring, follow her.'   25
I walked not finding Maper
Until I reached her home far away.
When I courted Akuol
She accepted
She never refused me on the river Kir   30
We would not have gone into the hut
We would not have gone to her house;
But it was for Ajok who castrates men
That she took me in.
As for me   35
Only the skin holds my testicles
The roots of the testicles are gone
The feet of the testicles are gone
They are severed
They are broken by Ajok.   40
As for me
I have become impotent
Even before I have founded a family;
Daughter of Arob, beware of a curse
If I should be sterile before I found a family.   45
Ajok saw me and attacked me
As though she had something with which to lure the girls[4]
She has gone beyond her role
She has pushed her role aside
You have protected the vagina of a person you cannot manage;

[1] Unmarried.   [2] The people of that area.
[3] His own tribe.   [4] He accuses her of penis envy.

The girls of the *toc* will be left for the Great Majok[1]   50
The Great Majok Arob
The person who has become aggressive on the Lol
The person who watches over Akuol.
They have killed me   55
The woman held my legs and pulled me
Like a long canoe,
Consider, O Col Agoth,
The girls of Maper scorn us
It is the girls of Maper.   60
Ajong Arob has burned me with fire
That is why I abandoned Akuol Aduot
Great Majok, you will pay the price.

22. *It's Only a Club* [Ngok]

(Extract)

A Ngok Dinka in Arabland seduced an Arab girl and was attacked by
her relatives. It is not clear whether he was in fact beaten. Of course, a
man would not sing this way about a girl he respected. The fact that she
was an outsider and that the sexual relationship was only a casual one
must be behind the singer's tone.

Hold yourselves
I have not hit her with a spear[2]
It is only with a club, a club,
Girl of the Baggara, we are on the ground
'Dinka, gently, gently.'   5
I do not know 'gently',
I put it right in.
I caught her back and cries arose at Jaabatein.
Mine does not sleep
It tosses the thighs.   10
We were in haste
And when my shorts were wasting my time
I tore them,

---

[1] A pun. The male equivalent of Ajok is Majok.
[2] Spears are used only in major fights between sub-tribes or tribes and clubs
are used in less serious fights.

We were in haste
I laid her on the ground   15
I put it in again
My ox, curve-horned Magak, I have caused an accident.

23. *I will not Swear* [Tuic]

(Extract)

A man whose courtship was resented by the girl's relatives went into
a hut with her for the night. They attacked him, and he ran away leaving
behind his spears and his wooden seat which is also used as a pillow.
The seat is something carried by Dinka men when travelling on occasions
when they do not expect seats to be provided for them, that is, when in
the cattle-camp, courting in a deserted hut, etc.

> I will not swear never to see your land
> I shall attend the dances
> I will not swear never to see your land
> I shall continue to herd in the summer camp
> As for the courtship of girls, I no longer know   5
> If it were in our land
> O if it were in our land
> The spears would not have remained
> And the seat would not have remained.
> I shall meet girls from other tribes   10
> But I will not court them again
> I am a man taught a lesson.

24. *May the Creator be Cursed* [Ngok]

(Extract)

Our herds destroyed the crops of the Tuic
And a girl from the Tuic insulted us;
Sister, do not insult me
Daughter of my mother, we are age-mates.[1]
Do not make me insult you with a big insult   5
You will make me insult you with what the Creator gave me

[1] Because she is courtable he calls her age-mate.

Even if it be small, you will not blame yourself[1]
You will not scorn it, it is a thing created by the Creator;
The Creator has bewitched me
He gave my age-mates a good share and then gave me a poor
    share,
The Creator has bedevilled me, may the Creator be cursed.   11
I would have taught the girl of the Tuic a lesson
I would have stuffed her with my thing
She would have hated the Ngok for ever.

25. *Yours is Yours* [Atuot]

(Extract)

In my move to the *toc*
I began early in the morning
We slept on the way
We slept at Jarweng
The gentleman begins the move between day and night.   5
Those of you who own the *toc*
Do not show contempt for other people's land
No one is bad for what he has,
Yours, even if it be bad, is yours
Yours, even if it be good, is yours.   10

26. *A Son's Wish* [Ngok]

(Extract)

If only I could turn my father into steel
To remain over the ages
And the age-set of the Decorated One to be strong
To remain over the ages.

[1] She will be so satisfied despite the size of his penis that she will not regret having slept with him.

27. *The Fatal Spot* [Ngok]

(Extract)

Arob, a son of Chief Kwol Arob, is proud as the most influential son
who gets what he wants from his father. He sees the secret in knowing the technique of approach, which he likens to knowing his father's
fatal spot. He also likens being able to persuade his father to having untoothed him.

Those of you begotten by the son of the White One
Who among you knows his fatal spot?
Is it the older Deng[1] or the younger Deng?[2]
Is it Allor Maker,[3] or is it Biong?[4]
I have found the fatal spot of my father,   5
I hit it with ease.
What will vex me
When I untoothed my father last winter?
When I fetched him from Abinangui
I found Pied One a joy of the heart.   10

28. *Noong* [Ngok]

(Extract)

Also by Arob Kwol, the previous singer. Noong is the traditional home
of his older brother, Chief Deng Majok.

What is given goes on
What is swallowed is wasted
Bellow my curve-horned.
It is the bell of the sweetness of my heart
The bell chimed loud.   5
Guests came to our home at Noong
There was the curved-horned guest[5]
And the hollow guest[6]
Ring yourselves out.

[1] Deng Majok, the Chief.
[2] Deng Abot, one of Deng Majok's deputies.
[3] Deng Abot's full brother who is next to him.
[4] Deng Majok's full brother next to him.
[5] An ox.   [6] A bell.

Our Noong is booming like a market place¹   10
It is looked forward to by a traveller on the road
Like a place which the vultures descend on.

29. *My Guest Moved On* [Ngok]

(Extract)

People came to the cattle-camp and the singer was honoured to receive
them as his guests. Bol, a member of the Pajok clan, was one of them.
The guests wanted to move to someone else's place in another part of
the cattle-camp. To the singer, it appeared that they wanted to stay with
a richer man. This song is directed against what he sees as snobbery.

> Though my herds are few
> I, the son of Guiny,
> I invite a guest
> Whose heart is unsettled
> He is after the red ashes of the wealthy   5
> O Bol, the Swarm of Bees
> Even if my cows were only two
> Like the teeth of a rabbit,
> They would save you
> I will ease your hearts with a chant²   10
> 'I bartered a bull for my grandfather's camp'³
> So that your hearts may be assured.

30. *A Guest Must Stay* [Ngok]

(Extract)

The singer brags about the hospitality of his family and their determination not to let a passer-by go without spending the night.

¹ Showing that there is meat.
² *Mioc*, an exclamation in which he indirectly tells them his material ability
to provide hospitality.
³ The bull here is representative of his wealth. In other words, his being in
a position to barter a bull meant that he had cattle and therefore was not too
poor to show hospitality.

A guest, a guest
He will never leave
Without cleaning his mouth with our ashes[1]
Our maternal kin are on the peak of the tree.[2]

31. *All Must End* [Ngok]

(Extract)

Nothing does not end
O Carrier of Water of the Grey Bustard[3]
How I used to sit with my father!
Who departed in front of my eyes.

32. *A Magician* [Ngok]

(Extract)

The Dinka believe that 'black magic', which they loathe, will eventually
return to punish its user. Blisters on the eyes are used metaphorically
to represent such a punishment.

A magician, a magician
However handsome he may be
Will one day bewitch a man.
I heard an ancient magic denied at Maker
Man, you may go   5
But one day your eyes will have blisters
Like those of your ancient fathers.

33. *The Land was Spoiled* [Ngok]

There is an unverified story among the Ngok of how Arob, the grandfather of Chief Deng Majok, saved his land during the Turco-Egyptian
rule or the Mahdist revolution which overthrew the Turco-Egyptian

---

[1] In addition to using the branches of certain trees, Dinka clean their mouths
with the ashes of burnt cow dung.   [2] Of class structure.
[3] Carrier of Water: the bee, which is often seen swarming over water, and
hence the bee-patterned, speckled ox of the singer; Bustard: the praise-name
of his father's grey ox.

regime. It is said that a governor desired to test Arob's commitment to his tribe in order to decide whether he was the legitimate authority to be recognized by the central government. He challenged Arob to have his son sacrificed to prove his claim. Arob, in the face of tribal opposition, surrendered his son. It is not clear whether he actually killed him or gave him in slavery. Recently, I asked Arob Kwol, an elder of the Pajok lineage, to inform me more on the story. And although he himself mentions the story in one of his songs, his response was, 'Those are the lies of songs, no child was killed.'[1]

It is a chieftainship for which there is death
The land remained with Arob de Biong, my ancestor;
The old are asked about the distant past
Ask your father about the distant past
Governor from foreign land, have you heard the word of Arob?   5
He returned the word to the Ngok
Come, hear the word of the Mahdi;[2]
The land was spoiled and did not hold
And when it did not hold
Arob said, 'Sacrifice the child.'   10
But the death of the child astounded the tribe
All raising their hands cried,
'Killing the child will spoil the tribe
It will spoil the tribe.'
We are the Ngok of Kwol   15
My father called the word[3] all night
'It will spoil the tribe.'
We are the Ngok of Kwol.
In the Ngok of Kwol,
The Tuic come asking for a chief;   20
One day we shall take over the whole
As Gogrial[4] includes the whole
And extends to Mading Aweil[5]
It extends to Mading Aweil
[Subjection] will not reach Abyei.[6]   25

---

[1] The story is also covered in songs 82, 84, and 85.
[2] Although it might have been during the Turco-Egyptian rule, the Dinka tend to confuse the periods and the non-Dinka personalities involved.
[3] He prayed.
[4] A Dinka district in Bahr el Ghazal Province which includes many western Dinka tribes.
[5] Another Dinka district.
[6] The administrative centre of the Ngok Dinka.

If you displace Jong Yom[1]
People will burn;
Ask your father of the distant past
The thing will spoil the tribe
We are the Ngok of Kwol. 30

34. *Longar was Spearing the People* [Rek]

The singer presents two opposite themes. The first concerns a wrong
committed by an ancestress leading to the poverty of her husband's
descendants. The second concerns the cattle-loving attitude of an
ancestor, leading to the clan's being rich. According to the first theme,
the singer's ancestress, Adut Akol, felt that she had too much milk. She
threw it into the river, angering God so that he deprived her descendants
of cattle.

Although the milk wasted is said to be that of goats, and the animals
lost are said to be goats, it would be obvious to the Dinka that the
singer is speaking of livestock in general (cattle, sheep, and goats). It
may be recalled that the word *thok* covers both goats and sheep and
that the Dinka sometimes speak of *thok* as *weng*, cow.

In his second theme, the singer not only demonstrates his ancestors'
love for cattle as a factor in their wealth, but also explains his family's
wealth and power with a legend which tells how their founder fought
with Longar, a culture hero of the Dinka who was conceived by a river
spirit, and who had good and evil mystic powers. (See Lienhardt,
Divinity and Experience, the Religion of the Dinka, 1961, chap. v, p. 171.)
As part of the myth, the singer tells the story of how the Pakuec came
to be chiefs among the Rek and became entitled to the hips of sacrificial cattle according to the order of seniority established by Longar. It
should perhaps be pointed out that this is an unusual song in so far as
it criticizes an ascendant; normally Dinka praise ascendants, whatever
their past.

Adut Akol, wife of Kueng Angok
Our ancestress went into fire like a flying ant[2]
If death were a visit from which she could return
There would be things she would see and repent,
Adut, taking ropes[3] into the river was your wrong 5

[1] A praise-name for Deng Majok, the chief.
[2] When ants swarm they fly into fire. 'Ancestress' symbolizes her whole
lineage in the same way. To make this even more apparent, the singer uses a
plural verb with 'ancestress'.
[3] Taking ropes means taking the livestock tied by the ropes.

Yes, Adut, it was a wrong on your side
Adut Pakuer,[1] it was a wrong;
Adut who enjoyed the riches of my ancestor Kueng Angok
Then she thought big
It was a thought disliked by God   10
The word of a fool is disliked by God;
She poured the milk into the river
And the smell of the goat's milk remained
That is why we had no goat's dung
We had no goat's dung in the kraal of the sons of Angok.   15
Maluil of Great Kueng went into the marshes[2]
And when he went to visit
He stumbled over the sacred grass and fell.[3]
Ring Giir, the Great Flour-White
My father Ring was called by his father   20
He seated him down by his side
And affectionately rubbed his head
And left him these words,
'Son, Ring, there are the cattle.'
He said to him, 'O son Ring, there are the cattle   25
Cattle are the wealth of man.'
My great father had a cattle-camp
His house became rich with herds
The cattle-byres were full.
My ancestor Akol Kuec is an elephant   30
And Thiik Ring is an elephant
Kiro Riiny is an elephant
And Ring, my father, is an elephant;
An elephant.
My ancestor, Agoth   35
My ancestor was in conflict with Longar about a spear
Longar speared the people
Longar speared the people with a harpoon
Longar speared the people with *atom thok*[4]
And the cowards ran away   40
The cowards stampeded away

[1] The name of her clan.
[2] Presumably to fish, as they were now poor.
[3] Presumably unable to fish as his background did not include fishing. The 'sacred grass' refers to clumps of the grass *deel* which grow on the banks of rivers.
[4] A kind of spear.

But my great ancestor came and caught the spear;
They fell wrestling in the river
And the Dinka crossed.
The spear of the master was shafted with *peny*-wood   45
And the bull exclaimed, 'There goes my spear.'[1]
But the spear became a lie.[2]
They fell and struggled under the water in the river
And the Dinka crossed.
The day the meat was divided   50
The day Longar divided the meat
The day he gave it to us
Agothcithiik was allotted the thigh-bone[3]
He gave the Kuec people the thigh-bone.
We are the clan Pakuec   55
The clan Pakuec of the thigh-bone
Pakuec of the thigh-meat
Pakuec of the thigh-meat
They call the words
To hold the clans together.   60

35. *What Misery* [Ngok]

(Extract)

Chief Deng stopped the police from flogging the singer, who praises him,
mourns his father's death, and criticizes people's unsympathetic attitude.

When they almost flogged me at Abyei
If it had not been Deng the Designer of Rial Pattern
Who would have saved me?
Is not the Chief the father of orphans?
What misery   5
That I should be shouted at:
'Man whose father is dead.'
O Dinka, I did not eat my father
There is no one whose mother cooks for death.[4]

[1] A *mioc*.
[2] That is, was ineffective.
[3] As his clan-divinity.
[4] Death is envisaged as an eater of people who cannot be propitiated by any
other food.

36. *Not My War* [Ngok]

(Extract)

In 1951, the Ngok were given the option of joining Bahr el Ghazal Province or Upper Nile Province, rather than be the only Dinka group in the North. Chief Deng Majok threw in his lot with the North. A member of the opposition, named Biliu, an associate of Deng Majok and a famous warrior, composed this song against the decision to remain in the North.

In the future, should we fight the Tuic
I will take my shield and be among the people in the front,
In the future, should we fight the Rek
I will take my shield and be among the people in the front,
In the future, should we fight the Nuer   5
I will take my shield and be among the people in the front,
But in the future, should we fight the Arabs
I will take my water-gourd, and call my wife,
'Come let us leave,
This war is the war of Acuil and Deng and Can Dau   10
The people who made that choice.'

37. *Lonely as though I Never Had a Father* [Ngok]

Deng, a young man whom the court had held liable, had not paid the judgement creditors, the sons of Kur. The court sent a state policeman, as opposed to tribal policemen normally sent for such tasks, to summon him or seize his personality ox, Miyan, to compel him to appear in court, where he was arrested and detained in prison, awaiting trial. Later, the case was settled in his favour. In the song he appraises various court members by names direct or disguised.

Sons of Kur, Sons of Kur
Mijong de Kur, Jok Yom
And Mayol de Kur de Deng,
I tell you my word:
Should my Miyan move a step away   5
We shall fight
We shall parry spears
And our sweating heads will shine to the village.

The chief's heart is troubled
Troubled with hot words fanned by gossipers   10
Like Acol de Kwol[1]
O Chief Marial, help me.
My ox has a shining head
Miyan white-headed like an elephant.[2]
Has Deng[3] become a man without a father   15
That a special law is made for him?
That I should be summoned by the state police
When I did not kill a man
And the ox unpegged when I was away?
They tied him to a *nim* tree.[4]   20
When I heard the news of Miyan
My heart fell apart like an ending dance.
O Wacker, Mareng de Malek
My heart is a worn coin.[5]
This case I will bring again   25
Like a man chewing the calves.[6]
Even if I be thrown into a well of maggots
For Miyan I will forget myself
Like those Arabs who held each other's hands
And threw themselves into fire[7]   30
If my case is not seen well.
It will be seen by Deng de Kwol
It will be looked into by Deng de Kwol
It is a case which is snarled as a creeping plant
As tangled as entanglement;   35
Marol de Kwol, the Honoured Pied One, tracks the case like game
Until he finds my truth:
I do not speak a lie
I, Deng de Juacbong,
The word I say   40
That is the word people all come to

[1] A court member.
[2] He is indirectly insulting Acol de Kwol who is bald.
[3] The singer's name.
[4] Dinka normally use pegs and to tie his personality ox to a tree was degrading.
[5] In rural Sudan, worn coins are not accepted in trade.
[6] The singer's image is that of taking his case to a higher court, continuing with it in the manner of a Dinka eating a honeycomb. There are two parts to a honeycomb: a main part and 'the calves'—the brood comb which contains the very young larvae surrounded by royal jelly.   [7] A legend.

Like a place where beer is brewed.
Only a man who has always hated me spoils my case—
In the court there is a cross-eyed man.
Brother-in-law, Madat d'Akoc,[1]   45
Let me tell you
A man learning to judge
Does not learn with new rules.
My Miyan roams with cows
He has nowhere to sleep[2]   50
People, lend your ears,
A word is said by someone,
Someone with teeth as red as the soil of Tuicland
He says, 'Miyan, the ox of Deng,
Let us take and give to Deng de Dau.'   55
How amazed I am!
My Malou has grazed all over the land
Even with the cattle of the Rek in the *toc*
Eating grass, his teeth have turned red
Like the man at Alal of Ciere.   60
The man at Alal has no dignity
Even when written as head of a clan
He will leave the chieftainship at Abyei
And go to pick the roots of water-lily[3]
The day Ador[4] fetched me   65
He found me away from the camp
He did not wait for me
I do not know how these days the police of the Government unpeg
When the man is away;
The thing is fear,   70
It is fear which made him steal my ox
While I was still away.
I left in the dark of the morning
Still following my ox,
Even if he passes the chief's fence[5]   75

[1] Another court member.
[2] Metaphoric insult to Madat or another court member who came with wives to Abyei where he had no home of his own.
[3] Usually picked by needy people.   [4] The policeman.
[5] Ngok Dinka litigation often continues into the chief's private enclosure. Sometimes, a policeman stands at the gate to stop the public. Here, the singer expresses his determination to enter even though the enclosure be out of bounds.

I shall not stop, I shall follow.
I went and sat under the tree[1]
The Court Tree of Ayang d'Ajang
Of all the people that gathered,
Not a single man said, 'Good morning'[2]   80
So I sat with a twisted heart
Like Akol with his axe,[3]
I knew the court was against me
A court order was written in silence
Even my name was not asked   85
Fodul, the clerk, was silent.
Why do you write without asking my name?
Why do all people get angry when I state my case?
Do they mean to put me in jail?
'Yes, the law is strong   90
You will go into jail.'
Is that why people threaten me with anger?
Only jail?
Is that why people show anger?
So what? I will go myself right now   95
Without being driven by the police.
Even if there is a crocodile in jail which catches people,
I'll go inside.
I am locked in jail, I am locked in jail
And sweat hurts our eyes,   100
Sweat hurts our eyes, while bats stink
Like a dog covered with lice.
[See] what has befallen us!
Son of Pakir clan, Mayon de Dan de Kir[4]
The Government is not like the ancient times   105
When you lived by the arm,
Do not get angry when the police send you
You will be beaten,
You will be beaten, and there the face of great shame
Shame for the beating of an elder   110

[1] Abyei court-tree.   [2] Literally, 'Are you dawned?'
[3] Akol is said to have sat waiting with his axe ready to strike all day outside
the front door of his cattle-byre while a lion was eating his cattle inside. The
lion never came out through the front door. After having had its fill, it went out
through the back door. The idea is that Akol was too afraid of the lion to attack
inside the cattle-byre.   [4] A prisoner who is an elder.

While young men[1] watch him beaten
And do not take his place.
A victim of law cannot be replaced
O Mayon de Dan de Kir,
Let's tie our hearts, father of Nyannuer,   115
And go to grow cotton.
When we were driven to the field
I walked, tilting my head like a canoe
I almost refused to work.
What my grandfather once said,   120
'The pain of initiation',[2] came back to my heart
I almost did what I almost did;
My head rattled,
Mijang de Dak,[3] do not walk behind us
Do not follow us with the whip   125
You will not escape without a club on your head.
People do not enslave one another
When they are both initiated.
Mijang de Dak, leave that to Dhieu,[4]
Dhieu is a man known for lack of heart   130
He sides with the ways[5] of the Arabs
And flogs us.
The vileness of the Arab police
A Dinka must not join
To kill his own people.   135
I am ordered, Mathac Akenwai,[6]
The Arab ordered me about a dead donkey;
He ordered me to sit in the sun
And said, 'Guard the donkey from birds.'
All the birds that fly in the sky   140
Can I guard against?
I cannot, Micar Aroljok,
All the birds that fly
A man cannot guard against
Micar d'Ayuel de Jongkor.   145

---

[1] Including the singer.
[2] An aphorism bringing to mind the respect due to those who have gone through the pain.
[3] A Dinka policeman.
[4] Another Dinka policeman.
[5] *Cieng.*   [6] A fellow prisoner.

Because of an animal which will not be eaten or skinned
I sat all day in a burning sun
Then my case goes to court.
I do not vex myself when a case goes to court
Mithiang, the Flying Goshawk[1]   150
This case
If the Creator were near
I would call my father
I would call my father, the son of Deng,
To come and attend my case;   155
Each man comes with his father
And I brave the court alone,
I am lonely in my pleading
Lonely as though I never had a father.

38. *Sugar for Some* [Ngok]

Niim gal, singular *nom gol*, clan-heads, are now selected administrative officers primarily engaged in the collection of taxes, and to the Dinka the position has lost its traditional dignity of a clan elder. Clan-heads are therefore scorned. The singer, Deng Yol, however, has an ulterior motive. His sister was divorced by a clan-head and, according to him, unjustifiably. Although he generalizes, his real motive is known so that no clan-head takes offence, and indeed, they are not altogether unamused.

The song covers a wide range, and several people are appraised, but the focus is on the clan-heads.

Our chief is returning from the land of the Arabs
The Crested Crane is returning from the land of the Arabs
He returned with a pink car.
The chief is going to inspect the Ngol[2]
Our chief is going to inspect the Ngol   5
And Monydhang d'Amiyok remained behind.[3]
The chief is going to inspect the Ngol.
The land is in order, Abyei is in order.

[1] A type of hawk whose colour resembles that of Mithiang's ox.
[2] An area of the Ngok.
[3] A policeman whom he is belittling as too insignificant to be taken.

The chief is going to inspect the Ngol
Some people who wanted authority have remained behind 10
The chief is going to inspect the Ngol.
My ox is as noble as Pacir[1]
Do not call him Pacir d'Agu,
Do not call him the son of Agu,
He is our Pacir who carries keys to money. 15
Our Sergeant is not like the Sergeant of Wunrok[2]
Our Sergeant is called Deng d'Angok
He is a man who makes feasts
Malith of my father, when our herds go to the *toc*
My heart becomes sweet like that of Dheel 20
Our Dheel of Ngor, our Ngor of the Left-handed.
Last year, my ox became fat at the *toc* of Anyel,
The hippo became fat at the *toc* of Anyel
It is the *toc* for our calves.
I asked the people coming from the land of the Arabs 25
They said: 'Sugar is not available to all
A court-member is entitled to rottles[3]
A Sheikh is entitled to rottles
An Omda is entitled to rottles
But the clan-head has no share in the rottles.' 30
I, Deng Yol, I am better
I have my gourd of honey.
Who is the man who prohibits going to the *toc*?
It has always been our chief, Jok Yom[4]
He is the one who prohibits going to the *toc* 35
He will not open our borders.
If only prison could be made like a rope[5]
We would have made our own prison
And put it on the river Kolakuoc
Then the area of Malual Agaak would be ours. 40
The years we were recalled[6]

[1] The singer is honouring Pacir son of Agu.
[2] Wunrok is a town of the Tuic tribe, whom the Ngok consider stingy.
[3] A unit of measurement, approximately a pound.
[4] Another praise-name for Deng Majok. To increase agricultural produce, the chief sometimes prohibits going to the far-off grazing areas in the *toc*.
[5] The Dinka word for imprisonment is *mac*, to tether with a rope. But unfortunately a prison cannot be made like a rope.
[6] They had gone to the *toc* in violation of the chief's order.

O friend Kerdool, Akol of Malek of Padool,
We were brought to the end of Alal
There, we met people on the way
They said, 'We left Noong[1] yesterday   45
I heard that Deng de Kwol has said,
"The people who have taken their cattle to Tuicland
When they return, I will jail them and send them to Nahud." '[2]
And the cowards confined themselves to Alal
But we did not succumb, Dan de Kur Ajolgiet and I,   50
We insisted on moving from Nyalcuor
And the jangling of our bells was heard at Korrioc.
Nyang d'Arob de Mou and I, we are better
We have been called by the Chief Deng Majok
We have been called by the son of Chief Kwol;   55
He said: 'You, Deng de Yol and Nyang d'Arob,
Fetch water for the District Commissioner.'
And I said, 'Nyaak, let us go.
It is the Great Chief who has called us.'
If it were the word of a court member,   60
I would also go.
If it were the word of a Sheikh, the junior chief,
I would go.
And if it were the word of an Omda
I would run.   65
But if it were the word of a clan-head
I would completely refuse
I would entirely refuse
And let him do what he liked.
And if people say: 'Why do you refuse,   70
Is a clan-head not a noble man?'
I will say, 'He is a noble man
A noble man who does not give to people.'
O Great Curve-horned of Deng,
The clan-head is obstreperous   75
The assembly of tribes met at Tongliet
Deng de Kwol was our Warrior
Our Deng de Kwol the Decorated One

[1] The traditional village of Chief Deng Majok.
[2] The headquarters of Western Kordofan District which administered the Ngok Dinka until the Missiriya District was formed.

We gave Deng a helmet and a club
He fought with the chiefs of Bahr el Ghazal   80
So that we acquired some prisoners.
Clan of Adhaar[1]
Clan of Adhaar were not even dissatisfied with my sister's conduct,[2]
But I am dissatisfied with the clan Payaath.[3]
Why are people in turmoil against me?   85
I, Deng, what have I done?
Deng de Tiel Magak and I
We are full with people's hatred.
Kir of my mother[4] calls to me
'Deng, wait for me.'   90
And I answered: 'No, I will not wait for you.'[5]
I see the big-bellied gossipers of Anyiel in front of me.

39. *Listen then, Judge* [Tuic]

The owner of this song, a Tuic, appraises the attitude of some important chiefs of Bahr el Ghazal in a case in which he had been accused of
violating inter-tribal boundaries. There is no real contradiction in the
singers' saying that the chief saw him with the brink of his eyes and that
he gazed at him too much; both are abnormal and scornful gestures.

He is wearing the robe of honour in our land
And when I addressed him, 'Can, the Crested Crane'
He looked at me with the brink of his eyes
As though he had never seen me before.
O chief, why gaze at me so much?   5
Chief of the robe of honour, see into my eyes
Here I am, I have not killed a man.
Cyer Rian, let my words finish
And then give your opinion,
Why do you no longer appreciate words in your land?   10
Mawir Rian, let my words finish
And then give your opinion.

---

[1] The people who divorced his sister.   [2] *Cieng.*
[3] The same clan of the man who divorced his sister.
[4] His elder brother.
[5] He is proud that he is so independent and courageous that he will disobey
his elder brother.

Why do you no longer appreciate words in your land?
The chiefs make up their words
While the robes of honour remain silent.   15
Can Ajuong is the man on whom I lean
Lang Juk is also near to me.
So, being rich is a thing that invites problems,
Riches have invited problems for me
So that I quarrel with people all over Dinkaland   20
Even the chief of the Arabs, I quarrel with him.
I, Deng, the owner of one Mayom;
It is for my Mayom that I go looking for grass.
I am told, 'Stop herding at will'
And I said, 'It is not that I herd at will   25
It is malice against my search for grass.'
Deng e Kwol has said, 'The Rek will graze,
And the Tuic will graze
No one will stop them.'

40. *Clothes have Finished Goats* [Ngok]

(Extract)

The singer alleges that the court members, the *Makam*, buy expensive
clothes as status-symbols, and that because of their bad pay they cannot afford such clothes so that they must sell their goats and impoverish
themselves to support the image. He also alleges that, because of their
inferiority in the court hierarchy, they lack chairs and must sit on the
ground and mix with dust.

Because of a case seen by Deng the Saddle-bill Stork[1]
The court-members stretch themselves
As though they had claws.
What are the court-members about to do?
With eyebrows like the arms of a lion   5
Your clothes have finished your goats.
The case is seen by the court-members
There is a dust-storm in their clothes.

[1] Arialbek, the Saddle-bill Stork, is Deng Majok's ox-praise-name.

41. *The Arab Laughed* [Ngok]

(Extract)

A man who was jailed tells of his experience in prison.

The day we were jailed
The son of the Arab laughed at us,
He walked with pride
As though he had found permanent slaves.
O that we should chew groaning   5
Like a dog struck in a fatal spot:
I crush a grain of sand with my teeth
And I groaned like a man whose wounded foot is hurt,
My head hurts
I feel as though I were being initiated again.   10
The sand of Khartoum hurts
Almost like being hit on the head with a club.

42. *What Wrong have I Done?* [Ngok]

(Extract)

The singer tells of his arrest and of the policeman's attitude when he
was in jail.

When I heard the name, Abyei,
I collapsed
Worse than an unconscious man.
I searched my head
What wrong have I done in the land   5
That I should be escorted by Bol Col?[1]
Whose Bol is he?
Is it Bol of Biong's father?
No, it is not,
The policeman of Deng de Kwol   10
If you do not know him
Then you will meet him some day.

---

[1] A simile. The singer recalls the name of the Tuic chief, Bol Col, to indicate
the magnitude of his surprise at his arrest by the policeman, Bol.

The man with a hat does not joke
He says, 'hurry-quick'[1]
And we jump out in a group.   15
If the forest of Paan de Koor is far
We shall go to the forest of Manaweng
We are going to fetch firewood for those of Amel.[2]

43. *The Writer* [Ngok]

(Extract)

Nyong de Kwol, a son of Chief Kwol, was among the first from the
Ngok, and the first of the Chief's sons to go to school. This song is about
his assisting with the collection of taxes by issuing receipts.

Nyong de Kwol, the Honoured Pied One
Has put the land in order,
He writes four lines on paper[3]
And ends with a zigzagging road,[4]
And poll-tax comes to an easy end   5
Like the behaviour of a falling tree.

44. *Cattle are Finished* [Agar]

Because of collective responsibility introduced by the administration
in the payment of poll-tax, relatives of a man who has gone into town
are made to pay on his behalf. This is a song in protest.

Kelei[5] is annoyed, Kelei is provoked
He asks Malual and Majok of Derder and Makuac,[6]
'What will be done with the question of poll-tax?'
We are in conflict, we are in conflict with our chief,
There are three collections   5
There is the District Commissioner
And the new tax is still there
And Mangok[7] stands alone.

[1] Arabic, '*Yala, guam*'.
[2] Amel, one of the chief's wives, is the only one mentioned, but in a way which
indicates that she is one among others.
[3] A receipt.   [4] His signature.   [5] Administrator.
[6] Tribal chiefs.   [7] The chief.

Who has not heard the word?
You go to the land of Nyinyam[1]   10
Then people return in haste;[2]
The cattle are finished,[3]
They are finished for the sake of our people
Our people who have left the land.

45. *In Search of Money for an Ox* [Ngok]

Cash economy introduced urban labour and purchase of cattle.

> Maker, go to El Odeya
> Where money is in plenty
> Go as far as the White Nile
> Father of Athieng, go ahead
> Even as far as Omdurman   5
> O brother Malek, go ahead
> Until your pocket bursts.

46. *The Educated are Spoiling the Country* [Bor]

This song is a critical appraisal of the educated, who, while purporting
to represent their constituencies in the Parliament, sought their own
ends and kept allying with any political leader offering them the greatest
personal gain. The singer, himself illiterate, prefers that their seat be
vacant rather than abused.

> Kuorjok Akuot of my maternal aunt,
> What is the turmoil at Bor about?
> Why is the land in turmoil?
> This I will try to explore.
> Some are competing for the land   5
> Others are concerned with their mouths,
> I am addressing myself to the man of Azhari[4]
> Azhari who shot the people,[5]

---

[1] Non-Dinka tribes. More used to represent urban communities.
[2] After tax collection is over.   [3] Sold for taxes.
[4] Once Prime Minister and later President of the Sudan.
[5] As a consequence of the 1955 Southern revolt.

And to those who follow Abdalla[1]
Do not think that I am a child who does not know.   10
Alier [de Boor] went to the Parliament last year
Ajong de Mayom will go this year
To eat the good things of the town
Where people like him go to eat.
My ox Malith is mounting the bulls   15
Our educated are spoiling the country
Let the seat remain vacant
It is the seat of the ignorant.

47. *Gentlemen Beg* [In exile]

A Dinka in exile as a result of the South–North civil war in the Sudan
laments his experiences in the Congo.

Every day, when it dawns, the rain falls
Whenever it dawns in Congoland, the rain falls,
We follow Deng Nhial.
Gentlemen grind their grain in the land of the Congo[2]
The Dongolawi,[3] the Arab has remained at home   5
He has remained in our land.
We left our herds tethered in the cattle-camps
And we followed Deng Nhial.
Gentlemen beg in the land of Congo girls
The Dongolawi, the Arab has remained at home   10
We left our herds tethered in the cattle-camps
And we followed Deng Nhial.
Abur, the Egg-man,[4] left the land
He is a determined man,
Wol Majok, Wol Aleu, left the land,   15
He is a determined man,
Then we reached the land of the Congo
And when we reached the land of the Congo
The Congolese said, 'Dinka are *matata*.'

[1] The Prime Minister who handed over the government to the military junta
on 17 Nov. 1958.
[2] Normally, women grind the grain.
[3] A tribe in the Northern Sudan, here used to refer to all Northerners.
[4] Owner of a white ox.

I turned and asked Ngor Maker,   20
'What does *matata* mean?'
Ngor Maker answered,
'He says we are bad.'
My heart became angry
In the land of the Congo, my heart was angered   25
And I thought of Anger, the daughter of Wol Ayalbyor,
I wish I could find her to see her.
Ater, I have noticed something with Congolese girls
I must say it to you
Here it is: 30
They urinate while standing
O they urinate while standing,
Ater, I have noticed a bad thing with Congo girls
I must say it to you
Here it is: 35
They urinate while standing.

II

CATHARTIC SONGS

WAAK (which also means 'washing'), translated here as 'cathartic songs', are composed during a sort of retreat and whether or not the words for the songs and for 'washing' are connected, they play a 'cleansing' role. Hence the term 'cathartic' songs. There are periods when young men, and, occasionally, a few older men, isolate themselves in far-off camps and gorge themselves with milk supplemented by meat. As the word for this, *toc*,[1] literally, 'to lie down', suggests, they lie down, fatten themselves, and move as little as possible. They compose songs about matters of especial interest to them, usually pressing problems. The most frequent subject is marriage. A man may praise his intended bride and her relatives, urge his own relatives to marry her for him, or mourn her loss if they fail him. Inability to marry because of poverty may prompt a song even if the singer has no specific girl in mind. A man convicted of an offence he denies having committed may lament the injustice of the case in a song. The son of a chief denied the right to succeed his father when he believes himself entitled may complain in song. But the songs are not merely complaints. A man may exalt his father or his family, or may relate with pride the history of his lineage or certain incidents in it. In short, any topic of special significance, sad or happy, may be the subject-matter of cathartic songs.

During the first few weeks of their return, the men returning from their retreat have a great impact on society. They are seen to be attractive as a result of their being fatter and heavier, for, since the Dinka are generally very slender and tall, gaining weight can only improve their figures. They attract a great deal of attention as they move around in a group presenting their songs with a dance for the occasion, in which women do not take part. No musical instrument is used. The group forms a large circle with the owner

---

[1] To be distinguished from the *toc*, the dry-season grazing area. Though spelt here in the same way, *toc* in the present context has an open 'o' which does not exist in English alphabets.

of a song in the centre leading the group in singing and dancing. In
dancing one leg is raised and dropped with a jerk of the body in a
manner similar to initiation dances,[1] but done gently as the dancers
are too heavy to move vigorously. The dance is first done at the
homes of those addressed, but may continue to be done anywhere
and with a public audience. Sometimes, the effect of the songs
is striking. For instance, on the presentation of the long song
'The Wedding of Alai',[2] so moved were the singer's uncles that the
senior uncle, the chief himself, got on to his horse and had the
wedding arranged with himself acting as the principal 'father' of
the bridegroom, a fact of great significance for the status of the
marriage. Such songs requesting the attention of relatives to a proposed marriage attain their purpose more often than not.

48. *The Wedding of Alai* [Ngok]

Arob Allor, the singer, lost his parents when he was a little child and
became a ward of Deng Abot, one of the two deputies of Deng Majok.
Deng Majok and Deng Abot are half-brothers; both are therefore uncles
of Arob Allor. Deng Abot had been negligent in performing the wedding.
Arob therefore composed the song to complain; primarily to criticize
Deng Abot but also Deng Majok.
    After the presentation of the song, Deng Abot and Deng Majok
immediately arranged the marriage.

I have begun the wedding of Alai all alone
And when I turned my face to see
No one followed me into the byre.
Deng Abot, Deng de Kwol
Is it misconduct,[3] have I misbehaved?   5
Man, Uncle Deng the Saddle-bill Stork, hear the word.
Father, Great Majak,[4]
You are the man sitting on our head
We the orphans of the clan,
If you see me in the wrong   10
Lock me in jail,
If the wrong is my uncle's
Then tell him gently, gently

---

[1] See Initiation Songs.
[2] The first of the Cathartic Songs.
[3] *Cieng.*   [4] The oldest member of the Pajok lineage.

The word of an elder should not be rebuked
Keep it soft;   15
My father will think alone at night
If he rejects the word of a son
I will cry inside myself
The sons of Kwol d'Arob have thrown me to the Ngok
They have thrown me to the Ngok of Arob   20
The Ngok gossip about me and say,
'Arob d'Allor is a man without a mother
Do not give him this only girl
He is a man who does not know to hold the hoe
Do not give him this only girl   25
Do not give him Alai, Alai.'
Alai is like Alai of a lion[1]
People, you will not take the daughter of Ajuong of clan Payath,
The woman will be seized by the crocodile[2]
My father is the crocodile of the river Lol   30
He is the crocodile of the river Lol
He is the crocodile of the open lakes
My father is the crocodile of the lakes
Gossipers of the Ngok, step aside
You will be attacked by the mighty beasts
You will be killed by the mighty beasts   35
Beasts, beasts are coming
See the elephant[3] on the move.
I have Deng de Kwol, the great man
And I believed if I had too big a problem
I would let my uncle, Deng the Saddle-bill Stork, the chief, hear.
The bride is provoking a feud   41
Deng de Kwol is pushing me away
He has pushed my back into fire
He turned me into the orphan of Kur;
Great Kur was crying for his own life   45
And said, 'Looking after an orphan is bad.'
O, looking after an orphan is bad.
I am a man left alone with the rope.[4]

[1] Alai appears to him as difficult to marry as it is to defeat a lion.
[2] A symbol of his clan's power.
[3] Another symbol of his clan's powers.
[4] Because cattle are tethered, the rope symbolizes them. No one is giving the
cattle they should provide to assist him.

Deng de Kwol points at the court-tree
The court-tree of the chief   50
I am told to complain to the court,
Because of the marriage of Alai, I will never go to court.
If the Ngok have feared the son of Kwol d'Arob de Biong
Then, let my bride remain
I will gaze and wait   55
I will alert my ears,
Why are the Ngok afraid, even Deng d'Arob de Biong, my uncle?
My grandfather Kwol d'Arob, the bull to whom the tribe belongs,
The bull on whom the Ngok call,
Is hiding from the marriage of the son of his mother.[1]   60
I shall make the daughter of Ajuong sever our blood ties
To sever the blood of the birth of one family
I am severing ties with Deng of my mother[2]
He does not honour my word
As though I were not the son of his mother.   65
If Alan d'Ajuong should disappear
If the daughter of Ajuong should go away
Deng de Kwol will move from the Seat.
Who will honour him with the Seat
Who will give him the ancient chieftainship of Arob de Biong   70
The chieftainship for which my grandfather ate an afterbirth?[3]
My Great Father was fed with the afterbirth of a donkey
When he sought to hold the tribe of his father.
If it were Deng and Deng
The land would not have been held,   75
People who do not know even their own sons.
When my Great Father ate an afterbirth
It was not for the sake of his son
He ate it for the sake of his tribe, the Ngok;
Is that not the chieftainship?   80
Was that not the chieftainship?

---

[1] He puts his grandfather into his uncle's place and himself into his father's place.

[2] Placing himself in his father's shoes.

[3] At the early stages of the Mahdist revolution against the Turco-Egyptian rule, Arob went to Jebel Gadir, as did many chiefs of Kordofan, to visit the Mahdi, believing that he had appeared to free them. Arob is said to have eaten donkey-meat. The point is dramatized in songs by specifying the part he ate to have been the guts, or, as in this song, the afterbirth.

I am thinking out aloud
Let me think out aloud
To what shall I liken my fate
That my bride should be led astray   85
When my father is the chief of the Robe?
I am thinking aloud in the Great tribe of Kwol d'Arob
It is the tribe of Deng Majok.
In the tribe of my father Kwol d'Arob
I will cut my throat   90
Deng and Deng of my father
Will they not blame themselves?
My father Kwol d'Arob is known to the land
The chief is known in Dinkaland;
They were two—they were two   95
The ancient chiefs were two
There was Bol de Nyuol in Tuicland
And Kwol d'Arob in Ngokland
They were the people who saved the land
Yes, they saved the land   100
I shall not add a lie.
Father Deng the Saddle-bill Stork
Are you not the God of the land
O son of the chief?
Deng is the son of the chief   105
Deng is the son of Kwol d'Arob de Biong,
Kwol d'Arob is lying across the Ngok
Even if a man found Alai lost in the wilderness
He would not touch her,
Who would hold her?   110
Will he not fear Deng de Kwol?
He would be holding a scorpion
He would be holding fire
If it is Deng the Saddle-bill Stork.
Father, great Deng Makuei,   115
Uncle, do not hide it any more
I will tell the word to the Ngok to hear,
I will show the word to the Ngok to see,
They will uphold the law on our quarrel over a bride.
My father, Allor de Kwol, left me   120
In his last word, he said to me,

'My son, you will remain
Deng, the brother of your father,
Will marry a wife for you
Deng, the brother of your father,   125
Will marry Alai for you.'
When I ventured the daughter of Ajuong
I could not succeed.
The treatment of an orphan!
That is why Deng Makuei started   130
And even accompanied me
Like a catfish followed by eels
And then dodging them
He dodged me leaving me alone in the cattle-byre;
I remained alone in the cattle-byre of Alai.   135
I am beginning to see what is behind
When I speak, he turns to marry for the son of his stomach
The sons he bore from his own stomach
Deng Abot, admit the truth.
Deng d'Arob, you have turned me away   140
And you Deng the Saddle-bill Stork, son of Arob, please
    get up
You are the weight
You are the rock of the land;
He is the rock, Deng is the rock
If anything should go wrong   145
Deng can always mend it to be strong
A thing is going wrong near to you.
Deng de Biong, the Stork of the Marshes,[1]
Never mind, it is all the same;
A son of man should not be left alone to struggle with people 150
Like a black bull of the buffalo
This marriage, the marriage of Alai,
Has been dug out with words of feud
The marriage has provoked a feud
Between me and my uncles.   155
Do not take it lightly;
If it is because my father is gone
If it is the absence of my father, Allor, the son of Kwol,
And I am blind to the fact

---

[1] Biong's ox-name, derived from the black-and-white Saddle-bill Stork.

Then please say it in haste   160
That I may know the truth
To stand and face the elephant
To fight a lonely war with the elephant
But should he fall one day in the future
Please, forget his tusks[1]   165
Do not ask for the tusks.

49. *Equals* [Rek]

The singer, a Rek, compares the importance of his father to that of Deng
Majok, the Chief of the Ngok Dinka, and complains that by not marrying
a wife for him his father is not giving him the chance to maintain the
name of the lineage.

Deng Kwol Arob is the equal[2] of my father
He is the equal of my father
If the songs of the things equal to the great man are counted
All animals will be left
But the elephant will be counted.[3]   5
Deng Kwol Arob is the equal of my father
He is the equal of my father
If the sons of the things equal to the great man are counted
All birds will be left
But the ostrich will be counted.   10
The son of Kwol Arob is the equal of my father
He is the equal of my father
If the sons of the things equal to the great man are counted
All fishes will be left
But the giant catfish will be counted.   15
Deng Kwol Arob is the equal of my father
He is the equal of my father
If the sons of the things equal to the great man are counted
All trees will be left

---

[1] If he must pay the whole bride-wealth, he will not share his daughter's
bride-wealth with his uncles.
[2] Literally, the singer says 'age-mate' since status is partly determined by
age.
[3] Here, as in the lines to follow, the singer equates his father with the largest
creatures and objects of their kind.

But mahogany will be counted,   20
Mahogany, mahogany, the mighty mahogany.
Kerjok, son of my father, son of Mou
The name of my father is big
The name of my father is big in the tribe
His name always is on people's lips.   25
Father, that is right
Great Chief, that is right.
Father, you will make me lose the name in Marial[1]
You will make me lose the name among the tribes
You will make me not be known by our girls.   30
Let me go into the tribe
To observe the girls of Marial.
Father, that is right,
Great Chief, that is right.

50. *What will the Orphans Do?* [Ngok]

(Extract)

Yai Kwol, the singer, a half-brother of Deng Majok and Deng Makuei
(also known as Deng Abot), both of whom are Chiefs, indirectly requests
their attention to his marriage by mourning the death of his father.

Jipur d'Allar d'Ajing[2]
My father is not inside the clay in vain;[3]
Clan of Biong,[4] Clan of Biong the Stork of the Marshes
Has not our father left us in misery?
Deng Makuei, what will the orphans do?   5
I think of loneliness, O Deng Majok.
Nyanluak,[5] I only mourn the absence of my father
Leaving me grieving in the clan of Biong, the Stork of the Marshes,
The spirit that took my father while still strong
To leave me grieving in the clan of Biong   10
I mourn my father all alone.

[1] Their rural area.
[2] Chief Kwol Arob's deputy who survived him.
[3] Meaning that his death has not left them unscathed.
[4] His ancestor.
[5] His proposed bride.

51. *Ayan of Pajok* [Ngok]

(Extract)

Pajok, the clan into which the singer wants to marry, is symbolized as
God, the Creator, because of their power in the tribe. The singer mourns
his father's death to influence those concerned with the marriage to sym-
pathize with his claim.

I follow after ivory[1] into the byre of the Creator
I creep under the bosom of God
I am trailing the clan Pajok
I pursue the clan Pajok
Begging them to give me Ayan   5
Deng Abot, I am begging for Ayan.
But who will give her to me?
Has not my father entered the earth?
Ayan, daughter of Allor,
If only my father had lifted the earth,   10
My father would bring her to me,
So that my father would be a bull of three horns[2]
So that my father would be a bull of spreading horns.

52. *The Good Thing called Woman* [Ngok]

Kwol Tiel, the younger brother of Jipur Tiel and a maternal relative of
Chief Deng Majok, was herding the cattle of Deng Majok, whom he
refers to as Majok. When he went to 'lie down', Acol Kwol, Deng
Majok's half-sister, and Nyanbol d'Arob, Deng Majok's first wife for
whose cattle Kwol was more directly responsible and whom Kwol
normally helped with cultivation, contributed milch-cows for him.
Apart from praising Deng Majok and these women, Kwol addresses
himself to his older brother to procure for him Aker, the daughter of
Allor, a wealthy man from the Pajok clan. Being related to Deng
Majok through Deng's mother, the fact that the girl was Deng's agnate
did not violate the rule of exogamy.

[1] The bride is symbolized as being valuable as ivory.
[2] While nothing specific is indicated, the singer means that his father's power-
position would be enhanced.

Acol, brown girl
Pack my gourd
With it, I shall search for that of my father;[1]
We shall praise Acol in songs
My ox Maker, we shall praise Acol de Kwol d'Arob   5
Acol, brown girl, released a cow
The ox, Maker, has brought us to Amet.[2]
I am courting a young beauty in Abyor
But the gossipers say to her; they say,
'Is Kwol Tiel Magak the right man to marry you?'   10
I am after an orphan with black hair[3]
I shall tell Jipur that I am a man wanting a wife
Aker d'Allor Majok
Even if you run from me to Nuerland
I will not say a bad thing about you.   15
O the good times[4] when big people talk of little things
Then the woman holds her man calling him
'Father of so and so!'
Then I say, 'Yes, yes',
While I put my spears away   20
I put my spears away after a journey
Aker, I do so without words.
Then she takes the pestle[5]
There is hunger
And I sit in a conversation.   25
Nyibol d'Arob Majok, pack my gourd
I will gorge myself, pack my gourd.
Kur Aker,[6] Kur Aker, is like a chief.
The chief, Majok, does not need persuasion[7]
Because of honour[8] he released the cows;   30

[1] It is not clear what is meant by this line. It may be that by going to fatten himself to be attractive, he is preparing to search for a wife who will bear daughters who will bring cattle here seen as those of his father. Or it could be merely wanting to marry in order to maintain the lineage—his father's.

[2] Grazing area.

[3] Young men and women normally dye their hair reddish-gold in colour, but when mourning a dead relative the hair is left unbleached for about a year.

[4] Of marriage.   [5] To grind grain for food.

[6] A young boy looking after their herds; those 'lying down' are not supposed to work at all.

[7] The chief sometimes forbids *toc* so that all might cultivate. Here, he apparently permitted it and therefore will not punish them.

[8] *Dheeng.*

Majok does not need persuasion
Honour is a very good thing.
Majok does not want persuasion
I am afraid of the court of the chief.
A man wanting a composer is not hated   35
We went after a composer
Allor Manyiel we went after a composer
Allor Manyiel
Morning rain thundered and shook the men
My milk-gourd resembles Col Mong.[1]   40

53. *The Thing is Mockery* [Ngok]

Allor Manyiel, the man mentioned in the previous song, sings about the same occasion, mentions a number of companions (including Kwol Tiel, the owner of the previous song), praises Chief Deng Majok, and criticizes his elder brother's attitude to his intended marriage.

We went after a composer with a gentleman called Kwol, 'the Back
    Shaded',
We reached Magak[1] of Kwol, Kwol d'Arob[3]
We were with Allor, Allor de Deng, the Python
Ours is a camp in which Amenh e Yor Kerjok[4] is present;
We met with the Ajuong,[5] Ajuong of Yor[6] Maker.[7]   5
Ours is the camp of Deng de Kwol
Deng de Kwol is our chief
It is for him that we go to Abyei.
I asked for Nyibol when she was a baby in her sling[8]
When she was still small,   10
I asked for Nyibol when she was a child before she grew
When she was small.
The marriage is kept on the ground by Paguiny[9]
The marriage is kept on the ground like a sacrificed bull
O people, do not keep the marriage on the ground!   15

---

[1] A legendary man known for his greed. Here he is proud that his milk-gourd was large to indicate that he drank much milk.
[2] Cattle-camp.   [3] Deng Majok's father.
[4] Son of a Malual Dinka chief.   [5] A branch of Malual.
[6] The chief of the Ajuong division.   [7] The colour-pattern of Yor's ox.
[8] The leather sling in which a mother carries a baby on her back.
[9] The singer's clan.

Malual Gitjok,[1] Malual de Kat
Your brother[2] is muddling up the marriage while the cattle are not
    finished!
He tells me, 'Look for a girl
I do not like this girl for your wife.'
Have you not seen Abyor, our tribe?   20
The thing has become a mockery
My ox Marialjok, the thing is mockery
That is what the older brother has done:
He tells me, 'Look for a girl
I do not like this girl for your wife.'   25
He sent me, saying, 'Look for help'[3]
But I was embarrassed; what should I say?
I did not tell my paternal uncle
He sent me, saying, 'Look for help'
But I was embarrassed; what should I say?   30
I did not tell my maternal uncle
He sent me, saying, 'Look for help'
But I was embarrassed; what should I say?
I will grow old with cows
I, Arob, Madien Yom,[4] have grown old with cows   35
I have grown old with cows,
People ask, 'Do you hate women?'
O I love women
Why would I hate that noble being?
The good thing called 'woman'   40
Who will feel your chest
Then ask you, 'Is anything wrong?'
Then I am cunning and I say
'Yes my own, something is wrong.'

54. *O Ajok* [Ngok]

O Ajok
My Ajok whom I asked for when she could not even dance
O Ajok
My Ajok whom I asked for when she was still carried in a sling

[1] His brother.   [2] His eldest brother.
[3] Relatives and friends assist in the payment of bride-wealth.
[4] His ox's colour-pattern.

O Ajok   5
My Ajok whom I asked for when she looked after goats with a
    stick;
O Ajok
My Ajok whom I asked for when she was not yet a tribal beauty;
Alas, when she grew
Another man waited to take her from me.   10
What cruel treatment:
The Creator has speared me
Mareng[1] has speared me
The sons of the son of Kon[2] have speared me.
Because of the daughter of Kat Atem   15
I think of the misery of loneliness,
If it were your father Kat Atem[3]
And my father Kateng[4]
They would have reasoned
Ajok, daughter of great Kat, they would have reasoned   20
They would have reasoned.
I am mourning the loss of Ajok, the brown girl
Alas, when she grew
Another man waited to deprive me of her,
What treatment: 25
Man who has been given Ajok
Divinity[5] has given unto you.

55. *Awut, Say 'Yes'* [Ngok]

Because of Awut,[6] I have become lean like a child
I say to my father
I have become lean because of Awut.
I am a man with a confounded mind
I do not know to whom to give the seat of my father   5
To go and sit on the discussion-bed
I do not know to whom to give the bed of my father.
Our words have ended with the times he used to send me for water
And the times he would say 'Go and bring a mat from the cattle-
    byre.'

[1] A sub-tribe. Either his competitor's or his own people who did not compete
successfully for him.   [2] His rival's relatives.   [3] Who is dead.
    [4] Also dead.   [5] Literally, 'the Earth'.   [6] His intended bride.

I would bring them in front of my father   10
That is the good of a person's son
People have now confused us
So that I am like the son of a stranger,
My father has tapped his chest in refusal
O clan of my father, shall I be only a fellow tribesman?   15
I love Awut of the clan Panoi
I will compete with any man who wants to marry her
I will give the people of Awut a shop
The shop of Gagrial of Aguok tribe.
Awut, say yes,   20
People of Diil[1]
I will give you the shop of Gagrial of Aguok tribe,
Awut, say yes.
My people, you gave me a shield,[2]
And gave me a helmet   25
Then you became afraid,
A bride is like a buffalo
A bride is like an elephant
So that my father feared to enter the cattle-byre.[3]
O Awut, do not touch him[4]   30
Awut, girl, do not touch him,
Who was the first to court you?
Who courted you first?
Awut, my heart has not surrendered;
Awut, advise the suitor to go   35
O Awut, advise the suitor to go.

56. *O that my Father were Alive* [Ngok]

This song concerned the marriage of the singer to Abul, Chief Deng
Majok's daughter, who expresses her resentment of the marriage in
song 103, 'What Misfortune'.

[1] Her sub-tribe. Of course, this is only a figure of speech since not the whole
sub-tribe shares the bride-wealth.
[2] In this and the following lines, he means that he was first encouraged to get
married and then let down. The helmet is made of black ostrich feathers or horse-
tail or giraffe-tail on a hand-woven base.
[3] To discuss the marriage.
[4] A competing suitor.

Silence, silence
I greet you all
My mother[1] and half-mother[2]
And Acai, the daughter of my father
If you find Adau,[3] tell her,   5
'Good morning[4] my relations-in-law
Good morning people of Abul
Tell my father, Deng Majok
Tell my father, Deng Makuei[5]
I am not frivolous about the proposal   10
My father Deng Majok
My father Deng Makuei
I am coming into the byre of the Creator;
O that my father Gitbek were alive
I would not be in misery.   15
Abul of Mangar[6] with the robe,[7] I will strive for you.
I know of no bull taller than you
I meet men with missing teeth[8] from Alei[9]
And meet men with missing teeth from Abyor[10]
I know of no one taller than you.   20
I wish I could fly to the home of Abul
To take an aeroplane and reach her in the sun
I would reach her in the sun
I would go as far as there
Mother of *ajiec*,[11] and mother of the moon—   25
There will be a man to be cut by the throat:[12]
Gentlemen are not the same
Crocodile-like man[13]
You are deceived by conversation.   29
Some men will wait to marry during the plenty of the winter
    beer[14]

[1] In law.
[2] Dinka, *dhiamdi(e)*, comprises any female relative-in-law; but is more often
used for stepmothers-in-law or anyone of that status.
[3] The eldest daughter of Chief Deng. Adau was in fact angered by the song
and had to be appeased because while the eldest, she is simply to be told if found.
[4] Literally, 'Are you dawned?'   [5] Deng Majok's half brother.
[6] Praise-name for Chief Deng Majok.   [7] Of chieftainship.
[8] The singer insults his competitors.   [9] A Ngok sub-tribe.
[10] Another sub-tribe.   [11] A small blackbird.
[12] Defeated.   [13] Ugly as a crocodile.
[14] He insults his competitors again by alleging that they are too poor to afford
bride-wealth before new crops ripen when cattle are needed more for survival.

Some men will wait to marry during the winter with plenty of
fried flour.[1]
Abul, O friend Abul, tall girl
Daughter of the Dinka
Even if I lose my way, I shall not surrender.
Mangar, my age-set, do not fear my father Deng Majok, the Chief
I have chosen Abul like ivory in the clan of Arob.   35

57. *Marriages of Schoolboys* [Ngok]

In a competition with a literate Rek Dinka over a bride, the singer, a
Ngok, scorns the educated and considers them as beneath competition
with him. The term used for the educated is 'children of the father',
'father' being the missionary.

I will frighten the Aguok[2]
The people who buy lamps
The people who buy with *Taarifa*[3]
Move away Ajong Yuot[4]
Will you be married with lamps?   5
Those lamps [torches] of yours
With them, you see the hyenas on the fringes of the open plain[5]
I will take Ajok away
I will take her to the plains of Abyei.[6]
When I see a man who kicks a bicycle[7] *garow*[8]   10
I see him as adopted
You are not the son of the father
The father is not your father.
My wife,[9] Ajok, forget him
Do not put shame on yourself   15
His proposal will end under the trees[10] called *abyei*[11] and sycamore

[1] *Akop.*   [2] A division of the Rek.
[3] A Sudanese monetary unit. There are 200 *taarifas* in a Sudanese pound (£S).
[4] The bride.
[5] The implied insult is that when they go to empty their bowels, they do not
go as far into the forest as a Dinka gentleman should. But although the animals they are likely to encounter at such distance are less dangerous ones
like hyenas, so cowardly are they that they need torches for detection and
protection.   [6] The administrative centre of the Ngok.
[7] Associated with the educated.   [8] The sound of a bicycle.
[9] A betrothed girl is referred to as 'wife'.
[10] Trees are a place of courtship.
[11] A kind of tree from which Abyei, the town, derived its name.

The cheap marriages of schoolboys,
Their marriage is easily shaken by the wind[1]
The marriage is waved by the wind.
Forget the daughter of the chief   20
You will never fulfil the marriage.
For the daughter of Giir Mayuot
I shall compete with the people of bicycles
And they will swarm away like bees.

58. *That of the Frog* [Ngok]

(Extract)

Unable to marry because of lack of cattle, the singer, being without
a sister, wishes he were a woman to assist his aged mother in housekeeping.

I call upon the Creator
Give me the vagina of a frog
That I may save my mother from the mortar
That I may save my mother from grinding the grain.
When my guests come home   5
O, when my guests come home
My mother is in the house
Only grain is boiling.[2]
I wish I were born a girl in the clan Pajing[3]
So that I might save my mother from the mortar   10
So that I might save my mother from grinding the grain.

59. *I Want a Little One* [Rek]

(Extract)

The objective of the requested marriage is to beget a child.

Uncle, uncle, I want a little one who will hold me
Uncle, uncle, I want a little one to whom lullabies will be sung[4]
One who will cry *e ngee ngee* while his mother makes his food.

---

[1] The image is that of his clothes being blown while cycling, combined with
the fact that betrothal without enough cattle lacks stability.
[2] His mother is too old to grind grain into flour.   [3] His clan.
[4] Singing lullabies connotes a woman singing any kind of song, shaking a
gourd with grain in it as accompaniment. No men sing lullabies in this sense.

Then I tell my sister-in-law,
'Come and see what the little one is doing.'   5
O our age-set, then I would say to my sister-in-law
'The son of your sister is crying
The son of you sister is crying.'
Uncle, uncle, I want a little one who will hold me.

60. *The Ancient Curse* [Ngok]

The case from which this song originated concerned alleged incestuous
adultery by the singer with his half-brother's wife. The allegation was
made by the woman, and the man denied it. After making the woman
take oath on the ashes to affirm her allegation according to Dinka rules
of evidence, the man was held liable.

Abyiem,[1] the Black-headed Cattle Egret, comes in haste
And asks, 'Have you settled the case?'
'Yes, we have cut it all through.'
Deng Jokngol d'Allor
Each man thinks of his father.   5
The chiefs stood together,
'Kur, Kur, have you admitted your fault?
Kur if you have admitted your fault
We shall put you in jail.'
Youth of our land asked me,   10
'Kur, Kur, how could you think of it?
O Kur of great Deng,
Are you cursed to seek the wives of others?
If you have done it, admit it,
A gentleman does not fear.'   15
They have crossed me with girls,
'Kur is spoiling the tribe,
O he is spoiling the tribe
True, he is spoiling the tribe
Great Chief, write him an order   20
Great Chief, write him an order
To be jailed for ever
And your head will be at ease in the land
Banish Kur to a foreign land

---

[1] The chief, *omda*, of the singer's sub-tribe, who is also a relative.

And your head will be at ease in your land.'   25
The Big Chief said, 'No!'
The Big Chief said, 'No!'
The Earth is refusing[1]
The Earth is refusing
The Earth is poised between death and life,[2]   30
And my father pointed at me, 'Kur'
My father blamed me
'How could you think of it,
How could Kur think of it
To be brave about a married woman,   35
When it is an ancient curse of mankind?'[3]
O ancient curse of mankind
The kind called women
They lead you into the wilderness
It is an ancient curse.   40
'Kur it is an ancient curse
Kur, son of Deng of the Women's Camp[4]
O Son of the ancient curses.'[5]
O I am the son of ancient curses
Has not the woman confounded me?   45
Has not the woman cheated me?
She said, 'Let us do it',
She said, 'Let us do it.'
Then came and confused it
She confused it all alone   50
After she tried to mislead a man
She was no longer she[6]
And when I said, 'Drink the ashes',[7]
I said, 'Drink the ashes'
She accepted evil, she did not refuse;   55

[1] Earth has religious significance. He means that the chief, through his Divine Wisdom, is refusing.
[2] The harsh treatment he might receive if the chief should be persuaded is metaphorically expressed as death.
[3] Adultery is believed to invite a curse that may cause death.
[4] The singer comes from a clan believed to have been founded by a woman.
[5] Women are believed to be the source of evil, and since he comes from a clan founded by a woman he calls himself 'son of the ancient curses'.
[6] She changed.
[7] Normally people are sprinkled with ashes to take an oath. She probably did not drink the ashes but he says she did to indicate the gravity of the case.

Sister, are you never ashamed?
Your vagina will kill you.
O son of the ancient curses
The woman has confounded me.

61. *Fish are not Cows* [Gok]

The singer's wife committed adultery with a fisherman. Fishermen do
not have cattle and are considered inferior. He wonders how the fisherman can pay his bride-wealth should he divorce his wife and demand
the return of his cattle.

> The girl, Acol the Brown
> Has indeed pierced me.[1]
> Will my cows be collected from fish?
> Has a fish ever borne a cow?
> Acol e Kooc   5
> Has a fish ever borne a cow on the river?
> Do fish have mothers?
> Padhol,[2] I do not blame you
> She is a child built by her mother
> The child is captured by her mother.   10
> Our hearts have missed
> The daughter of Kooc and I
> Her mother once rolled her sleeping skin
> And moved across the river.
> The child is captured by her mother;   15
> Acol who remained with her mother.
> Even her mother is better than Acol;
> The heart of Acol the Brown is seized by her mother
> And taken to the riverside.

62. *Husband of my Wife* [Gok]

This is an insult song against a competitor in marriage, whom the singer
refers to here as husband of his wife. According to Dinka custom,
the highest bidder wins, but if the girl loves the loser, she might elope
with him.

[1] *Woor*, piercing through something, the symbolic act by which magicians
destroy their victims.   [2] Her agnatic lineage (clan).

Makol, son of my father
My heart is at Makuac in Ayiel,[1]
Son of my father
My heart is at Makuac in Ayiel.
The man is a dog with a heart like his father's,   5
For my girl, I will pluck the bottom of the suitor
Like the hummer-headed Stork plucked by the Saddle-bill Stork.[2]
I am in conflict with a hummer-headed Stork over a woman.
This girl I will never leave
What you have laid down[3]   10
If you do not stop, I will say it now
Husband of my wife, I will say it now:
Are you not the son of Dir Riak?
We shall meet, we shall meet,
Dog whose father went into town   15
Dog with a trotting heart
You will return into your cattle-byre;[4]
The ancient deeds of your father,
I am leaving out a big thing here
I know it, but I will not say it,   20
It is suitable only for you.[5]

63. *What shall I Do with Tomorrow?* [Rek]

(Extract)

A lamentation by a man deserted by his wife who wants a divorce but
whom he still loves.

My wife, Acok of Great Malek
O Acok
Have you hated me
When I have not hated you?
How can the marriage spoil?   5
The woman wants my cows returned:[6]

---

[1] Presumably the home of the girl.   [2] Story unknown.
[3] He has provoked the singer into threatening to reveal scandalous information about his family.
[4] Defeated, he will be forced to take back his cows.
[5] So bad that even his saying it or its being heard is not becoming.
[6] His bride-wealth cows to be returned on divorce.

A man after a woman is not simple;[1]
What shall I do with tomorrow?
Shall I go to drink beer?[2]
What shall I do with tomorrow?   10
Shall I go to drink coffee?
What shall I do with tomorrow?
Shall I go to drink tea?
What shall I do with tomorrow?
I am bewildered by what Acok has done to me   15
I have not understood it.

64. *Long Gone are our Days* [Ngok]

Since the Ngok Dinkas and the Baggara Arabs became incorporated
into one local government council, the Missiriya Rural Council, a
struggle over power has marked the relationship between the Pajok and
the corresponding Ali Gula ruling families of the Ngok and the Baggara,
families which had for generations been on very friendly terms. The
ambition of Babo and Ali Nimr, grandsons of Chief Ali Gula, is that the
Ngok be included under Babo's Paramount Chieftainship as are the
Homr Baggara Arab and Nuba tribes. Deng Majok, the Ngok Chief,
on the other hand, insists on his tribe's remaining outside Babo's paramount leadership, and all successive governments have maintained his
leadership separately, though incorporated into the council. Tensions
between the two families continue and worsen.

   In the following two songs, the singer, Arob, the youngest brother of
the Chief, reflects these tensions, the history of his family's leadership,
and his resentment of the inclusion of the Ngok in a council in which the
Arabs must always predominate, if only by virtue of their overwhelming
majority.

The great Ngok of Kwol is spoilt
The great Ngok of Kwol is spoilt;
We are victimized; we are sacrificed like a bull,
Deng the Chief is harried over his land.
O that my father were here, the great White and Black of Arob![3]   5
I shall tell my father, the great White-Black of Arob

   [1] He means that he is too determined to be discouraged easily.
   [2] In this and the following two lines, the singer sees beer, coffee, and tea as
outlets to his emotional crisis. While beer is drunk traditionally, coffee and tea
were unknown to the Dinka, but the singer apparently sees their functions as
similar to that of beer.   [3] Kwol d'Arob.

And tell Biong, the Stork of the Marshes[1]
Shall I not tell my father?
You, Ali of Nimr
Who is causing confusion?   10
The man causing confusion?
What of the robe of Kwol, the Chief?
Take the case to Madibok,[2] Deng Majok, my brother.
Deng de Kwol is wearing the robe[3]
He is like God; like God the Creator.   15
In the time of Ali of the former days
When you, Arob, were installed Head of the Land
That was the land.
Alas, long gone are our days,
Alas, numbered are our days.   20
If the chiefs are wanted, then call the Great Bol[4]
If the chiefs are asked for, then call Kwol, my father.
When confusion was caused
O when confusion was caused
The great man wore the robe of red[5]   25
And Nuerland was the land of his father's[6]
Yes, Nuerland was the land of his father's.
How great was Ngok of my father Kwol Arob!
Ali then had his byre   30
From it he released a horse
It was to propitiate Arob
It was to conciliate the father of my father.
And whenever Madibok asked
His power ended at Denga[7]   35
The man we have lost was the bull who guarded us at the peg
The bull who protected us at the peg.
He was the bull who guarded us at the peg.
Should the Arab from far off Nahud be the bull to guard us to the peg?
Should the Arab from Muglad be the bull to guard us to the peg?

[1] The grandfather of Kwol.
[2] It is not clear who Madibok is. It probably refers to the Mahdi whom the Dinka revered though they opposed his political leadership.
[3] The modern symbol of office.
[4] One of the important chiefs of the Tuic.
[5] The red robe symbolizes seniority of chieftaincy.
[6] The singer assumes that the traditional power of his family extended over Nuerland.
[7] Muglad, the administrative centre of the Homr Baggara Arabs.

What misfortune has now reached our land   41
Ali the bull of the brown
Is wearing the tassels of the land
He has extended his power into the land of Arob.
He will meet with the facts of the distant past   45
When one man ate even the rib of a donkey[1]
One man ate it to survive the pain of evil
He surrendered his child to death
To save the land of his father.
Misfortune has now spread over the land   50
Ali, the bull of the Brown,
Is wearing the tassels of the land
He has extended his power into the land of Arob.

65. *The Bull Tethered Across the Head* [Ngok]

(Extract)

Abyor and Manyuar are the bulls of the land
Jipur Allor Ajing,[2]
And my father,[3] the Bull Tethered Across the Head[4]
My father was the bull tethered across the head,
A bull like Ariath Makuei.[5]   5
A man who will not recognize Kwol Arob
Will have nothing else to say
He will meet with the clan of Biong[6]
And will have nothing else to say
The world will hear.   10
My father, even if a disaster were that of the Tuic,

[1] See story in note 3 of Song 48, p. 162, 'The Wedding of Alai'. There is a play over what Arob actually ate: some say merely donkey-meat; others, as in the song cited above, dramatize even more by saying he ate the afterbirth of a donkey; yet others specify other parts of the donkey, as the rib in the present song.

[2] The late chief of the Mannyuar sub-tribe who was Kwol Arob's assistant and whose successor is now one of Deng Majok's assistants.

[3] Kwol Arob.

[4] *Muor Ngak Nhom*, 'the Bull Tethered Across the Head', is used wherever the English word 'King' is applicable because only the most powerfull bull is tethered this way to keep it under control.

[5] A Prophet who resisted the British. He was finally overcome and imprisoned for most of his life.

[6] Kwol's grandfather.

He considered it that of all
Now we are joined to the desert,[1]
When my father held his land from Ali[2]
Deng Majok is our Chief, Deng Majok is the Chief.[3]   15

66. *Defiance* [Ngok]

In this song, Nyok expounds some of the incidents in his family's
history and appraises the recent political developments *vis-à-vis* the
Arabs. Nyok, being the full brother of Deng Abot who competed with
their half-brother, Deng Majok, in the succession-case discussed under
Power and the Law, has another objective in the song. He believes that
the Sacred Spears, the symbols of authority, were wrongly given to
Deng Majok by the Government he calls *jur*, foreign, which he sees as
spoiling the tribe of his father.

The Sacred Spears possessed by Kwol were not stolen
They were bequeathed to him,
Son of Madibok,[4] they were bequeathed unto him.
Great Bol Nyuol, Great Bol
Allor d'Ajing;   5
Father, Father, son of Arob
Father, Father, Father, Great Chief
The Government is destroying your man.
The man who ate the ribs of a donkey[5]
Is it to him that the land belongs?   10
It is to Biong, my great-grandfather, that the land belongs
It is to Arob that the land belongs
It is to Kwol that the land belongs
It is to him that the Ngok belongs
It is to him that Abyor[6] belongs.   15

[1] Another way of saying that they are joined to Arab administration in
Missiriya District, Kordofan Province.
[2] The grandfather of Babo Nimr the Paramount Chief of Missiriya.
[3] While praising his brother there is a tone of criticism that, unlike his father
who was totally independent, his brother has given in somewhat by joining a
Council in which the Arabs are in the majority.
[4] See No. 64 n. 2, p. 181, of 'Long Gone are Our Days'.
[5] See 'The Wedding of Alai' (No. 48, n. 3, p. 162), and 'Long Gone are Our
Days' (No. 64, n. 1, p. 182).
[6] The sub-tribe of the singer and therefore of the Ngok Head Chiefs.

When he reached Noong[1]
Horses were trailing the man
He went as far as El Obeid[2]
The Governor came and Arob was defied
'If we are fighting over power   20
Bring out your son
And the land will be yours
And your things will be four.'[3]
He cut the throat of his son
And the land of the Ngok held.   25
Our land was saved
The land of my grandfather was saved,
Our land was saved
Arob cut his son
And the land of the Ngok was saved;   30
Arob split himself
And the land of the Ngok was saved.

[1] The traditional home of both Deng Majok and Deng Makuei. The latter later moved altogether to Abyei while the former moved to Abyei but maintained his traditional home at Noong.

[2] The Headquarters of Kordofan Province. It was because Arob, and later Kwol, registered their allegiance to the colonial regimes in El Obeid that the Ngok became officially incorporated in that Province.

[3] Not clear, but presumably his power will be increased.

III

INITIATION SONGS

INITIATION songs basically describe the introduction of the initiate to the warring period ahead, his elevation to a more respected position in consequence of his courage, and his conflict with the older generations because of this step towards emancipation. The period of a young man's life after initiation, but below the 'eldering' age, is one of the most dramatic in Dinka life. It is a period in which physical courage is emphasized as manly virtue. Initiation introduces a young man into this period. The bloodiness of the occasion, the recognition of its pain, and the pride in endurance are all symbols of the adventures ahead. Despite its physical pain, the occasion of initiation is characterized by pride, joy, and lavish festivities.

As initiation songs in this volume were collected from the Ngok, our account and commentary on Dinka initiation should be seen in that context. Initiation among the Ngok begins with the designation of a 'father' and a name for the emerging age-set a few years before their initiation. This 'father' is usually an elder member of one of the chiefly lineages. The intending initiates then request their father and the chief to permit their initiation. Their request granted, a period of festivities precedes the cutting of some seven to ten deep, well-ordered marks across the forehead. The day before the operation is particularly festive, with beer, meat, and other kinds of food in plenty, and the sound of drums in the air. On the last night, no one sleeps. They dance all night and there is a feeling of tension. Early next morning, the operation begins. In proper order of seniority of birth and clan the to-be-initiated lie on the ground with a small hole under each one's head to hold blood. As the operation proceeds, relatives and friends of the initiates display great pleasure. Both men and women dance a special ballet, known as *goor*, and nowadays, gunshots fill the air in expressions of joy.

The initiation period (which goes on for several months) is the most colourful in the life of a Ngok Dinka. They live collectively by lineages ('Doorway, or mouth, of the house') in special villages. They have few responsibilities and a lot of privileges. Their special dress, their initiation songs of bravery, and their dances in which lineages and sub-tribes compete are a great attraction to men and women, especially to girls.

Initiation is much more complex than a uniform source of pleasure. The initiates are in a kind of accepted conflict with the older generations, since initiation is a step for the younger towards replacing the older. Every step of the initiate towards equality in seniority is a further limitation on the authority of the older generations. But with the resentment at this curtailment of tutelage goes the pleasure of seeing one's child or relative rise in age and status. The initiate in turn combines his zest for greater freedom with the gentle submissiveness required of a younger man. This concurrent conflict between, and harmonizing of interests of, different generations are symbolized in initiation and articulated in initiation songs. The initiator, who represents the older generations, is seen with both affection and enmity. He is pictured as one with the upper hand who must be faced with courage. Most references to the father are those of conflict over whether the son should be initiated or not. The son wants to be, but the father refuses. The father's argument usually revolves around such statements as 'You are still a child', 'You will run away', or 'You will fear'. The conflict is seen in the songs as a war, for initiation is a step towards the establishing of the son's own role in the lineage. The father is ambivalent because he is pleased to see his son rising to perpetuate their lineage, while at the same time recognizing that it signalizes a loss of parental control. Those who are often presented as un-reservedly glad are women: mothers, sisters, and other relatives. This is because females are perpetually under tutelage, and partly depend on their sons and brothers for influence. The sister does not stay long to pursue this, but the success of the mother as a wife is so dependent on her success as a mother that her status rises in direct correspondence with the number and the ages of her children, particularly sons. Initiation is a promotion for her.

Among the Ngok, the initiation dance in which initiation songs are sung consists of a lifting and dropping of the legs with a jerk of the body to imitate the movement of a horse under tight rein. This is accompanied with exclamations (*mioc*), such as 'I blunt the knife'. The singer, representing the horse and the rider, makes sounds as though subduing an unruly horse. Sometimes he portrays the whipping of the horse with the reins held tight so that the struggle becomes more marked. These are symbols of their coercive power, their pride in their forthcoming status as powerful warriors, and, it would seem, their desire for emancipation. It is, however, important to stress that this symbol of the rider and the ridden represents the conflict and harmony in a lyric fashion. Dinkas did not traditionally own horses—Southern Dinkas still do not. Because of their long association with the Arabs, the Ngok have horses but think of them as belonging to people of wealth and authority.

In initiation dances, the drums are not used. The dancers beat the ground together with their bundles of canes, and also decorate themselves with anklet and bracelet bells which produce a variety of jingling sounds as they dance. Added to this is the cry of joy (*kieu*) of women dancers. Generally, men and women share the dance, but each person dances as a member of a group without any special partners. The only exception to this is a variant of an initiation dance called *ruaath* which is usually danced by men of all ages with women of older age-groups. A man and a woman hop around with one leg raised up and held across the leg of the partner while the dancers chant:

> My father throws a war club[1] at me
> I shall cut my feet
> My father throws a war club at me
> I shall cut my feet.[2]

Ruaath is the only Ngok Dinka dance in which bodies, that is, legs, touch, and in that sense is the sexiest, even though it is danced with women whose sex-life would have ended, for once her children reach maturity, which for sons is signified by initiation (for girls by marriage), the mother should stop bearing children as

[1] What the Ngok call *ñuer*, presumably because it originated in Nuerland.

[2]
> Wa ya biok e nuɛr
> Yɛn ba acok teem ee
> Wa ya biok e nuɛr
> Yɛn ba acok teem ee.

'*Acok teem*' means literally 'to cut my feet'. Dr. Lienhardt suggests that it may refer to the division of one sub-set from another in which the juniors (*cok cien*) become the leaders of another series.

well as having sexual intercourse, it not being decent for the
mother of a 'gentleman' (*adheng*) to do so.

Once fully acknowledged as an adult, an initiate changes
dramatically. Correlative to his newly acquired privileges is a high
standard of individual dignity and responsibility which distinguishes the initiated from children.

67. *Redemption from Slavery* [Ngok]

I greeted the initiator in the middle of the night
The morning has not come
Ajiec,[1] has the world not yet dawned?
Friend, Col Marial[2]
The knife became red like leather tanned by the Arabs   5
Our Mangar[3] will lie for pain in the home of the Dancing Crane[4]
Isn't it the good thing which redeems a man from slavery?
I will not run.
Our Python-like Stork[5] of Circling Fish-Eagle[6] will lie on the
     flank
The flank is held strong as a bridle
We lay still in the home of the Sacred Leopard   10
Even though it hurts, I did not feel its pain
The gentleman lay red with bloodlike a firefly
Red and White Spotted Fish[7] go to the flank.
Tawny daughter of the lion[8] ran wild   15
A goat struggled with a spear[9]
The spear of Col 'the Python'.[10]
Woman dancing the *ruaath*[11]
What do you say?

[1] A small black bird which sings at dawn.
[2] A co-initiate.   [3] The age-set.
[4] The praise-name of the elder in whose village the initiation took place.
[5] The ox-name of a co-initiate. The association is between the frequenting of
the river by both the python and the stork.
[6] The co-initiate's father's ox-name. Fish-eagles, black and white in colour,
circle over the river like dancers in the *gor* dance.
[7] An initiate, in Dinka called *Apoklek*.
[8] The corresponding women age-set.
[9] In celebration, a relative may kill anybody's goat knowing he must repay
more.
[10] Col's ox-colour-name.
[11] A variation of the initiation dance.

She says I have endured it   20
Yes I have endured it, it is only the pain of the aftermath
Ngol Akol,[1] lead the songs.

68. *A Determined Heart* [Ngok]

In 1955, Nyangateer, an age-set of Abyor sub-tribe of the Ngok, was just
about to be initiated. The singer, Deng Biong, was then about 130 miles
away from Ngokland in school at Muglad. He wanted to be initiated.
Since educated Dinka normally are not initiated he was refused permission by both his relatives and the school authorities. He got into a
lorry loaded with sacks of grain, put himself in an empty sack, and hid
among the sacks until the lorry was close to Abyei. His initiation was
still opposed by his father, Biong Mading. Deng Biong appealed to his
uncles Deng Majok and Deng Abot, both of whom are Chiefs.

I heard the news in the land of the Arabs
Even if Arob[2] tries to stop me, I will not agree
The war is waged against the veins
If Kulang[3] is gone, Ador[4] is there
Ador and Bol, the Victim of the Arabs,[5]   5
The noblemen of the tribe unite against me
But I did not move.
Because of a determined heart I crossed the *goz*[6]
I hid myself in a sack
I turned into grain.   10
I appeared at Alal[7]
But what could be done?
The head is bewildered[8]
I ran after the knife
A knife that was sharp   15
I will not combine veins with my ox Mabil.[9]

[1] A co-initiate.
[2] His educated cousin, then Local Government Executive Officer.
[3] An initiator brought from Ruweng tribe of Upper Nile.
[4] Another initiator.
[5] An initiator whose ox-colour-pattern is that of the giraffe, hence 'the
Victim of the Arabs' who hunt giraffes.
[6] High sandy land in the North.   [7] In Dinka territory.
[8] The people with him did not know what to do.
[9] Only after initiation may a man publicly display or sing over his ox and be
known as the official owner and by the metaphoric name or names of the ox.

I am blamed by my father, Mading de Yar[1]
Mine is a determined heart
Mading de Kwol, it is a determination you will not stop
You will never.   20
The Chiefs[2] are allied against me
But they will never succeed.
If you leave it unresolved
I shall discuss it with my uncles, Deng and Deng
Uncle and Uncle, I will not agree.   25
Nyankat[3] is running at the ancient speed
The ancient speed after which she was named.
Abul[4] is dancing with joy
Acai[5] is dancing with joy
Gik, gik,[6] the knife has gone deep   30
Old man, Ador Gagrial, son of clan Pajing.

69. *Sentenced Veins* [Ngok]

Ayong Monyyom, then at school, was prevented from being initiated
to the extent that he was detained in jail by the chief, his maternal uncle.
Determined as he was, his relatives ultimately allowed him to be
initiated. He claims that only cowards argue that education is inconsistent with initiation.

I greet the town with the coming of dawn
Micar d'Allor,[7] it is dawn
I refuse to remain uninitiated
Bol, Follower of Twins,[8] it is dawn
I am locked in jail   5
A knife as red as a firefly
Stained with blood eating the veins
He pulled it across the forehead and the skull rattled
My head fell, a knife which leaves no veins.

[1] Praise-ox-name for the late Chief Kwol Arob.
[2] His father and his uncles.
[3] A cousin whose name literally means 'Running Girl'.
[4] Another cousin.
[5] Yet another cousin.
[6] The sound of the knife as it cuts the forehead.
[7] His age-mate and friend who, like him, was initiated while attending school.
[8] Any male born after twins is named Bol.

Each year comes, and with it the knife of Bol   10
Cowards will remain in the land of Babo[1]
And in the land of Mangar de Cap of Kiec and Agar[2]
I said to Bol Athieng de Mangol
Do not hurry
Arrange them[3] well.   15
My head lay still
The knife was raised
And the wounds were traced[4]
I hate a vein to escape
Bol will sentence the veins in the morning   20
The metal drum[5] will beat all night
I hate a vein to escape.

70. *The Gun of Deng* [Ngok]

We are provoking the war with Deng and Deng and Agok[6] the
   Pied One
The big age-set is held back like a fleeing swarm of bees[7]
The carrier of the Shields hides the knife from the eyes of the sun[8]
And the guns of Deng roared.[9]
A war we started with the father of Acai[10]   5
The carrier of the Shields hides the knife from the eyes of the sun
And the guns of Deng roared.
A war we started with our uncle, Jaklek,[11]
The carrier of the Shields hides the knife from the eyes of the sun
And the guns of Deng roared.   10

---

   [1] Chief of the Homr Baggara Arabs.
   [2] Here, the song reveals Dinka ignorance of other Dinka tribes. Mangar Cap was the chief of Atuot Dinka and not of Agar Dinka.
   [3] Initiation marks.
   [4] During Dinka initiation the veins must be cut.
   [5] The name of the drum was *Ayang weeth*, literally, 'Ayak [a feminine name] of steel'.
   [6] Father of the age-set.
   [7] Their initiation had been delayed.
   [8] The first man initiated, whose blood covered the knife so that it could not shine.
   [9] In happiness, guns are shot into the air.   [10] The initiator.
   [11] Yellowish-white and brown, the colour-pattern of the giraffe and his ox-name.

The Great Bol is spoiled[1]
He is like Awek[2]
He goes around running
Cries of joy arose, heard by all
The son of the Chief of all the tribes is lying.   15
Jokrol and Deng Miyom,
Sacrifice the bull on the shrine of Jok[3]
That the son of the clan of the initiator may lie first.
We have divided Abyei[4]
The Pollen Grabber[5] of Pabil clan wants to be a Dinka on his head
While he remains a *jur*[6] carrying the pen in his eyes.   21
Pollen Grabber of Pabil
Will remain a *jur* with a pen in his eyes.
Mading de Ngol is taking the girl[7]
Count the marks like the money of the *jur*   25
Count them as seven.

71. *I Hate Being a Boy* [Ngok]

I hate being a boy
And I shall not remain[8]
The Great Vulture[9] flew to Puduonythiek
We met, and the place turned red like a firefly
The ram is tethered for the invocation.[10]   5
The ram is tethered for the invocation in the home of Dorjok[11]
Kwol of clan Pajok
I will not bring shame on you.
The knife turned red with blood
Jipur, have we said a word?[12]   10

[1] The initiator inflicts harm without reprisal.
[2] A human being who was believed to have turned into a lioness and to
have eaten a girl before she was killed.   [3] The founder of Pajok lineage.
[4] Abyei, the administrative centre of the Ngok, symbolizes their modern
sector, which no longer adheres to tradition. Here, however, some of the educated
Dinka have chosen to be initiated.
[5] The bee colour-pattern of the educated initiate.   [6] A foreigner.
[7] The cuts are compared to cattle used as bride-wealth in competition for
marriage. The initiator will win if the initiate does not have sufficient cuts.
[8] A boy.   [9] The age-set.
[10] A ram sacrificed to ensure a safe initiation.
[11] Praise-name for Chief Kwol Arob.
[12] The initiate must not move or utter a sound during initiation or he will be
considered a coward.

The thrust of the spear of the tribe of Majuan[1]
The age-set of Deng, the Dancing Head,[2] came like locusts.
If pain is not endured
A man is not a man
Veins bled like a stormy rain   15
The head of the bull[3] is torn apart.

72. *Brew the Beer* [Ngok]

Brew the beer
The moon will appear
O mother of the Hawk of Deng
Our Abyor has rejected darkness[4]
I tell Makuany de Mijok[5]   5
We cannot remain for another year.
Makuen e Kwol has consulted his heart[6]
'The moon will appear
Let the Hawk come with Agok.'[7]
We met with Monyjur[8]   10
Monyjur with a stained arm
He has covered himself with blood
I will not wait vexing myself
Bol has turned wild
Bol has become a lion   15
He is killing men
In clan Pajok, a lion has appeared.

73. *The War Begins* [Ngok]

Coward, run away, people are killed
People are killed by Malek[9]
People are killed by Ajang
People are killed by Ador

[1] Rurweng Dinka tribe from where the initiator was invited.
[2] The Crested Crane—an ox-colour-pattern of the 'father' of the age-set.
[3] The initiates call themselves bulls to symbolize courage.
[4] The moonless part of the month.   [5] An age-set.
[6] Chief Deng Makuei who was at first refusing his consent to initiation that year.   [7] The age-set's 'father'.
[8] Literally, 'the Arab man'. Bol the initiator's ox-name derived from the colour of the giraffe hunted by the Arabs.
[9] An initiator; so are Ajang and Ador in the next two lines.

Initiators have attacked Magak[1]   5
I ask the Big Chief
Why was I not told of the attack[2]
O Deng, the Saddle-bill Stork?
The junior Magak lie in the morning
Bol[3] sat on the right flank   10
And Marial[4] on the left flank
They met in the centre *Tum!*[5]
The war begins!

74. *If I Fear, Slaughter me* [Ngok]

When the morning star appears, I will not run
I will kneel and sing a war song
Grey[6] of the Dancing Head,[7] I scorn its pain
Son of Col, Ash-painted Crested Crane, Ajang[8]
If I run from the knife, slaughter me   5
Grandfather, son of the clan of Kon d'Ayong
Grandfather of Deng, Swimmer over the Reeds[9]
Son of the clan of Kon d'Ayong
My head will be ploughed in the morning
Man, endure the pain   10
Your father is dancing
The whole of Abyor is dancing
The wife of my father is dancing
The mother of Deng is dancing
She approaches us burning houses[10]   15
Monitor Lizard, Bol, on the right flank

---

[1] The initiator's age-set.
[2] A mock-complaint. The singer's metaphor is that initiation is a war in which he has been ambushed.
[3] The initiator whose ox name is Malek.
[4] The initiator whose real name is Ador.
[5] The sound of banging heads.
[6] The ox-colour-pattern of the man praised—the singer's age-mate.
[7] The Crested Crane—the colour-pattern of the ox of the father of the man mentioned in note 6.
[8] The colouring of the Crested Crane, associated with a particular pattern of black and white in oxen, is likened to the decoration of patterns in ashes put on the body for dancing or similar displays.
[9] The pelican—also an ox-colour-pattern.
[10] A customary destruction which she knows will have to be compensated for.

I defeat the people
I will not fear
Marial de Col advises me pointing into my eyes[1]
I hate being a boy   20
I will not remain a boy this year
Father, Marial, O Father Marial
The knife sharpened by the son of Rialjok,
Cut my veins for the sake of pride
Our girls, the Tawny daughter of the Lion will stand and watch 25
Girl-friend of the Lion,[2] I greet you.

75. *My Mother is Dancing* [Ngok]

The woman, my mother, is dancing the *ruaath*;[3]
Sister, if you see Ajiec[4] dancing with a shield
It has begun,
Have you seen that the moon has appeared?
If you see Ajiec dancing with a shield   5
It has begun.
Uncle, Ajiec, why does the world refuse to dawn
So that we may invoke Miyom[5]
That the dawn may come?[6]
God knows the words,[7] it is dawn.   10
If it is dawn, let us kneel,
The war has begun, we have met
There is a spear on the forehead
No one will fear the knife to shame his father.
It is said that we may run from the war of the knife   15
Acai has jumped into the river[8]
Acai is swimming,
People, rescue Acai
Acai nearly followed Acai who was drowned.[9]

[1] He shakes his finger in admonition.
[2] The age-set symbolizes itself as a lion.
[3] A variant of initiation dance.   [4] The initiate's uncle.
[5] A bull to be sacrificed so that initiation may be safe.
[6] With a blessed initiation.
[7] 'Knows the words' means he knows the right thing.
[8] A customary female expression of joy at initiation.
[9] Sacrificed to the powers of the river in a legend.

The girl of Pajok nearly followed Acai who was drowned;   20
Acai of the Shining Stars[1] and Acai of Macngol
They nearly followed Acai who was drowned.

76. *Are they Skinning the Man?* [Ngok]

(Extract)

I have subdued the father of Acai with my forehead
He is a man initiating a bull
Even if the knife is sharpened to be like a sliver of cane
Shield Man[2] I have blunted the edge[3]
You let Bol go, and did not say 'No!'   5
I have stopped him
The knife wore out on the brow of my eye.
Is Magwith Jok Adol not yet done?
He is still on the right side.
He has not reached the left side   10
What is the matter?
Are they skinning the man?
Why has it taken so long?

77. '*You Will Run*' [Ngok]

(Extract)

My father said, 'You will not lie
You will run away',
I do not care for my life
I shall lie down under the shrine of Kwol Marial
It has dawned   5
I shall lie down under the shrine of Kwol, the Chief
O it has dawned.

---

[1] An ox-colour-pattern: dark body spotted white.
[2] The giraffe-colour-pattern—the praise-name of the first man to be initiated in the group.
[3] A hard head symbolizes strength.

78. *No One is Saved* [Ngok]

(Extract)

Akwol is dancing away
Our Akwol is dancing in the river
She says: 'Herd of Wild Dogs!'
Wife of my father, why do you call me?
I am here   5
She says: 'Carrier of shades'
Wife of my father, why do you call me?
I am here
No one can be saved from initiation
Even a father cannot replace his son   10
It is the desire of each man's heart.

79. *Blood and Smoke* [Ngok]

The Twin-Oxen will lie
He is leading the Great Vulture[1]
Blood will flow into the pool with smoke[2]
Abyei is smoking with the shots of guns
The holes[3] red like the forest of red trees   5
My right forehead with five
My left forehead with five
My head will carry twelve.[4]
Nothing will ever be the same
The ancient dance, to which the birds came   10
Even dogs and lions came
The great time when sparrows killed the hawks.
Nothing is known that can subdue man
Dust covered the sun
Jipur[5] could not be seen   15
We shall fight with the father of Ayom[6]
Dust covered the sun

---

[1] Name of the age-set.   [2] Of shotguns.
[3] In which the blood flows on initiation. There is one under the head of
each man.
[4] On his head. Figures chosen for merely rhythmic purposes.
[5] The initiator.   [6] Another initiator.

Jipur could not be seen
My holes are like the holes of flood
The Great Vulture of Deng lined their feet.[1]   20

80. *Is All Well?* [Ngok]

A man from Abyei is asked before he sits
'Is all well, is all well?'
It is for noble display that guns are shot
Mustafa has left the town
To celebrate our honour.   5
Sheikh el Din,
Have you loaded the gun?
Sergeant-Major,[2]
Have you loaded the gun?
I lay   10
The bedding of the government[3]
Marial, Dancing with Girls[4]
Dancing with Girls did not fear.
Bung d'Alok, striped black and white ox of Jok   14
The Arabs are like hunters of elephants[5] in the home of the
Honoured Pied One.[6]

81. *Dogs are Lapping the Blood* [Ngok]

(Extract)

The Bird[7] feeds in the land of the Arabs
And feeds in the land of the Rek
And feeds in the land of the Nuer
The Grey One circles the world like a plane.
Nyandeeng de Kor, please help chase the dogs away   5
And fill in the holes
The dogs are lapping the blood
In my war with the Pelican, there is death
Chief Dorjok, bless the hand of the father of Ayom.[8]

---

[1] They lie in a row.   [2] *Shawish* (Arabic).
[3] The chief sometimes honours a relative by providing bedding for the
ceremony.   [4] The Crested Crane, which often dances.
[5] Carrying guns.   [6] Praise-name for Chief Kwol.
[7] Vulture—the name of the age-set.   [8] The initiator.

IV

AGE-SET INSULT SONGS

AGE-CONFLICT is also shown by a type of song known as *diet ket*, which is an attempt by the age-set immediately preceding the last initiated age-set to hold back the rise of the younger age-set by defamatory songs. Insult songs in general are common in Dinka society, but the category under consideration is peculiar to inter-age-set conflict. The immediate expression of this conflict is over girls. Dinka women also have age-sets. Because of the earlier maturity of women, the members of a male age-set usually go below their age-sets for girls. This means that their mates are nearly always far younger than they. Since in theory corresponding men and women age-sets mark potential husbands and wives, they are supposed to be exclusive. In addition, the younger age-set often have more influence over the girls who are closer to them in age.

In *ket* songs, the older age-sets explore any incidents involving members of the younger age-set which would shame them if disclosed in a song. Usually individual conduct is the subject-matter. The songs are not always about facts, and even when they are, the facts are exaggerated or distorted. A dominant theme portrays the younger age-sets as children still attached to their mothers. The mothers are often insulted. Even if a brother of the younger man be a member of the older age-set, so institutionalized are the songs that he would not oppose his mother's being defamed.

When presenting these songs, the older age-set dance the women-dance to represent the younger as womanly. The result is an institutionalized fight (*biok*) between them. Such fights are not only provoked by songs. They are a general manifestation of the conflict between age-sets. In the eyes of the Dinka, they are mock-fights. Only clubs or sticks, not spears, are used, but severe injuries are often inflicted. The effect of the insults is rather to encourage the younger group towards aggression than to deter them from it.

82. *Deem Stinks like a Hyena* [Ngok]

(Extract)

This song was composed by an Aliab age-set against members of the Cuor. The facts concerned a hunt for meat undertaken by the Cuor in a far-off cattle-camp. They found an animal the identity of which they mistook. Having killed the animal, they roasted it in the forest and ate it, as Dinka hunters often do, bringing back to the cattle-camp some meat to the elder in the camp. This elder doubted that the animal was edible, and, after close inspection, it was proved to be a cub of a hyena.

> Dogs bark at him between the poles
> Deem stinks like a hyena
> I do not know an animal of eight sausages[1]
> Deem stinks like a hyena
> In the hearth of Pieng Mangar,[2]   5
> Dogs bark between the poles
> Deem stinks like a hyena
> *Ngu, ngu,*[3] Monyluak[4] has become wild.

83. *They Beat him like a Dog* [Ngok]

(Extract)

> Women are tired at Noong
> They beat him with sticks like a dog
> White-striped bustard[5]
> The nobody-man who cooks with women
> White-striped bustard.   5

84. *Buying and Selling* [Ngok]

Until very recently the Dinka considered buying and selling shameful and that they should not be engaged in by a decent person. This is largely still the case, but trade has been introduced and accepted, and

---

[1] The Dinka make sausages from the viscera of animals. Eight would be an unusual number of sausages.   [2] Deem's brother.
[3] The cry of the hyena.   [4] Another member of the age-set.
[5] The ox name (*Bilou*) of the man who is being insulted.

some people, especially women, now engage in it with less consequent
ostracism. But sometimes insult songs are still composed for such
people. In this, the mothers of members of the younger age-set are the
target of insult. Because of their alleged selling and buying they are
presented as talking Arabic and, since selling and buying are said to be
their heritage, they are by implication insulted as originally non-Dinka.

> Buying and selling is the ancient heritage of the
>   mother of Gon
> And Abuk
> Abuk in particular is in the lead like a beer-filter[1]
> Followed by Akur,
> The girl fond of saying in Arabic   5
> 'Come, come![2]
> You see[3]
> I buy salt.'

[1] Which precedes the people who follow for the beer.
[2] The text is in Arabic.
[3] The text is a mixture of Dinka and Arabic.

V

WAR SONGS

WAR songs are usually about the courage and the power of the age-sets. They may concern forced labour on the roads, or in the fields of the chief, and such tasks, all taken to symbolize the adventurous spirit of the age-set and its implementation. They may also be about more obvious adventures like fighting ferocious beasts: lions, buffaloes, hippoes, and the like. By and large, they concern fights which have actually occurred. Sometimes this may be indirect. For instance, although war songs may commemorate a confrontation with a wild beast, it is usual for an age-set to hunt an animal bearing the name of the corresponding age-set of the enemy, and then compose songs about an actual war with this enemy under the guise of the hunted animal.

A conspicuous feature of war songs is that the group collectively refer to themselves as 'I', thus emphasizing their unity and identifying each one with this unity. Power, courage, and ferocity are primarily symbolized by the bull, but also by the lion, the buffalo, and similar beasts. The Dinka allege in their songs that they are never the aggressors. The worth of an age-set as warriors lies not in provoking wars but in halting aggression, though what they consider aggression is only too easily conceived.

War songs are used in a war dance, known as *loor*; this is not a dance during a war, though it might provoke a war. It is usually attended by members of sub-tribes which are warring units. The dance is a combination of types of dances. A theme which runs through them is that the man represents an aggressive bull and the woman a submissive cow. While dancing apart, for in most Dinka dances bodies do not touch, the man facing the woman forms the horns of a bull with his arms and the woman raises her arms, joining her hands to form a circle over her head. Thus, while the horns of the man symbolize danger, the horns of the woman appear harmless. This is maintained in another variation in which the man chases the retreating woman and symbolizes the victory

of the bull. On the perimeter of the dance, men circling in single
file dance the *goor*, a war ballet, in which they jump and dodge as
though fighting with spears. Other men in mimed duels jump up
and down, twisting themselves in the air with amazing skill, using
spears to imitate an actual fight between them.

The different sub-tribes dance together to each other's songs.
During or towards the end of the song of one sub-tribe, another
sub-tribe withdraws from the dance singing its *dor*, a special
type of war song in which a leader, followed by his group chorus,
excites peace- or war-demonstrations. The sub-tribe which has
withdrawn then returns singing a *dor*, and, running into the dance,
outsing the previous chorus and people begin to dance to *their*
songs. This is part of the dance, not simply a demonstration of
aggression. It sometimes happens that particularly enjoyable songs
are interrupted in this way, or a particularly provocative song is
introduced. Then a tension develops in which opposing groups
begin deliberately to introduce war songs.

For security in modern days, chiefs must watch the dancers to
prevent fights if necessary.[1] But the provocation of songs does not
have to wait for dances. A sub-tribe may learn of a war song newly
composed to defame them, and may take up arms and attack the
composing group. The trial that follows, in which the court usually
wants to hear the songs sung by the groups, is usually well provided
with a police force in anticipation of more trouble.

A war dance may be on a smaller scale and directed towards a
particular objective. An example of this is where an age-set has
been assigned a job, and, after completing it, seeks formal discharge
by the chief; or where the age-set seeks permission from the chief
to move to far-off grazings during cultivation period—a practice
which is nowadays restricted. After such a dance has lasted a while,
the chief, assuming that he grants the request, will ritually sprinkle
them with blessed water as a token of discharge or grant of the
request. The dancers then point their spears up saying together
nguoth, a word used when a person has speared an enemy, an
animal, or a fish. This custom probably originated in the blessing
which the chief would give the warriors before their going to war,

---

[1] It may be that the apparatus of modern government has in fact increased the
expression of aggression, since it is now known that at some point there can be
intervention to stop unrestrained fighting. In the past, more self-restraint was
necessary.

so that with the help of divinities they might be victorious. Nowadays, it has become associated with any formal blessing of the age-set by a chief, an elder, or a holy man, presumably to demonstrate success of the granting of their request, or expectations of future victory against any foes, human or non-human. War dance in all its variants is the main standard dance of the Ngok Dinka and as its name *loor* (drum) indicates much drumming goes on. There are at least two drums in a dance, a large one about three yards long with a round top about three feet in diameter and a narrow bottom about one foot in diameter, and a small one known as *leng* which is approximately one third the size of the large drum. The two are beaten simultaneously and their sounds are co-ordinated. Beating the drums is a skill which all Dinkas share, but not all perform on such dancing occasions, for a high standard is required.

War songs are owned by the warring unit—the sub-tribe—and are transmitted from generation to generation. Some of them are so old that their origin is unknown. War songs are therefore of historical interest.

There is a special type of dance which follows the war dance among the Ngok but which has somewhat different characteristics and might be more appropriately termed ox dance than war dance. The Ngok call it *agaar*, *atoor*, or *dany*,[1] while the Rek and the Tuic, with whom it is the main dance, call it *agaar* or *loor*. The songs sung when dancing *atoor* are not generally about war or courage; they are about girls and cattle. They are almost identical with ox songs except that they are shorter and less concerned with poetry than with a rhythmic quality to accompany the dance.

The dance itself conforms to the theme of man/bull–woman/cow symbolism, but although the dancers, in a most striking unity of action, stamp the ground with tremendous vigour, the symbolism is more peaceful than in war songs and no spears are used, nor are there symbolic duels between the men.

85. *From Where is the Enemy?* [Atuot]

The facts of this song date back to the time when the Dinka resisted alien domination. The aliens are not specified, but presumably it was during the Turco-Egyptian period. In the face of superior weapons they

---

[1] *Atoor* in Rek is however a different kind of dance, and *dany* is a women's dance. The Ngok call their women's dance *tueng*.

met with a destruction far beyond their comprehension which they
attributed to the anger of their ancestors. Atuot, the singing tribal
group, unlike the Ngok of Kordofan and the Western Dinkas of Bahr el
Ghazal, do not circumcise, and despise circumcision as much as the
others despise non-circumcision.

> The circumcised is throwing his gun away
> The circumcised is throwing the gun away
> Things are bad on the mount
> I am tired of the words
> The words of the foreigners   5
> Malual, our tribe is cursed
> The land is cursed by the youngest son of Cherjok,
>   our father[1]
> Let us unite the land that our words be one
> Arol[2] too have their claim
> Eat your grain;[3]   10
> I will remain.[4]
> Where has the Creator gone?
> Save our land.
> From where is the enemy?
> The one with strange eyes whom I do not know   15
> If it is me, take care!
> Move your teeth[5] away from me.
> Cries of war were heard at Agher,
> I killed the foreigners
> And I killed their slaves[6]   20
> That people may sleep in peace;
> The circumcised has troubled us,
> One with a mouth full of teeth, rise
> Return to your land
> The evil-eyed has troubled us   25
> One with a mouth full of teeth, rise,
> Return to your land,
> Return to your land.

[1] The text is in Arabic, *aba*.
[2] Another enemy—a separate Dinka tribe.
[3] 'Think you are doing well'.
[4] Implying that while he will remain as he is he will prove himself to the enemy.
[5] The Dinka extract their lower front teeth. The enemy are insulted here because they do not have the custom.   [6] Negro mercenaries.

86. *Left Alone* [Atuot]

During the Turco-Egyptian period, Thany, the riverine Dinkas who own no cattle and who must live on fish along the Nile, were often exposed to the enemy, whose only throughway to the South was the Nile.

According to the story, another cattle-owning tribe called Awan would begin a fight with the government troops and then disappear with their cattle into the hinterland, leaving the Thany to fight the war alone. In this song, they mourn their fate.

> I am left alone
> The words find me alone
> I am the poor man without cattle
> I find myself amidst the enemy.
> O foreigners again!　　　　　　　　　5
> Ancient hatreds are falling on me.
> The enemy whose mother's vagina is pink.
> I have a word with father.[1]
> The enemy is coming again
> And I am left alone　　　　　　　　　10
> The words find me alone.

87. *Can Abyor Abandon the Land?* [Ngok]

(Extract)

This is an old song of Abyor, a sub-tribe of the Ngok, concerning their wars with the invading Arabs, referred to here as the Fur.

> The brown horse of the Fur
> Says I should abandon my land
> Beware of my spear shafts
> In my fight with the brown horse,
> Have we not both suffered in the fight?　　5
> And has not the horse of the Fur fallen?
> What is it that the man wants?
> I am a ferocious bull.
> And the tribes cried out,
> 'Can Abyor abandon his land?'　　　　　10

[1] *Wa* (father) and *Ma* (mother) are sometimes used in reference to a man or a woman in a way comparable to the colloquial use of 'daddy-o' and 'mama'. The Dinka use them to address an equal or a subordinate, and sometimes, as in this case, sarcastically.

88. *The Heart of a Buffalo* [Ngok]

The Grey One[1] flies in the *toc*,[2]
I killed a man[3]
And his mother got into a mourning skirt.[4]
I gathered my spears.
And I killed a man.   5
There is the Bird!
The Bird with a heart has killed a brave warrior
The Bird of Deng, Designer of Black Colour,
The Bird with a heart has killed a brave warrior.
I am a bad man   10
I fly in the *toc*
My heart is like that of a buffalo.
I danced around the herds I captured
And vultures followed my spears.
I do not honour the spears of the *Door*.[5]   15
We met while Miyom, the chief, was away
What is lacking when I have protected the river
The River of our chiefs?
Miyom[6] is away,
I will not wish he were here;[7]   20
The Star Man[8] is away,
I will not wish he were here;
The Assembly of the chiefs is away,
I will not wish they were here;
I am a big bull.   25

---

[1] The Vulture—the name of the age-set.
[2] Grassy plains in the Savannah region.
[3] Literally, *ajiec*, a small black bird.
[4] *Gutgut*—the way in which leather skirts are worn when a woman cries in distress on death, or when she runs, fights, or does any activity which requires keeping the skirts in tight position. She draws the skirt up between her legs and tucks it tightly at the waist.
[5] Sudanic peoples in the South—Bungo or Zande, sometimes called *Nyinyam* or *Nyamnyam*.
[6] Praise-ox-name for Chief Deng Majok.
[7] To protect the land by law since they have protected it by war.
[8] Praise-name for Acuil, the sectional chief—*Omda*—of Abyor.

89. *Ancient Feud* [Ngok of Upper Nile Province]

Chief Beek has spoken:
I will tether the spotted goat myself[1]
We Malual have made peace with the Nuer;
Our ancient feud with the Nuer
Is known by Jekeny[2] and me   5
I will remain silent, I will not say it;
My cattle have never been captured
And I have never been assimilated into other tribes
I, Lual, have refused,
It has always been known to the Ajang   10
Even if a man should injure me
And he has not cut out my heart
He will see with his own eyes
My wit has not been captured.

90. *People Slept with Twisted Necks*
[Ngok of Upper Nile Province]

(Extract)

We danced to the drums with apprehension[3]
Like people mixed with lions
What the chief of the Nuer once said
The chief Wun Deng spoke and said
We shall drink out of one gourd[4]   5
People slept with twisted necks[5]
But I, Agoor Minyang, I do not turn.

91. *I am Bad* [Ngok of Upper Nile Province]

A man threatened me at the borders
I thought we were at peace
Do not provoke me, I am bad[6]
If I should make it bitter one day
I will be bad   5

[1] To be sacrificed for peace.   [2] A tribe of the Nuer.
[3] Sarcastic reference to the fear of the enemy.
[4] To be at peace.   [5] Keeping a watch on the enemy.
[6] If provoked, he would retaliate badly.

And I will not be passed by
All people will avoid me.
Awaknyang, chief on whom the tribe depends,
Do not vex yourself
I remain, I have not displaced my heart   10
I knew the tree had destroyed us[1]
Branching tree, did you not go with earlier groups?
There aren't other generations to spare
I wish you would travel alone
In your nature as a tree   15
Go and a new forest will grow.

92. *My Spears do not Fall on Fish* [Ngok]

The subject of the next two songs is a hippopotamus killed by Cuor,
the age-set of the Abyor sub-tribe.

I quilled his back in the evening
And held the end of the spear shaft;
I have an animal in the river
He will not leave
He is kept by the Flesh of Jiel[2]   5
And manhood showed itself.
Age-set of Deng, the animal is capturing the land
I have skewered him
The Animal with an open anus
We are competing with gunners over the beast[3]   10
The Animal with an open anus
I have turned into a lion
I am tangled with spear-shafts
My thrusts are paining the beast
My spears do not fall on a ball fish.   15
The Vulture is going into the river
The Grey One is going into the river
The Grey One is attacking the river at dawn
The river of divinities

[1] The sacred tree had begun to die and attendant disasters were attributed
to it.   [2] A clan divinity.
[3] Although guns were available, Cuor used spears to demonstrate their
courage.

I saw something last night   20
I will attack it.
My shaft has skewered the animal
My shaft is blessed with sacred cows
The animal is taking the shafts away
The animal is taking the spears away.   25
I am not an imbecile
I am not like the imbecile tribes
The people who hunt small animals at home
I will pierce the anus of the animal in the river.

93. *The Beast in the River* [Ngok]

The age-set of Maker is boiling
The spear shafts have criss-crossed
Let us hunt the wild beast.
The beast in the river
We surround him like a fishing-party;   5
And the spears had a bath
I threw the water-lily[1]
There is my spear.
The Great Vulture flies with his spears
I have hit the big beast   10
The Great Vulture flies with his spears
The hyena in the forest knows
And jumps away
I will not leave the animal
I am known by the tribes   15
I rose against the animal of the forest
I held the head of the spear
And I held the tail of the spear
I swore by Mohammed[2]
Mohammed the Prophet of God   20
Let us be gone.[3]
I hacked him apart.
The animal of the river came with reeds on the head

[1] Throwing the water-lily seems to have a war-ritual significance.
[2] The singers use Moslem invocations as exclamations.
[3] The text uses the Arabic word *arah* in the same way as in note 2.

I pierced him with the big spear of the Arabs
His head full of reeds;   25
I first speared him in the dark
With reeds on his head.
I filled his back, and my spears broke
I swore by Abuk.[1]
I swore by Abuk   30
Abuk, the girl in the river[2]
I hunt like the Manangeer[3]
The river beast bends the spears
And disappears under the water
Then reappears carrying my spears.   35
The Great Vulture is assembled
The month of November[4] attracts all things ashore.

94. *No Word in the Stomach* [Ngok]

Anyar, Buffalo, is the age-set of Bongo sub-tribe, which wars with
Abyor, the sub-tribe of Cuor, Vulture, the age-set which owns the
previous song. Cuor, in order to disguise their defamatory attitude,
hunted buffaloes, and then composed this song, essentially aimed at
Anyar age-set about an attempted fight in which it is alleged that
Anyar refused to confront them.

My father said, 'The Vulture has no heart[5]
If they attempt to hunt a buffalo.'
I have no heart, but let him wait for me.[6]
I chased him with the spear-shafts I carried
And a dust-storm covered the sun.   5
The Great Tribe of Deng, the Saddle-bill Stork
Do not leave a word in their stomach.
He is dragging the spears away
The bush steams with his torment
I filled his eyes,   10

[1] Female divinity—the Dinka Eve, mother of Deng.
[2] They associate her with the powers of the river.
[3] A riverine tribe famous for hippo-hunting.
[4] When the floods are subsiding.
[5] Doing something reckless or stupid to the Dinka indicates lack of heart.
They see the mind and the heart as linked.
[6] Though it is reckless or 'bad', after they have defeated the buffalo they will
be admired and considered 'good'.

I will tear him apart;
I filled one side
I will tear him apart.
The buffalo has turned wild
Like the animal in the river.[1]   15
I like hunting like the Thuri,[2]
The Grey One has a frightening fame.
I speared the animal myself
I got him at Amenhaguok
He wears medicine[3] on his head   20
The medicine of the buffalo
He buys medicine
The Vulture[4] is like the Governor
I am the bird who flies in the sky
The Vulture flies armed with his spears.   25
The lion of Deng[5] has subdued the buffalo
He is sweeping away the grass[6]
He is competing over *gok*[7] with Arabs
The Grey Bull is competing for *gok* with the Arabs
Arabs with canine teeth[8]   30
The Arabs who ride their oxen.[9]
I hate killing cows for meat
But I do not leave the buffalo in the forest
And if I find one, I shall mount him.

95. *The Flying Lion* [Ngok]

In order to demonstrate their courage, the singing age-set disregarded
the chief's order that the lion be left to be poisoned instead of hunted.
After killing the lion, they composed this song.

I threw the water lily[10]
And dodged the spear;
He is a flying lion
A flying Grey One.

[1] The hippo which they had hunted.
[2] Riverine tribe who live on fishing and river-hunting.
[3] The opposing sub-tribe is believed to wear purchased magic.
[4] The age-set.   [5] Their age-set's father.
[6] Chasing the animal.   [7] High wet-season grazing land.
[8] The Dinka extract their four lower teeth, not the canines; but the insult
here refers to 'toothiness' in general.
[9] A custom the Dinkas loathe.   [10] A war ritual.

'The Brown with White on the Head'¹ of Kwol   5
Said the lion should eat the cow
He should be left for poison
The tribes who will fear will wait for poison
I will not.
We have a feud with the lion-bull   10
The lion that comes finishing the people
I do not like.
The news was kept from me
Our Mangar age-set does not fear.
We and the son of Aguengbaar²   15
We have a feud.
Did I not kill you last year
And now you have come again,
Have you ne heart,³ lion of Aliab?
Even if you thunder like rain   20
I will not leave you,
I will tear you apart with my spears.
Did I not kill the lion last year?
Did I not kill him with my own spear
I the son of Angok of Deng?   25

96. *Wol* [Ngok]

Sometimes, after tribal wars, individuals from the enemy side may be
criticized in song whether they were notable cowards or dangerously
brave. In this song, a man called Wol is insulted for his alleged greed and
cowardice which the song claims to be true of all people named Wol in
the enemy sub-tribe—Mannyuar.

Wol, son of Ayong,
Has picked reeds from the river.⁴
Wol, Carrier of the Serval Cat.⁵
Has the thing turned into a mortal disease

---

¹ Dinka, *Athokyom*, ox-praise-name of Chief Deng Majok.
² The lion is believed to come from the country of Chief Malual Aguengbaar
whose people though Dinkas (*Atuot*) are believed to turn into lions.
³ As pointed out elsewhere the functions of the mind are associated with the
heart by the Dinka.   ⁴ Presumably for food, a shameful act.
⁵ Wol's ox-colour-pattern is spotted white-and-black, the pattern of a leopard-
like serval cat.

Which can bless people with *duony*?[1]   5
A beast which gorges himself
And even keeps his left-overs for tomorrow,[2]
I hate you.
You whose brother has left to settle in the land of the Fur.

97. *Manyang Wet Himself* [Atuot]

The subject-matter of the song was a fight between the Atuot and the
Cic. In the trial that followed, Manyang, a member of the Cic, was
reputed by the Atuot to have defecated like a coward on the announce-
ment of the death sentence. 'Cic killed our people,' said an Atuot in-
formant, 'but despite the fact that they killed our people, our people
did their best to compose very insulting songs about the Cic.' This
illustrates the Dinka conception of war songs as a form of warring.

The tribe of Kuer has reached Ajak;
O Cyer
A man who was once a victor does not fear.
Who says that I fear?
The tribe of Ajak never fears   5
I do not fear.
Have you forgotten the war of Yem Ajou
Where I held the end of the bamboo shaft?
I will release my herds into the meadows
Where I shall meet the tribe of Kuer.   10
Son of a witch, do not cry when you began it.
Things have gone bad
Manyang has wet himself
Defecating near our cattle-camp
The sorcerer with four eyes   15
The inside of the man is falling out
He defecated with a red anus
Defecating like the young of a locust.
People died without making wills.[3]

[1] The disease of the back which causes hunchbacks. Having recovered from
a serious disease may sometimes qualify one and one's lineage to bless and cure
a similar disease.

[2] Among the Dinka, only children and women may eat left-overs. Gentlemen
are not supposed to.

[3] Hanged in execution of the death sentence with no chance to talk to members
of his family.

Riak sent word to the town,   20
'Send me back the things of my father.'
But there was no one left to bring them
The possessions of the man were left alone.
People who did not know the meaning of feud;
Manyang has wet himself   25
The man has defecated
The sorcerer is frightened
Where has your magic gone?
I am told to abandon the *toc*.
The land of my forefathers   30
I will never leave the *toc*,
Better dead
Let the people meet with me
If you have forgotten Yem d'Ajou
I shall wait.   35

98. *Peace is Gone* [Gok]

Give word to Arol Kacuol[1]
You have never seen the heart of the Agar
We are at war; he refused;[2]
Harmony is gone; friendship is gone.
The ancient word of the man of Amuk,[3]   5
'If you find a man lying sick, do not raise his head,[4]
But if you find a gourd, put it upright
You will drink out of the gourd.'
I took care of Maliet e Tieny.[5]
I speared the enemy, and his bowels moved   10
Like the sheep of Khartoum.[6]
Liet Tieny is both blind and lame
We met on a stream
The bowels of the man ran like the first-born of a crested crane,
The man cried like a goat,   15

[1] Chief of the Gok.
[2] Presumably to make peace.
[3] Another section.
[4] The sense is that people often turn against their benefactors.
[5] Who has turned against him.
[6] Which is so fat that its belly shakes like the thick fur of Northern sheep.

'O Ayai of Clan Padol, do not kill me
We have marriage ties.'
The man with an open anus like that of an animal
Maliet e Tieny exposed his teeth like a dog in a burning byre.

99. *The Army in the Jungle* [In exile]

May it be heard in Torit[1] which we have left behind
That the army of Deng Nhial[2] is in the forest;
The army of Deng Nhial will seize control of Akot[3]
And will seize control of Rumbek;[4]
The army of Deng Nhial is in the forest.   5
Tell my lover[5]
Girl, has the country changed after me?
Tell my lover
If I had wings
I would seize your hands.   10

100. *We are the Dinka* [In exile]

William, feud is the task of man;
O Deng Nhial,
The feud, the feud
The feud of the Southerners[6] with the Northerners[7]
Our feud will never end   5
The feud, the feud of the Southerners and the Northerners.
The army of Deng Nhial and Morwel
It is called the Anyanya.
In the Rek of Mou, we shall shoot
In Bahr el Ghazal,   10
In Agar of Marel we shall shoot

[1] A town in the Equatoria Province where the 1955 Revolt first began.
[2] One of the leaders of the Southerners in exile. He later returned to the Sudan where he was assassinated.
[3] A Dinka town.
[4] Another Dinka town.
[5] The text uses the word *abib* derived from the Arabic word *habib*.
[6] Text based on the Arabic word for South.
[7] *Mundukuru*, a rather contemptuous term used in the South for the Northerners.

With the Northerners—the Arabs
The brown Arabs.
Bahr el Ghazal
We shall cut through it,   15
Bahr el Ghazal
It is the land of Morwel Malou
And William Deng Nhial.
We shall avenge the evils of the past,
And if we succeed in our vengeance   20
We shall be praised by God;
If we succeed in vengeance
We shall be praised by God
Bless us
We are the Dinka of Bahr el Ghazal   25
O feud, O feud.

VI

WOMEN'S SONGS

WOMEN'S songs (*diet ke diar*) are usually a form of ox songs centring on the oxen of husbands or dancing-partners. In this respect, the fiction of the unity of the spouses is applied to the extent that the singing woman keeps shifting between referring to her husband as 'I' and as 'he'. Her identity is thus reflected through him.

The singer often praises her husband and through him herself, with surprising snobbery. The praises are usually exaggerated and the husband overvalued, so much so that this is only possible in songs.

Women's songs are by no means confined to their husbands' oxen. Like men's ox songs, they may concern matters unrelated to cattle. In one case,[1] a girl was betrothed to a man who suddenly decided to 'divorce' her (to use the Dinka terminology), and this for no obvious reason. The bewildered and distressed girl, though perhaps not meaning to influence the future conduct of the former fiancé, composed a song of sadness which so affected the man that he instantly reinstated the marriage by handing over to her relatives his personality ox as a bride-wealth token. In another song[2] we see a somewhat similar complaint by a divorced woman. A wife may herself claim divorce in a song.

Women's songs go beyond oxen and husbands, and concern any experiences of significance to the singer. She might honour a present, praise a stepson, mourn the death of a relative, recollect an illness that nearly caused death, oppose a proposed marriage, and so on.

The presentation of women's songs is done in a woman dance called *tueng* (*dany* in Rek). Dancers form a circle, and the owner of the song, or someone else, leads. In the centre are usually several who are related to the people praised in the song. While all sing and clap (the only musical accompaniment) those inside the circle

---

[1] See song no. 102, 'Sleepless Nights'.   [2] See song no. 101, 'Divorce'.

jump to the rhythm. Simultaneously, some people, and particularly those whose relations are mentioned, make such loud cries (*kieu*) that it is sometimes impossible to hear the words. These piercing cries are an expression of joy, though to a foreigner they might sound like the cries of a woman in distress.

101. *Divorce* [Ngok]

Agorot de Biong of Pajok lineage was divorced for dubious reasons by Micar of Col's lineage of clan Padeek. It was alleged that she had caused the death of her child by concealing some wrong. She herself felt that she was divorced because of her fading hearing ability. The situation was altogether uncertain. This song was composed to state her case, but the marriage was dissolved.

We are agitated, the man of the house Shining Dark-Light[1] and I,
We are a sparrow and a hawk in chase at home
Neglected girl,[2] remain in peace[3]
O abandoned girl left all alone
Unheeded girl, remain in peace   5
O girl neglected.
It is rumoured that the son of Jok has left his wife.
'No, we have no conflict with Nyantiwit,'[4] [he said]
'We have no conflict with the daughter of Biong.'
Do not deny it   10
Micar, I will leave to the astonishment of our people.
'Thank God'[5] were the words he sent to the sky
Grass of the Pelican has gone to the river, the river of spirits[6]
He has gone to wash away the evil spell;

[1] A praise name for Micar.
[2] Signifying the neglect of her family and his—that is, failure to give prompt attention to the settlement of her case.
[3] Dinka way of saying sarcastically 'never mind'.
[4] Agorot's nickname.
[5] *Thithiey*, here translated as 'Thank God', is an exclamation of gratitude used in many circumstances. For instance, after a hard labour when a baby is born, the Dinka might say '*Thithiey*', or when a man has been out of tobacco for long and has been given some, he might say '*Thithiey*'. Incidentally, the Dinka do not say 'thank you' though they express gratitude in various ways and this is the closest to the English. In anger, Micar reacted in a manner amounting to 'so be it'.
[6] His purification ritual implies that she had committed some sin endangering the well-being of the family—a fact she denies.

Have you now spoken with the spirits?   15
Mijak, have you and the spirits untied the calves?[1]
It is a thing that did not occur[2]
In the family of Col, only old age kills men.
Stand bewildered, daughter of the son of the White One.[3]   20
People say a big thing has befallen us
The son of the clan Padeek and me;
What the left handed[4] of Jok Anguek has done is bewildering to
    people
Even to the brown Arabs;
We met on the way, Deng Thokloi and I[5]   25
Deng de Rahma of Dhakam tribe;
The Arab said to me, 'Why have you left your home?
What have you done wrong at home when you have given birth?,[6]
The case of the daughter of the left-handed[7] is painful
Even to the Arab friends of the clan of Arob de Biong[8]   30
Deng de Rahma paces back and forth
The Arab paces up and down,
'Alas, there is nothing good that does not spoil.'
O Deng Thokloi, there is nothing good that does not spoil.
Word is spreading over the land: the daughter of Biong is di-
    vorced.
'Which one of the girls?'   36
'Is it not the girl for whom sons of noble men unpegged their herds
    to cover the plains?'[9]
Leave the wife of 'the Meek'[10] to walk in peace
The wife of the man with no words
She will find her home.   40

[1] Untying cattle signifies action in execution of a court sentence. Here she means that her husband and the spirits judged her guilty.
[2] The evil imputed to her.
[3] Her grandfather Arob's praise-name.
[4] Micar—her husband.
[5] Dinka name for an Arab, Ali Rahma, whose family is friendly with the Pajok lineage. The praise-name 'Thokloi' is that of a Pajok elder called Deng and it is applied here to praise the Arab called Deng.
[6] Procreation being the fundamental purpose of marriage, it is almost un-heard of for a Dinka to divorce a woman with more than one or two children.
[7] Her father, Biong, was also left-handed.
[8] Deng Majok's and singer's grandfather.
[9] Competing for her in marriage.
[10] Used sarcastically because while appearing so gentle in public he is so rough in private.

He is a gentleman who never feared his tongue
Nothing will cross his path,
Even if he travels to reach the land of the Arabs
He will remain the husband of the Noisy One[1]
Even if he travels to reach the land of Agar[2]   45
May the husband of the Noisy One go in peace.
The gentleman has divorced the daughter of a chief:
I will explain to the people of our country
I am divorced because of 'Yes'[3]
'Yes' has severed us, my husband and me   50
The marriage is spoiled for an empty cause
The marriage is spoiled for nothing
It is finished,[4] it is over
All is ended between us, the bull of Ajak[5] and me.
I never quarrelled with the people of the house   55
I was a girl attacked holding my peace.
I did not quarrel with the praised man of the house
I was a girl attacked holding my peace.
People ask me, 'Daughter of Biong
What have you done wrong in your house?'   60
Theft, there is none in me
The daughter of Biong is self-composed
O our people, nor have I been seduced
To have a case taken into the court-byre or under the tree[6]
A woman dismissed from the house with no fault   65
I walked away like a hyena surprised by dawn.
It is said that I am carrying a disease
I am carrying the medicine of the Falata,[7]
The evil pushed away by the tip of a shaft
Like the black viper.   70
Cobra-spotted[8] of Kwol, the Honoured Pied One

---

[1] Nyankieu—a nickname for herself.   [2] A distant tribe of the Dinka.
[3] *Wee*, feminine form of 'yes', used in response to being called. Men answer
with *wo* or *woi*. She alleges that she is divorced because she cannot hear well
enough to respond.   [4] Text, *kalaath*, derived from Arabic *khalaas*.
[5] The bull is Micar, her husband, and his father is Ajak.
[6] Since the court often sits under a tree or in a cattle-byre, going to court is
sometimes expressed as 'going under the tree' or 'going into the byre'. Here, the
two are combined in a rather unusual way.
[7] The Dinka believe that the Falata of Nigeria possess black medicine which
the Dinka loathe so much that they will not touch it.
[8] Her cousin, Deng Makuei (Abot).

Do not believe what people say,
Do not believe that word of the Pattern of Saddle-bill
The word of the father of Arek,
A healthy person is not beaten into sickness.   75
And what now that I have left him to his home until the star goes
    to Alei?[1]
Daughter of the camp of Milang, leave the house
The marriage has refused itself.
Col[2] said, 'Are you leaving before I go to court?'[3]
O Cobra-Spotted of Ajak,[4] I am leaving;   80
What a thing we have started with the son of my father[5]
Dancing Head, Lueth, the Shade of the Crested Crane
O Marial of Clan Padeek, do not preach to me[6]
I am as though I were burnt by fire
The words of the land are burning me,   85
O Pattern of the Saddle-bill, I am trapped with a trap
Flames have burned my face;
O brother,[7] I do not hate you.
A woman begins her quarrel with a child but will reach the man.
Because of my quarrel with Lueth[8]   90
I cannot leave with no one at the cooking hearth
Awien,[9] daughter of Rial, please kindle the fire
Daughter of the clan of Agueng de Kwol
We are the blood of Monydhaang de Kwol of Jok's clan
We are not orphaning ourselves[10] daughter of Biong d'Acuol. 95
It is ended between us, the bull of Ajak and me.
He charged at me, the man behaved like a rhino
We divorced in the moonless part of the bad month of August[11]
What will he eat?

  [1] Since the indicated star cannot go to Alei, a sub-tribe of the Ngok, this
means for ever.
  [2] Her husband's brother who objected to the divorce.
  [3] The text simply says 'cattle-byre', by which is meant 'court'.
  [4] Col's praise-name.
  [5] A Dinka woman refers to her husband's father as 'father'.
  [6] *Kuen*, literally, 'count to' a person, means 'to advise', but *kuen* connotes
a rather lengthy talk while advice can be given in a few words. 'To preach' to a
person, divested of its negative connotation in common usage, is a closer translation of *kuen*.   [7] Her husband.   [8] Another name for her husband.
  [9] Her agnatic relative married to her husband's kinsman living near them.
  [10] Not separating for ever.
  [11] The roughest time of famine when last year's crops are exhausted and the
new ones not yet ripe.

He will live on[1] Yom,[2] the Cow of Dau Dancing Leopard   100
Akol,[3] cow of my sister Abul.
Abyei,[4] Crossing Wild Dogs, fetch the cow from Maker, the camp
    of Abyor
The Great Camp of Deng, Reverberating Drums,
Fetch the cow Yom, from the son of the girl of our clan Pajok,
Tell the son of Makuany de Deng d'Ayuel   105
To give me the cow, Yom,
Our relationship is spoiled with the family of Baar Shining-Dark
    Shade
In the clan of Col, the Hairy, brave men do not die
I have brought death to the family of Baar;
But I do not know the wrong I have done   110
O mother, daughter of Ajing, the Spotted Leopard,
O Arob de Monytooc!
Our great clan of Biong d'Allor has always perished
We are the ancient victims of death;
Our clan of Allor de Monydhang has always been mortal   115
We are the ancient victims of death.

102. *Sleepless Nights* [Ngok]

The girl who composed this song was betrothed to a man she loved.
Then the man suddenly, and for no obvious reason, broke the betrothal.
In this song, she expresses her sadness over the breach. When this song
was presented in a dance attended by the man, he is said to have shed
tears and reinstated the marriage.

Will it not be the same with the tale of the horse of Ajak[5]
O brother, the Crested Crane, Matem?
My heart, do not remain perturbed
And twist your horns[6]
It was you who pushed my head into the bush [of love]   5
If only I could pull you out to stand like a man

    [1] Literally, 'eat', meaning 'live on' by 'drinking the milk of'.
    [2] Also received from her bride-wealth and must be returned on divorce.
    [3] Also received from her bride-wealth.
    [4] One of her relatives.
    [5] Ajak is said to have jealously and carefully trained and maintained a horse
that was suddenly killed and eaten by a lion before he even got to use it.
    [6] Be vexed.

I would pound you with a pestle and burn you with fire
Mine would caution the tribe to abandon marriage
Even the milk of goats would be abandoned.[1]   9
What about the beautiful thing which smelt like ghea at Monymau
    camp?[2]
Now I spend my nights thinking, vexing myself with a confounded
    heart;
We have bestowed a curse on ourselves, O Kerieth of clan Pajok.[3]
O Kerieth, son of the clan Pajok
A man of your age once said
The legendary man who blamed God said,   15
'Divinity is blamed and yet is not blamed';
I will not blame you
You were persuaded by others
To come and break our marriage.

103. *What Misfortune* [Ngok]

In song 56, 'O that my Father were Alive,' it was mentioned that Abul,
the proposed bride, refused her consent to the marriage. In this song,
she states her case. The marriage, however, took place notwithstanding
her resentment.

I run after a diviner as bitter[4] as a gourd
I say: 'This I will pursue to the end'
I will go as far as Malual.
Our Akok of Jiel of Baggat
Have you seen what I seek?   5
What is sought in the family of Beek
O Adau[5] of the Crested Crane, I hate
That is what I hate;
I will ask Deng,[6]

[1] People would not believe in marriage even though through it you received
cattle for milk. Furthermore, goats' milk is associated with fertility.
[2] The beauty of their courtship is compared to the smell of ghea, which the
Dinka find beautiful.
[3] Because their conflict is without good cause, she believes they have provoked
their ancestral spirits and therefore invited their curse.
[4] Spiritually powerful: the gourd-flesh is bitter.
[5] The singer's stepsister and the eldest daughter of her father.
[6] Her father. Though people refer to their fathers by names in song, as a sign of
respect it is normally not done except when father's name is specifically asked for.

'Father, am I not like Adau?'[1]   10
What wrong have I done to my father?
We shall look for judges;
I say: 'Deng, I refuse to go to a home where I shall be a hind wife.'
A daughter of the chief known to the Ngok and the Tuic
And even to the Arabs and the Rek   15
A brown beauty which has amazed the tribes
Abyor, people of Kwol de Biong, I am drowning
I fell into the depths of the river
And the mother of Adau[2] cried, 'O
O I am mourning;   20
Is this a person buried or married?
Deng, so chieftainship is such a big thing
That you give away a girl where you will not hear of her?[3]
What has he done?
I have refused my daughter   25
She will not go to a home where a man has another wife
And she to be the last.
I will ask you all, our Akok, and Thior
How could the chief think of it?
Is it not he who is lumping things together?   30
He has begun it like a dance
And now that he has begun it
Will each person not speak with her own tongue?'
When Deng heard it, he said to me,
'If you have a heart, never hide.'   35
It is a thing that will never be helped.
I tell you people of the family of Dhang
The only thing which holds me
Is the sake of our chieftainship and the danger to my father
I would have done it my own way.[4]   40
Adau, have you heard what has occurred?
I am told to go to the clan of Dak

[1] Adau was married as first wife.
[2] The first wife to whose daughter she compares herself in line 10.
[3] The implication is that because he is the chief, he is giving his daughter without asserting her higher status. She realizes that it is a paradox, since for the very reason that he is chief he should also care about the marital status of his daughters. This point is made in line 30.
[4] She implies that she might have committed suicide which would bring her father into disrepute and maybe criminal liability, which would also endanger their chieftainship.

And the wife of my father[1] will remain with her doubt
She has not blessed me with ashes[2]
The ashes of the clan of Dhang have not touched my skin.   45
Deng, Government, chief[3]
Must the girl fall *culub*[4] into the water?
Is the river of Acai[5] the best for me?
For this, I will seek judges
I will not let it pass;   50
It will be seen by Lual, and Cyer, and Acien e Yor,[6]
And my father, Marial,[7] and Bol Biliu.
Of all the many things in this land
What will surpass my bad luck?
It is far in the lead   55
Like the chair for installing a chief.
The clan Paguiny[8] are to blame
The people who had allowed their daughter[9] as a second wife.
Was it because of chieftainship that the girl was given?
Has the thing become a permanent scorn?   60
A continuing scorn falling on me.
Even if I remain behind
It is the fault of Paguiny;
Daughter of my mother, Acai-jur[10] of the Silvery One
Your maternal kin are to blame.   65
A misfortune which cannot be washed away
I would wash it away with the water of the Nile;
Bad luck which cannot be washed away
I would wash it away with the water of Acai;
A grievance which will remain to be buried with me.   70

---

[1] The mother of Adau, who objects in lines 19–33.
[2] A ritual which indicates consent and best wishes.
[3] Arabic *Nazir* used.
[4] Sound made by something like a stone falling into water.
[5] The girl who was sacrificed to the powers of the river by the founder of Pajok clan.
[6] Chiefs of various Dinka tribes.
[7] Against whom she is complaining.
[8] Her mother's clan.
[9] Her mother.
[10] Because she is lighter than the average Dinka, Acai is referred to as Acai-jur, *jur* being the term applied to foreigners and more particularly to the Arabs. Acai has a stepsister about her age who is referred to as Acai-monyjang, *monyjang* being the Dinka word for Dinka—applied to her because she is much darker than the other Acai.

104. *The Quarrel of Wives* [Ngok]

(Extract)

In a case with her co-wife, Awel Bol, the singer, a relative of the Chief,
Deng, was found guilty and punished.

I walked talking to my head
I nearly went out of breath,
'Deng, is it true, you have jailed me?
Is it true have you fined me?
There is nothing,[1] son of Jok, the Decorated One   5
I have come under the court-tree ready for death
I will not stop
I will not disobey the words of the Koic[2] of Allor.'[3]
The quarrel of co-wives is an ancient thing
Woman, do not trouble your heart any more   10
Deng of the Decorated One has pleased you.

105. *Is That a Husband?* [Bor]

The singer sought a divorce after having had an illegitimate child
whom she named Dhala, literally, 'I am scorned'.

Why is the case not decided?
The case of my supposed husband, Awer Rial?
So that I defeat the man?
Why does he gaze into my eyes
As though he is about to escape?   5
'Aluel, the man still considers you his wife.'
'Decide the case, his words are lies.
He knew I was his wife
Yet, he went away as far as Anyaar
Do you call that a husband?'   10
O my son, Dhala,
I am scorned for a right cause.

[1] Meaning 'Never mind'.
[2] The Ngok is vaguely divided into two main groups, the *Koic* and *Paan cien*.
According to Howell, the Koic were the original settlers of the Ngok and therefore have a higher status. The division is not discussed under the social organization of the Dinka because it does not have any particular significance today. 'Koic'
is used here to mean the public, which, together with the chief, constitutes the
court.   [3] Deng Majok's great-great-grandfather.

106. *I Hate Such Things* [Agar]

There are women who say,
'What shall I do with the husband of another woman?'
Women, do you say the same?
We are not all agreed
Each person has her own mouth   5
True, we are a group
But all are different and yet they fall into groups
There is the army, the police, and the prison wardens
They are all part of the government;
Mangok and Monynuer are both part of the government.   10
When he returned, he stayed for five days
A bewildering thing has appeared in my family
I do not know what is killing the man
He sleeps until it dawns;
I will leave   15
I hate such things.
'Man, get up,
There is something knocking at the door.'
But he will not wake
He falls back to sleep,   20
I will leave
I hate such things.

107. *Gossip* [Malual]

The song is against the singer's relative, whom she accuses of gossiping,
a habit she cannot find a source for in the family's heritage. Indeed, she
implies that the gossiper's mother, who associated with men of power in
town, was made pregnant by a District Commissioner. The woman's
child also took to town and the singer argues that one day they will be
forced back into Dinka life.

Girls, I gazed
I gazed and stood aghast,
What the child has done
Is not a thing of his father
And not a thing of his mother   5
Nor is it a thing of my mother, Awin Akol,

The gossiper spends the day with my name.
When people went looking for men of power
The District Commissioner did not fornicate with anyone's
    mother here,
People, you will return to our land.   10
I am the daughter of Lual of Pagong
Gossiping is bad
It is like the hyena
Gossiping has enlarged itself in Mading[1]
That is why the word was thrown to the court.[2]   15
Our gossipers of our Mading
Your insides will fall out with words
Your insides will meet with disaster at our Mading.

108. *Do All Things End?* [Ngok]

I went and sat,
'Uncle, I am without an ox.'
My uncle said to me,
'You have said no lie, son of Jok the Decorated One.'
White-Spotted Flanks,[3] black ox of the girl with whom I was
    born[4]
The black one finds a cow and pushes her   6
He has turned into a devil.[5]
The man called Wel, son of Deng
Striped One[6] of clan Pajing
The gentleman herds like a lion[7]   10
When the age-set, Ajong de Ker, has released the herds.
They were born—girls[8]
First born was a girl called Duoot,
She fell[9] into the family of Kir, the side-spotted white
The camp of the mother of Thon   15

---

[1] Mading Awil, i.e. Aweil, the District Headquarters of Aweil District.
[2] Literally, 'tree'.   [3] Praise-name, *Ruokbil.*
[4] The ox was acquired through the marriage of her husband's sister.
[5] Text from the Arabic *Sheitaan,* a term the Baggara Arabs use for a madman, implying that he is possessed by the devil; here used to indicate a maddened ox.
[6] Wel's ox-colour-pattern.   [7] In the forest.
[8] From whose marriage her husband acquired cattle including the ox.
[9] Got married into.

The camp of the cattle of Nyanwiir[1]
O Abek that is a big camp;
Next born was a girl called Adeel
The girl was brown like the snake, *biaar*,
She has gone into the family of Padeek.[2]   20
Ajeer, Marial, I breed you like the fish of the fox.[3]
In the camp of the Stork of the Marshes of Padeek
Bil turned into an ox of beauty[4]
A man asks me, 'Son of Mijong de Dhang
From where did you get the ox?'   25
He is from the herds of the age-set[5] of Maker Monitor Lizard.
He gazes at cows with penetrating eyes
Spotted-Black of Mijok of the Brown does not put down his
    spears.[6]
I have a tall[7] mighty black beast
He disturbed the herds last night, he did not sleep   30
And the One-Side-Patterned-Black asked,
'People, what is that? What is that?'
It is Shining Black Ox, the ox of the girl of clan Pajing[8]
He has again pulled out his peg
And a man cried, 'O Bil is spoiling the ropes.'   35
We shall herd, Low Lying Horns, Mijak of the Black Bird
We shall move to *gok* of Thigei
Ajuong,[9] we are going to build the road.
Makor, our age-set, what shall we do?
We have met with a big problem.   40
Every year comes and with it work on the roads.
Ajuong, Dark-Grey, age-set of Maker of Bil
Our Grey One is buzzing with *dor*[10]
Let us dance, Meeting-Animals of Makuei.
Brown-Mouthed, Roaring-Jok of Beek, we shall work day and
    night   45
Until the road is done.

---

[1] Female who presumably brought the cattle through her marriage.
[2] Section of Abyor sub-tribe.   [3] In a legend.
[4] *Dheeng*.   [5] Her husband's age-set is Aliab.
[6] He takes the cattle for grazing continuously.
[7] Arabic *Tawiil* is used in the text.
[8] Through whose marriage the ox was acquired.
[9] Another name for the age-set.
[10] Songs for exciting group-spirit in demonstrations or, as here, at work.

Why is it said that all things end?
Why doesn't work on the road end?[1]
The work of the government does not end
Our Ajuong age-set will move the herds to the *gok*[2]   50
Oxen went all night as we moved to Thigei.

109. *The Death of Mabil* [Ngok]

I sat moaning
I was not aggrieved by the absence of the ox
It was the sudden fall of Mabil[3] in one day.
The spirit which has taken Mabil away
Thinks I will not find him again   5
Mabil follows in file.
My ox has a voice like my grandfather, the son of the chief[4]
And like Cyer Deng, the Big Chief[5]
And Ariath Maker, the chief of the Rek[6]
And Bilkuei of Paan Aruw[7] is also like him.   10
Father, Decorated One, Honoured Pied One[8]
The Great Black One is as smooth as though he sleeps on a
    polished skin
A passer-by turns, Baak is bright.
Push him into the byre,[9] he is refusing the byre
The Side-Spotted White of the girl of clan Pajing is refusing to
    enter   15
Sons of the Pied One of the White One,[10] push him into the
    byre.
He bellows and vomits at Abyei
The home of the Honoured Pied One
The Maker of the Pied Pattern of the Brown of Beek.

[1] Tracks must be beaten every year to level them after the rainy season, which leaves them rough.
[2] The highlands in the Northern part of Ngokland. They will move the herds nearer to the working place.
[3] Her husband's ox.
[4] The singer is a wife of Mijak, stepbrother of Chief Deng Majok.
[5] In fact, a prophet.   [6] Also a prophet.   [7] A Dinka tribe.
[8] Praise-name of Kwol Arob, the singer's father.
[9] During the rainy season when mosquitoes and other insects disturb the cattle, they are put into the byres at night.
[10] Sons of Kwol whose father Arob has the white ox-colour-pattern.

The ox bellows with a thundering voice   20
And the trees in the forest reply[1]
His voice is like the Ship of the Sky.[2]
Why do you prevent the herds of my father from being served?[3]
You will let yourself be hated by the husband of the cows;
The ox with wide-spread horns misses bulls with his horns.   25
I sent Allor
I sent Allor, Allor of my mother
Allor like Allor, the Black Bird, I sent,
'Tomorrow, you go to fetch Ajeer
I hate his being at Panyom'[4]   30
O the ox of my father the Decorated One!
The big byre of Bung de Nyiel glitters with Mithiang
He is like the black bull of the buffalo
He is the display-bull of Bil of Akuei.

110. *Mijok* [Ngok]

Ox with diverging horns, the horns are falling
Like an overflow
They are reaching the ground
Like an overflow
My Mijok, the ground-hornbill.   5
I love the black pattern of Mijok of my father
I love it as I love the chief
I love it as I love our chief who is holding our land.
My Mijok, if no disaster befalls us
People will point at our camp because of you.   10
In the camp of my father,
The camp of my grandfather's clan
I possess a smooth one
I will never leave you
Even if people scorn you   15
Because of those horns, I love you.

[1] With an echo.
[2] Aeroplane.
[3] This is a praise-criticism of the bravery of the ox.
[4] e.g. because of lack of good grazing or because of the possible dangers from
wild animals.

111. *Kwol Arob* [Ngok]

(Extract)

A song praising the late Chief Kwol Arob, father of Deng Majok, the
present Chief.

> Adan de Ken cried in dismay and said
> 'Black Stork, what will spoil you
> When you are in an ordered land?'
> The case will be seen by Kwol with no bias.
> The word of the market is seen by Kwol   5
> And the case of a cow is seen by Kwol
> O Kwol, keep the people of your father
> And lead them to the people of the world.

112. *Friendship* [Ngok]

Before the deterioration of their relationships, as discussed earlier, Deng
Majok, the Chief of the Ngok, and Babo Nimr, the Chief of the Baggara
Arabs, were on very friendly terms, as were their fathers. In this song,
a wife of Deng Majok honours the gift of a horse by Babo to her husband.
The woman herself being Arabized sings about the horse as would a wife
about an ox.

> My friendship with the son of Nimr
> Is a friendship which will never end
> He presented me with a horse sprayed with grey.[1]
> The Governor said, 'Chiefs, race your horses.'   4
> The brown pied horse of the son of the Decorated[2] is in the lead
> And people gazed at the wonders of the horse of the son of the
>   White One.[3]
> Mithiang is hornless and will not wear the tassels of the Decorated
>   Jok[4]
> But tassels wave with grace on his back.[5]

[1] The Dinka use the same colour-names for horses and mares as they do for
bulls and cows.
[2] Meaning her husband.
[3] The White One being Chief Kwol Arab.
[4] Horses were not traditionally Dinka but were acquired from the Arabs. The
singer conceives of the horse in terms of oxen and their traditional decoration.
[5] The horse's mane.

The sheep of the sea[1] is exceedingly beautiful.
The tassels on your back, O ox[2] of the camp of Kwol Dorjok   10
A man wishes, 'When he falls, I shall skin him.'
Man, your eyes will turn black.[3]

113. *I Scorn the Chiefs of the Eyes* [Ngok]

A song of another wife of Chief Deng Majok.

Deng, Saddle-bill Stork, it is our land,
If it is death, all will go,
But if it is life, we shall wear bangles like mighty elephants.
Even if all chiefs meet, including the chiefs of the lions
I scorn the chiefs of the eyes.[4]   5

114. *Who can Surpass Deng?* [Ngok]

This song, and the two to follow, also belong to the wives of Chief Deng Majok. Among other things, they are an attack on people reputed to engage in plots or subversion against him.

Ox with spreading horns
Ox of the daughter of Yom[5]
Daughter of Yom Counter of wild dogs
Striped One,[6] you will mix with the bulls
And your father[7] will mix with the people of the Sudan   5
He is the expert on the words of the South
His words are as strong as *tiil*-fibre[8]
No one can surpass him in the land of Kwol.
Has not my name[9] travelled far to the land of the Arabs?
And to the land where the sun goes down?   10
I[10] have never said a word to be carried on

---

[1] As the sheep of the North, sometimes called the sea because of the Red Sea, are woolly, the horse is compared to them because of its mane.
[2] Meaning horse.   [3] Symbol of death.
[4] The evil-eyed who depend on magic for power.
[5] Received by the singer's husband as reverse payment in the marriage of her co-wife, 'the daughter of Yom'.
[6] The ox (*Mangar*).   [7] Chief Deng Majok.
[8] A strong fibre from which ropes are made.
[9] Meaning her husband's.   [10] Meaning her husband.

The Crested Crane does not
The Decorated One does not speak emptily
He does not speak the word of lies.
I have never found anything surpassing Marial   15
I have never found it in the land of Lual Amiek
The thing that can surpass him has never come.
Coward, you began it,[1] but you will not manage
It is a lie
The Flesh of Jok and Our Father Allor[2] are watching us   20
If we should need help
The Star Man[3] of Mangol will speak
Athian,[4] the chief who grew old with my father
And I will grow old with his son Leopard-Spotted[5]
The word said by Fishing-Eagle[6] of the Pied One[7] has hit my heart
Like the word of my friend the son of Ngol of Jok   26
The Star Man is like a man who writes with a pen
Patterned-Lion of Mabek Marol
Our country is spoiled;
Makuac of the father of the Decorator of Dancers   30
Let us hold the tribe.

115. *The Peak of the Land* [Ngok]

Akol[8] of my father is a joy of the heart
The *atuot*[9] with horns like a man's thigh
Miyan,[10] brought by Acok of clan Padool
Is roaring like a hungry lion.
Why does the man[11] hate me in the land   5
Star Man of Ngol,[12] does the man dare me?
We will lock his mouth like chests
And the world will stand still

[1] Referring to her husband's political opponents who had unsuccessfully raised cases against him to the national authorities.   [2] Deng Majok's ancestor.
[3] Praise-name for Acuil Bulabek, Deng Majok's relative and right-hand man who is the sectional chief of Abyor.
[4] A praise-name for Acuil's father.
[5] Another praise-name for Acuil. *Kuac* is leopard. *Ariok* is the spots of white porridge left in a black pot after the rest has been removed.
[6] Deng Makuei.   [7] A praise-name of Kwol Arob.   [8] An ox.
[9] Any cow or ox with long horns is called *atuot*, also the name of a Dinka tribe probably the origin of such cattle.   [10] Another ox.
[11] A political opponent.   [12] Acuil Bulabek, the chief of Abyor sub-tribe.

Words will hold the wind.
Man who conspires, are you not ashamed?   10
Star Man, why don't you advise the gossiper?
Our clan has never been in need
The clan of Ajong[1] de Monydhaang has never been in need of
    cattle
From our ancestor, Jok, now consumed by termites
To Acai, the girl of the River.[2]   15
Chieftainship is permanent with us.
Is Marial not the peak of the land?
I am the peak of the land
There is no one like Marial de Jok
The man who goes to the bottom of the earth   20
And returns with the glory of the land.
We shall run dancing the ballets with Nyanwiir[3]
O Nyanwiir of Mathiang, let us dance to the joy of Beek.[4]
The ox Miyar brought by Acol is raising his voice like an ostrich
The ox of the daughter of the clan Padol   25
I have bred Miyar in the camp of Biong Mabek
The great Black One moves like a cloud
The Striped One is an ox of the clan Pajok.
Women, come out
Wives of Ajong de Monydhaang, come out   30
Awut, Mother of Arob
Mother of Nyankoc, wife of Rial Pajok,[5]
I hear something like a cry of joy
Marial has come as near as Akuong.
'Who brought the news?'   35
It is the mother of Deng[6]
Awor who is like Awor de Mou
The daughter of Jong d'Arob.
When I returned to the land
I found plotters[7] spoiling the chieftainship   40
Plotters were spoiling the chieftainship, and I did not know
Plotters were spoiling the chieftainship, and Deng Marial did not
    know

---

[1] Praise-name of Deng Majok.   [2] Sacrificed to the river by Jok.
[3] A co-wife of the singer.   [4] The husband's ox.
[5] Another praise-name of Deng Majok.
[6] Awor, Deng Majok's sister.
                                                   [7] Political opponents.

They are causing disorder in the land
Star Man, tell the conspirers to stop.
A message is sent   45
It has gone to Khartoum
And it has gone to Juba;
Let him be reached by telephone
Abyei will hear and the Governor will hear;
The radio is talking   50
With a voice like anklet bells
It is saying the words of the land;
Deng, son of Kwol
Deng, son of Kwol the Pied One.

116. *An Only Child* [Tuic]

During the late forties, when woman's education was just beginning,
the singer's husband, Mawir Rian, then a chief,[1] wanted to send the only
daughter of the singer, his wife, to school. Her mother opposed him,
and after taking her complaint to the late Cyer Deng, a prophet,[2] her
request was granted.

I am trailing Great Cyer to Anyaar
He says: 'We shall meet early in the morning.'
I am a person tortured; I am a person killed
To give birth to a child now to be given to the *jur*.[3]
O our tribe, where shall I then go?   5
O Dinka, where shall I then go?
An only child like the stand of a drum
How can I hear of her in town?
I heard the name, 'Acol', and could not sleep
I could not sleep, but what could I do?   10
Son of Rian, O son of Rian
If you have left her to me,
We shall be on good terms;
Monywir Ajingker, if you have left her to me,
O we shall be on good terms.   15

[1] Later deposed.
[2] See Lienhardt, *Divinity and Experience: the Religion of the Dinka*, 73–4,
78–80.
[3] Being sent to school is conceived of as being given to the *jur*, i.e. foreigner.

VII

HYMNS

HYMNS reflect man's reaction to the cruelties of a world he does not understand, his attempt to understand what he cannot understand, his appeal to God, spirits, and ancestors for their assistance and their response to his prayers.

In order to gauge man's failure which has invited evil, or the capriciousness of the spirits which have unjustifiably inflicted harm, hymns embody the ideals of the Dinka as guaranteed by God and by well-meaning spirits and ancestors.

In accordance with Dinka religious expression, in which prayers are not a regular habit but a request for something specific, hymns are sung for the help of God, lesser spirits, and the ancestors. Thus, except for certain regular occasions of offerings and feasting, they are used as prayers during sickness, war, drought, famine, or any such tragedy, and may be sung by individuals or by groups, in public or in private. Divine leaders and other religious functionaries may also sing hymns alone or in company with others as part of their general prayer for the well-being of their people even though there may be no specific threat. Hymns are also sung as part of the inauguration ceremonies for chiefs or as part of the burial rituals of chiefs and certain holy men.

On whatever occasion hymns are presented, they are generally a means of communication between the ancestors and spirits and their representatives in this world, usually the elders. During war, when young warriors sing in prayer for victory, their hymns take the form of war songs.

In so far as they reflect situations of public significance, whether involving the public as such or some pivotal individuals or groups, hymns are of historical value. This is especially so because hymns of such public interest tend to be perpetuated even though they may be reinterpreted and distorted to present the viewpoints of interested groups. Even when they are new, hymns tend to build on ancient legacy and therefore on old hymns. Whether old, re-

interpreted, distorted, or newly composed, by referring to specific
clan-divinities, hymns may be of particular help in interpreting
mythology and understanding not only the roots of divine leadership, but also current political structure, in so far as it is based on
the traditional system. Other hymns may be found in Lienhardt,
Divinity and Experience: the Religion of the Dinka.

117. *The Lord Thunders* [Ngok]

The Great Lord Madhol[1] thunders in the byre[2]
Thundering in the byre, he is angry with the ants[3]
He is the Man who brings death.
The master whose heart has no grudge
He attracts all the ants   5
People gather on his feet
And also on his head
Great Lord of the Gourd[4]
Put right our land
The land is shaken   10
If the earth is bitterly cold
If the earth blows with cold wind
It is the wind of Divinity.[5]
If a man loves me
I love him   15
And if a man hates me
I hate him.
But not with all of my heart shall I hate
For am I not the prosperity of the ants?

118. *If I Wrong Him* [Ngok of Upper Nile Province]

If I wrong Him
I make it right.[6]
If I have wronged Him
I have made it right.

[1] Praise-name for God.
[2] During the rainy season, Dinkas normally keep their cattle in the cattle-
byres. God is seen as having a byre in the sky.   [3] Ants are human beings.
[4] Gourds are used in some religious rituals.   [5] The healthy season.
[6] Usually by sacrificing or consecrating an animal to the offended spirit.

I will not tire 5
I will not tire
I will not tire of Deng, the spirit of my fathers
Ayuel Longar,[1] Master of Earth,
I do not understand the doubts from above
If I wrong Him 10
I make it right.

119. *My Horns will not Break*
[Ngok of Upper Nile Province]

Ayuel Longar,[1] son of Jiel,[2]
I will appease you with a white bull.[3]
The Winter has come
The world has dawned[4]
My horns will not break[5] 5
I am no longer vexed.
The Winter comes
And I sleep with leisure.
O our Deng,
Deng, son of Garang,[6] 10
Deng, son of Abuk,[7]
The man has come with life.

[1] Ayuel, the son of a woman and a Power of the river, punished the people of the village in which he was born by spearing them as they tried to cross to the land of endless grass and water where there was no death. He was finally overpowered by a man to whom he gave the Fishing-Spear which is the source of the power of the clan of the Fishing-Spear. Thus, Ayuel represents a combination of life and death and is divine. For further reference see Lienhardt, op. cit. (1961), 171–206.

[2] The Dinka are not consistent about the genealogies of their clans or of their clan-divinities. Any descendant may be called the son of any ascendant. But the lack of consistency may also extend to such cases as this: Ayuel Longar was said to have no known father except the Power of the River. In Dinka logic, the relationship arises by virtue of Ayuel Longar's affiliation in Jiel's lineage or Jiel may well be a symbolic representation of the unknown father of Ayuel in this particular context.

[3] The colour of an animal to be sacrificed matters according to the spirit concerned, and the objective of the sacrifice. A white bull is often associated with God and usually a request for rain.

[4] The cool season is associated with good health and good health with dawn.

[5] A bull's horns sometimes break during a fight. Since this is a healthy season without epidemics or famine, they are secure.

[6] Garang is the Dinka Adam.   [7] Abuk is the Dinka Eve.

120. *The Man from Above*
[Ngok of Upper Nile Province]

If a thing subdues me
It will be solved by Deng, the man from above.
Awol Kerjok[1] and Deng[2] Acuny[3]
Praise Him Who Embraces the World.
Our River-Girl[4] and Wieu[5]   5
Come let us pray to Deng.
Kokbong[6] and Longar
The ants have been sad for eight years.[7]
Awol Kerjok, come and listen to the words I say
I praise Abuk and her son, Deng,   10
The face of the ant you created has become sad
Come let us pray to our Lord.

121. *Big Chief Pray to God* [Ngok]

Some years ago, a young man of the Pajok clan fell ill. After his recovery, he did not return to his normal life, but became 'a man of God',
who might have been an acknowledged prophet in traditional times. In
this hymn, he asks the Chief to turn to God to save the country from
disintegration.

We have become lean
Big Chief, pray to God
Our buttocks have wrinkled
Big Chief, pray to God
Our faces are sad   5
Big Chief, pray to God

---

[1] A clan divinity or an ancestor.
[2] A common clan divinity. Correspondingly, Deng is a common Dinka name.
[3] A praise-name for the clan divinity often used to praise people with the
Deng name.
[4] Either a girl sacrificed to the Power of the River (e.g. Acai) or a woman who
was conceived by the Power of the River (e.g. Ayuel's mother).
[5] Presumably another divinity.
[6] Yet another divinity.
[7] A similar line appears in a song quoted by Lienhardt, op. cit. (1961),
and presumably refers to the upheavals of the nineteenth century.

Will dances be held at night
As though they were dances of spirits?[1]
Doo, doo, doo, doo[2]
Big Chief, pray to God.   10

[1] Most adult male dances are held in the day-time. He means that they will
be too ashamed of their appearance to dance when they can be seen.
[2] Signifying the beating of the drums.

VIII

FAIRY-TALE SONGS

FAIRY-TALES among the Dinka are an important part of a child's growth. They are recited only at night, and, as their name *koor* (lion) suggests, are usually accounts involving the animal world with that of man. As a rule, they begin with *ke ghon ka* (this is an ancient event). But apart from communication with the animal world which justifies the attribution of their origin to the past, they are a presentation of Dinka life to a child, a revelation of Dinka conceptions of evil and good, in short, an educational method. As in any other phase of Dinka life, songs are an important part of this educational method.

122. *No Room for Words* [Rek]

A man ventured into a grazing area dominated by a lion. Having tethered his herds, he made a smoky fire to send flies away. The lion saw the smoke and heard the bellows of Miyar, the white ox of the intruder. The lion approached the camp, singing while the ox bellowed, and the man answered, taking pride in his might as symbolized by his ox, which he likens to a wall and considers too powerful to be affected by rain in the summer camp. The man won the fight.

> 'Yiboo.[1]
> Who dares make smoky fires in my camp?'
> 'It is I, Deng, the Mighty Wall in the camp
> With my ox Minyiel smooth and round.'
> There is nowhere for words to pass.   5
> Lion, lion, see the back of my Minyiel
> Where will rain fall?
> Where will it fall on my Minyiel?
> O Mijok
> Girls coming to the camp,   10
> Rain falls only in other camps.[2]

[1] The ox's bellow.
[2] Since rain does not affect them because both he and his ox are healthy and strong it is as though it does not fall in their camp.

123. *It Flashed with Lightning* [Ngok]

A lion sings.

It flashed with lightning in the land of Apuk[1]
In the darkness of the night
Lightning dazzled people's eyes
But it did not dazzle my eyes.
Gentlemen[2] rose,   5
Gentlemen rose to attack
I sharpened my own spear
And charged with it at Maleng de Giuny in a byre
And women cried,
'Our camp is left without gentlemen.'   10

124. *Increase Your Speed* [Ngok]

A brother and his sister were confronted with a lion; the brother engaged
the lion while he had his sister run ahead. They exchange these words
as she runs.

Acol of my mother
Increase your speed
Daughter of my mother
Increase your speed;
The lion is displaying   5
Like a young calf[3]
The animal is displaying
Like the young of a cow;
Madut of my mother
I am delayed   10
Son of my mother
I am delayed by anklet rings.[4]

[1] A section of Rek Dinka.
[2] *Adheeng.*
[3] When full and happy, young calves display amazing strength running and
jumping relentlessly.
[4] Often fixed and not easily removable.

125. *The River-man* [Ngok]

An extraordinarily courageous and handsome man who attracted the
attention of most girls was hated by his age-mates out of jealousy. They
spread false rumours that he was courting the lame ugliest girl in the
camp. The girl too told stories in which she was backed by the man's
sister who apparently liked her. In protest, he left the camp and
went into the river where a crocodile adopted him and made a river-
man out of him. His two personality oxen discovered his survival and
would come and bellow near the river. On such occasions, he would turn
into a human being and come ashore to sing to them.

Children who were herding one day heard him sing and reported to
the elders. Meanwhile all, including his age-mates, had regretted his
disappearance and wished him back, though they would not believe the
story of the children. After careful investigation and proof, a plan was
made to catch him and bring him back. This was done and, after a long
struggle in which he turned into a crocodile, he was overcome. He turned
human again and rejoined the camp. This is the dialogue as his oxen
bellowed and he sang.

> '*Hooboo*[1]
> There is our father in the river,
> *Hooboo*
> Our father who did not fear,
> If our father were not dead[2]   5
> He would be carrying a shield in the lead
> Taking us to grazing-grounds he had explored.'
> 'Here I am my Monitor Lizards[3]
> Here I am my Striped On the Sides,[4]
> If it were not for my feud with the Lame Girl   10
> I would not have come into the river;
> Bellow, Ivory Bangles herded by the Riverman
> Feud which has crossed me with the Lame Girl
> The poor single daughter of my mother
> Remained sad with a lonely face,   15
> It was you who spread the word
> That Guot and the Lame Girl are friends
> Bellow, Ivory Bangles released by the Riverman.

[1] Bellows of the oxen.
[2] It would seem that even after he started answering them his having turned
into a crocodile also amounted to death.
[3] The oxen are of the same colour.
[4] Maker.   [5] Praise-term for his oxen.

126. *Adim* [Ngok]

Adim was sent to fetch a goat to be sacrificed for a sick relative and contrary to the advice of senior men he returned by night with the goat, and was killed by a lion.

Mee[1]
What my father said
Mee
What my mother said
A man after life   5
Does not walk at night;
Mee
Adim, you did not hear
Mee
Adim, you let yourself be killed   10
Adim has left me alone in the forest
The forest of lions
Adim is eaten by a lion
And I exclaimed,
'O my Matem,   15
O my father's Matem,
There goes Adim.'

[1] The cry of sheep and goats.

IX

CHILDREN'S GAME SONGS

IN games, children act out such adult roles as age-grading, initiation, war, cattle-camp life, family life, litigation, and the like. Consequently, they have ox songs, cathartic songs, age-set insult songs, war songs, and women's songs (in the case of girls), though not hymns, which are presumably too serious for them. There is no substantial difference between the contents of such songs and those of adults. For this reason, it is unnecessary to include here those children's songs which would merely repeat the various classes of songs already covered. There are, however, songs which reflect the peculiar role of children both in content and in the circumstances of their presentation. Those included here are only a few examples.

127. *Sleep at Home* [Ngok]

Whose sister is this?
She is the sister of Diingthiy
And where is Diingthiy?
Diingthiy has gone to the cattle-camp,
He left early in the day   5
And young girls came
Young girls came, and evening came;
Abul where will you sleep?
Abul sleep in your home,
You are called Abul   10
You are called Abul.

128. *Do not Leave* [Ngok]

This is your home of marriage
This is your home, daughter of Dorjok;
You are a girl who found the home

Indeed, a great home
The great home of Ajang de Ker;   5
No, no,
No, daughter of Dorjok
Do not carry yourself away from a solid home.

129. *Hide-and-Seek* [Ngok]

In a game of hide-and-seek one child stays outside while the others hide.
They sing in a dialogue:

May I come now?
No, do not come yet.
You are still thinking of your mother
Your mother is married in the land of the Tuic,   4
The people with initiation marks running to the backs of their
    heads.[1]

130. *Bend your Leg* (*a*) [Ngok]

This song is sung in a game called *thiilim*, which must have as part of its
objective to train girls to sit in the proper way. Dinka girls and women
sit with their thighs together and their legs folded under them by their
sides. A girl is strictly taught from an early age to sit in this position.
A girl who sits carelessly is severely reprimanded. The game of *thiilim*,
in which boys take part, entails sitting in a row with outstretched legs.
One person sits in front of the row chanting mostly unintelligible words
while touching each leg at each beat of the chanting. The last person to
be touched at the end of the song bends the touched leg. Winning is
determined by bending both legs. It is not clear which language most
of the song is in; a few seem to be Baggara Arab words, more are Dinka
words, but the vast majority of the words are simply meaningless at face
value, although their sounds seem significant. I only translate what I can
and leave the rest in italics.

The fact that the boys participate in the game, rather than an argument against its educational objective, confirms the point since it creates
the circumstances where the need for sitting properly is greatest. The
fact that the one told in the end to bend the leg is a woman further
supports the point.

[1] Some Tuic (and also Rek) initiation marks fan out from the centre of the
forehead and run over the head.

Thiilim
Thiilim anyom
Anyom beerge
They are *thaabi*;
Thaaba yeey   5
Yaa dheen
Will enter *elek lek*
Will enter *enyam*
Dhaan akam
The word said   10
Mother of Ajak
Have you heard?
Bend your leg.

131. *Bend your Leg* (*b*) [Bor]

This version which accompanies the game described in the preceding
song is from Bor. The man who sang it did not explain the words which,
as in the Ngok song, he said did not really mean anything. However,
unlike the Ngok song the words are recognizable, and although they
may not be altogether coherent I have translated them.

Arol from where did you come?
I came by stealth looking for grass
That of the girl on the side is throwing itself down
And I shall go to Rekland
I shall go to show hospitality to Arol,   5
This Arol is like Arol of the Pied Crow
Better look for gum with which to glue your opening
You of honour, bend your leg
Your child will drown.

X

SCHOOL SONGS

THE position of schoolboys somewhat resembles that of age-sets, as their songs reveal, though the songs emphasize the boys' newly acquired skills rather than fighting potential. They often express the dilemma of a person asserting the value of his new wisdom and abilities as the means of progress in a yet largely traditional system. In consequence, he still has to appeal to leaders who, while recognized as leaders, are also regarded as lacking the new virtues.

School songs are formally presented on a variety of occasions involving schoolchildren's activities such as marching, dancing, church-singing (where appropriate), or celebrations of parents' day. They are of course very recent and relevant only to a small minority of all Dinka.

132. *I shall Turn the Land Upside Down* [Ngok]

The moon of December has appeared
Our age-set in white[1] sees it from all flanks
The age-set which obeys orders
We obey orders;
Our junior age-set in white gathers at Abyei   5
The school is opened;
The age-set in white knows the words.
I shall turn the land upside down
I shall change the land
I am small, but I am a man;   10
I sit in the place where words flow
O Wor[2] of the Brown[3]
Our mothers all cry,
'Our children have gone astray
The land has remained without a child.'   15

[1] Literally, 'the White Bull'.   [2] The headmaster.
[3] Wor's father's ox-colour-pattern.

Mother, I do not blame you
There is nothing you know
Nothing you know.
The word of the world is creeping on
It comes crossing the lands of all peoples;   20
In Khartoum, a child is born, and he goes.
Am I to appease you only with a white cow?
What about the white one in the market
And my pen?
I seized the spears,   25
I seized the spears
And raised my voice with a song[1]
And ran in a stampede;
I raised my voice with a song
And ran in a stampede;   30
Our age-set in white threw a water-lily[2]
And ran in a stampede.
I arranged the poles firm as rocks
And lay the foundation.
An age-set which is gathered and determined   35
Nothing subdues them;
I called our age-set
And we laid the foundation;
I pulled the lumbers
And laid the foundation;   40
I am building my home
I am building my home
The home of the children of learning
The home where words of children flow even at night.
To the age-set in white, jealousy is unknown.   45

133. *Do not Delay* [Ngok]

I seized the spears
And raised my voice with a war song[3]
My pen rattled against my books
I did not miss.

[1] *Dor*, a song for arousing group-spirit in action.
[2] Probably a war ritual.
[3] *Dor*.

The book is with those who write the word[1]   5
The ancient wisdom of the sons of Adam
Is known by our age-set in white[2] who write
Age-set who write, bring the words.
The lost child will not be looked for
The captured cow will not be looked for   10
If they be looked for, it is we who write
Age-set who write for the chief
Write the message;
The message which I shall write
The bearer cannot read   15
It will be seen by him who reads
Never by a pagan priest;
Your priests, I do not honour them
I am a big man
The age-set in white know the words.   20
Brother who is left behind
I will send a message to you
When you come, do not be late
Our age-set in white is going ahead,
Turn and see, turn and see   25
Turn your back—you are late
Turn, turn.
The display of the age-set of Wor
Is done with guns
The sounds of drill are heard   30
It is the ancient art of the sons of gentlemen.

134. *Father and Mother* [Ngok]

My father and my mother
Father and mother
You have bred me
Both of you, you have bred me.
I love you both[3]   5
If God has kept me for you both.

[1] Of knowledge.
[2] The school uniform, but more generally clothes. Traditionally men were nude.
[3] Since Dinka children, especially sons, do not express love to their mothers, this is certainly a new concept.

See the sweetness of a son
You, our fathers
We greet you;
Accept our greetings with all of your hearts   10
Our hearts are filled with the joy of seeing you.
God, Creator, master who created men
To you we pray,
Save for us our fathers
And all our brothers   15
Our chiefs who are holding our land
Our judges, and our people at large
And our masters of learning.

135. *The Bishop* [Rek]

We shall honour our Lord
We shall honour the Bishop
We shall honour Edward,[1]
He is the master at our head
Our master appointed by the Creator to keep us   5
He is given life to keep us
And given power to keep us.
We are the children of Mary
We are the children of Mary, the Immaculate
Our Immaculate Mother.   10
Let us honour the Bishop
Let us honour Edward.
May our master Edward sleep in peace
The master with life will sleep in peace.
He has put the land in order   15
The land is held by our master
The land is held by the master of the Christians
The Great Mason is the master of the Christians of Bahr el Ghazal
And he is the master of the world.
I honour the master   20
Ayom of my father, we have arrived
Bussere,[2] we have arrived

[1] Edward Mason was the Catholic Bishop of Bahr el Ghazal Province. He was later transferred to Kordofan, where he served until the expulsion of the missionaries in 1963.
[2] Which used to be a Catholic centre of education in Bahr el Ghazal before the schools were taken over by the Government in 1957.

Our big home, the mission of Kwajok[1]
Our mission will go to the big town
The followers of Father Fazzine[2] will bring the cloud.   25
We are honouring our Father
He is the master to overcome the evil that confronts us
When the evil spirits come,
Mohammed[3] comes to break our divine laws
Mathiang Guk[4] comes to break our divine laws   30
Our big Father is the protector.
Our Father Fazzine is showing us many things
The many things of God
Our father has spoken
Ecclesia   35
Our master will put the land in order by his Church.
The mission of Kwajok, we built with our hand
We built our home with our hands and our hearts
The Head Priest here
And our Mother Kapila here   40
She came with her own flank
Her girls who could not be counted
Then the people who lumbered in the woods
And those who dug the ground
The school was built   45
Kwajok was built,
Our home was built.

136. *The Tribe has Remained Behind* [Rek]

Who was the first to put the flank in order?
The man who governs the land
It was Can,[5] the Crested Crane, our chief,
Akol,[6] Hair on the Head, our chief.
Akol, Hair on the Head, our chief,   5
Do not let the tribe of your father stray.
Magot[7] is maintaining order in the land
Great Akol, Can e Nyal, our chief
Hold the flanks of the tribe, Awan.

[1] Another educational and missionary centre.
[2] The head priest in Kwajok.   [3] Meaning Muslims.
[4] Traditional Dinka black medicine.   [5] Chief of Awan Rek tribe.
[6] Praise-name for Can.   [7] Another praise-name for Can.

The feast of Aweil has begun
The feast of the Tribe of Lang[1] has begun
And the feast of the tribe of Giir[2] has begun.
The feasts are celebrated at Kwajok
Kwajok Mission is our summer cattle-camp
Kwajok is our home   15
It has become our home
The home of the Great Priest.
We kissed the Master
We kissed the Master.
Our group have become few[3]   20
I hate to be scorned by other tribes.
The Governor of Wau asked,
'People of Akol Mayuok,
Why has your tribe remained behind?
Your tribe has remained far behind   25
You have been surpassed in learning
Apuk of Jok have gone ahead,
And Kwac of Yot have heard the word.'
Ee—ee—ee
O what shall we do?   30
Deng Makuei,[4] our master, will teach us to write
Our master will teach us to write papers and books
In the Great Awan of Can e Nyal.
Let us go to sharpen the horns[5] of Great Can at Kwajok.

137. *Maria is Feared* [Rek]

Maria, our Mother, is feared by evil spirits
Cries arose in the middle of the day[6]
Mother
Help us
The war of evil spirits,   5
Our mother is feared by spirits.

[1] The chief of a faction of the Tuic.
[2] Chief of Apuk, one of the Rek Dinka factions.
[3] In other words, their tribe is behind in education.
[4] A schoolteacher.
[5] Meaning to make him proud.
[6] Cries of war symbolizing fight with evil spirits.

We cry and call you with a loud voice
O O O
And you come to save us from evil spirits.
The war is grave   10
The war against the spirits of the world.
We shall fasten our hearts
We shall bear no fear
When our mother is near.
Spirits fear your name   15
Maria our mother is feared.

138. *Dinka, Think* [Rek]

Who taught us to write and read?
We are the children of the Priest
Let us praise Great Giir Mangar, our chief.
Carrier of Animal, Governor of the Land
Carrier of Animal, chief of Apuk of a hundred divisions   5
Carrier of Animal, chief of Apuk of ten divisions
Our tribe is the maternal kin[1] of the tribes;
Apuk is the maternal kin of the tribes
And Giir is the maternal kin of the tribes;
Ador is the maternal kin of the tribes   10
And Giir is the maternal kin of the tribes.
We shall pray to God
To save our chief for us
Our chief, Giir Mangar;
And Mayuot Thiik, our chief,   15
We shall greet them every year
We shall greet them with the drums of the Turuk[2]
We shall greet the chiefs with the drums of the Turuk,
We shall greet them with the drums of the Priests
Music, the drums of the *Jur*,[3]   20
Apuk, our tribe, think
Monyjang,[4] think

[1] Another way of saying that theirs is a very important tribe.
[2] A carry-over from the Turco-Egyptian period used to designate the British
and such whites as may be associated with colonial power.
[3] Foreigners.   [4] Dinka word for themselves, 'Dinka'.

Dinka, think
Jenge,[1] think;
So that we may be like Malakal   25
So that we may be like Europeans
And be like the English
So that we may be like the Europeans.
Cyer[2] is the man
The person holding the pen;   30
Lang[3] is the man
The person holding the pen;
A person holding the pen is also the one holding the cows
He is also the one holding the goats and sheep
He is also holding the medicine,   35
People become miserable during the summer[4]
Riches are only heard of among the educated.

139. *What will the Christians Do?* [Rek]

In our tribe, people are at peace
In Apuk, our tribe, people are at peace;
People maintained by the robe of Giir
Keep your country high
Your country is about to fall   5
O Giir the Great Mangar.
Apuk, we are leaving
We are visiting Kwajok;
Apuk, we are leaving
We are visiting the big town, Wau;[5]   10
Apuk, we have arrived
Beat the drums
Let the drums be heard.
Our tribe has never been slow
We have never been late in the celebrations done in Awan   15
And in the celebrations done in Aguok.
We beat the drums for music
Piol, Grass-Man of Nyon, beat the drums
Even if you beat the drums and destroy them

[1] Colloquial Arabic for Dinka.   [2] A literate chief of the Tuic.
[3] Another literate chief of the Tuic.   [4] Lean season.
[5] The provincial headquarters of Bahr el Ghazal.

It is your tribe, led by Giir of Arek.   20
We are known among the Dinka
We are known among all the tribes.
Will Apok remain in the lead?
No, we have become disdained in the tribes.
O the scorn of the tribes!   25
Apuk has pulled its head behind
The bull has pulled his head behind
Who will remain with the lead?
With whom will leadership remain?
Even if tribes gang up against me   30
O Aguok, O Amuk!
O Amuk, O Aguok!
Our leadership has remained behind.
Giir the Great Striped One
He is the man who leads Apuk   35
He is the man who leads our tribe
He ordered the land
The land which his father Thiik had led.
The name of Giir is heard
The name of our chief is heard   40
He has united the tribes
He has united the great tribe of Aguok.
The name of Great Giir has been heard for long
The name of Great Mangar has been heard for long.
When they took Giir into the sky by a plane[1]   45
Women all cried in dismay,
'O O ee ee
Our chief is taken away
What will return him to us?'
The chiefs were asked,[2] 'What do you want?'   50
'Father, it is breath.'[3]
'What do you have to say?'
'Father, it is life.'
'What do you want?'
'Father, it is breath   55
It is what we, of Ajang, are seeking.
We heard of the Bishop

[1] A number of Southern chiefs flew to Rome to visit the Pope.
[2] Supposedly by the Pope.   [3] Dinka for 'life'.

We heard of our Lord
We heard of him who puts the land in order.'
The Bishop is the one who puts the land in order   60
The land of Bahr el Ghazal
Our land is ordered by the Bishop,
The land of Bahr el Ghazal
Our land is blessed by the Bishop,
The land of Bahr el Ghazal.   65
Father, our master
The land is threatened by pagans
The land is threatened by Mohammedans
O what will the Christians do?
I turn this way, and it is the fetish Mathiang Guk   70
And Mohammedans are facing East[1]
They are facing where the sun rises.
What misfortune, what misfortune!
We are entangled with bad spirits
Some are evil-eyed   75
Some inflict evil spells
Some are evil-eyed who disturb the innocent in the land
The land led by the Bishop
The land led by Edward
The land is confused   80
The land has its head in a knot.

140. *The Rays of Light* [Ngok]

Learning is good, learning is good
Brothers in learning,
Let us rise early in the morning.
Learning is good,
Open our minds, masters, open our minds   5
Our minds like rocks, our minds like rocks
Our minds like the earth, our minds like the earth
We shall enlighten them with rays of light.
Thanks, thanks to the Government,[2]
Thanks to the Government.   10

[1] In accordance with their prayers.
[2] Education among the Ngok, unlike most Dinka tribes, was provided by the Government and not by the missionaries.

141. *The Gentleman of the Future* [Ngok]

Learning is good
We have found it so,
Learning is the best
We have found it so.
I will not leave the school[1]   5
I am a man
I have liked it;
I will not leave the school
I am the gentleman of the future.
Those children who run away   10
They have no hearts
They do not even bid their masters farewell;
Those children who run away
They have no hearts.
Even if we tire   15
We shall endure
We shall find its sweetness later on;
Even if we tire
We shall endure
To find its sweetness later on.   20

142. *The World is Ahead* [Ngok]

Have you come?
Have you slept?
O our chiefs
We want to show you the sweetness of our hearts.
We greet you all   5
Our big chiefs
What you have done to us
Has sweetened our hearts;
We greet you all
Heads of clans   10
Heads of the camps
And the *omdas*.

[1] Before education was popularly accepted, many children used to escape
from school and return home.

Let us love ourselves
O brothers
Brothers in learning 15
Let us love ourselves all;
Let us leave jealousies
And love ourselves
And love education.
O brothers 20
All the world has gone ahead
Shall we reach them?
Can we reach them?
Let us pray hard to God our Father
And teach us well 25
You our teachers.
You our big chiefs
Learning is good
We have found it so;
We greet you all 30
And thank our government
For having opened a school in our land.
We greet you all.

143. *House of Knowledge* [Ngok]

We of class one
We have opened the door
We shall go;
We of class two
We have opened the door 5
We are in;
We of class three
We have searched the house
Except for the store platform
A B C   X Y Z 10
A B C   X Y Z

I

DIƐT KE MIOR

1. *Cil tuŋ adi wɛrwɛɛr?* [Ɗɔk]

Cil tuŋ adi wɛrwɛɛr?
Cil tuŋ adi ke kuar piny ɛɛ?
Tuŋ de Maŋar ala roor ee
Tuŋ de Maŋar ala roor ci raan ci
    maar
Tuŋ ka la nhial mɔɔth.   5
Anɔmkɛɛu dul ka cɔl 'Atuenywiin'
Abik ke win de rel ci many biok e
    bab.
Anɔmkɛɛu e guet acit rol mɔɔŋ
Ku agun e yom.
Ke ye Maŋar di bur theei   10
Ke ye Mijoŋ di bur theei ke mɛc
    weŋ
Ka kuoc e nan yen kiu bi teem
Ku nan yen kuɛth yen Ɗar wa yii
    nɔm
Ci raan ca-arega rueeth.
Ba weŋ wut aci thok e mim,   15
Ke rel oi miŋ
Naŋ thëëi ku ci weŋ thok e mac
Aboŋ dɔu Maŋar ke ci gau la pil
Rol tam-e-tam ci biak ci Deŋ Abuk
    cɔɔl ke maar.
Miak e dur be weŋ da luɔny tooc   20
Kic kuɛth waan thok
Maŋar akic biok thiɔn e liei
Ake kiu e thɔyɔɔŋ.
Weŋ da cok pial ci wut
Ci Mithiaŋ de Pajok,   25
Raan miir nuat

Ago ku thook e dɔl.
Weŋ nɔm tueŋ ke Makuany di war
Ci kɛny de Nuɛr tɔŋ nɔm tueŋ
Aci war,   30
Acak weŋ da bɛ liaap ka-aluony de
    wun Jameel
Ke Maŋar aci war;
Mijoŋ bɛɛr diir ci raan abɛr biaac
    piny
Ago biaac nuɔr Maŋar cok;
Aci bi nuat   35
Ke ciet ke cieŋ gaar e cok atam
Ake dhur baak weŋ nɔm ci lai.
Bɔk athiaak Mijoŋ di kɔu ka ŋuan
Ku ka cik ki ram athɛɛr
Kek ki waac ci ya-akol ke pɛɛi.   40
Ayɛɛr Jok
Biɔŋ e cieŋ e bany
Biɔŋ de raan e yath
Biɔŋ de raan de bith,
Yin bi tuŋ du gut thook;   45
Yɛn keek Makuac kek nyan Beekrɔl,
Mijoŋ tuɔŋ acɛŋ luac de Nyanaŋeth;
Biaac dit thier yen ba guɔt nɔm piny
Ayɔɔk Maŋar yin bi tuŋ du rom thok,
Ci biɔl e run ci piny de riak   50
Acen riny e dɛɛ yen.
Yɛn ci piɔu e piɔu e riny da bɛ piɔu
E tuŋ guɔt piny ci raan nin
Ajal kuen agua alaraan ka bi piŋ thin
Ku na wadaŋ ku la e nɔm guik   55

Ke duet ke many da-Aguen de Kur
 e ke go awɛɛc baai.
Mijoŋ ban tuŋ de gut nɔm wadaŋ
Agon dɛɛ beer mɔu ci pan randai.
Gua-abadaai daŋ ke beer,
Daŋ abi daai biak e Makuany di miɔl
 thin kek biith ci tuɛɛl mɛɛc   60
Ago riny bi wok ye liem tuŋ acɔŋ
 piɔu ci ke cɔŋ ruaath,
Maŋarker ago rin ki bɛ luɛɛl
Ci piɔu athan ci wa kɔn piɔu ke
 Matiɔk Arolbeek.
Jot pal rak ku cen ken ye luel rin
 Maker
Ci ŋuɛn raan cuer ke bi ye luɛl   65
Jot pal rak ku cen ken ye luel rin
 Maker,
Yen aŋoot e ban tuŋ de gut thook
 nyan Beekrɔl
Ke bi wo luɛɛl.
Aŋeth Aŋeth nyan Beŋ de Madiŋ,

Anyaar yɔl ke Makuany di teŋ ci
 nyum ka-agɔk.   70
Ayɔɔk Maŋar ke bɛ yɛn ye lɛc nɔm,
 ka luel Jok Maŋar;
Kan yi cɔl Jok Maŋar,
Buŋ tok arɛɛr e tɛɛn ken duɔl guuc;
Ke na Maker ku ke na Maŋar,
Na ceen ke ye guɔp Makuac,   75
Na wen tueŋ ke go ya Mijoŋ rɔl ci
 dhuny adol,
Ci weŋ athan miit awan tiɔp.
Mijoŋ di wien riɔk ke mac piɔu,
Acit thɔn ci dɛɛu yam.
Maŋar yen kan bak yol;   80
Ayɛɛr Jok yin ka muk lɛnlɛɛn,
Ci ke kuet acɔɔt raan daŋ.
Yɛn man rɔt wo wiin ci raan daŋ loc
 piat nɔm,
Ka kuoc maan ka ci wal nyuɔth;
Ke ku nhiaar piny bek-ku la gɔl, 85
Gɔl ku Maker ee bek-ku la gɔl.

2. *Wiic miɔɔl ci Deŋ jöt* [Ŋɔk]

Miyar di wo laaŋ ɛɛ,
Ka lueel, 'Run ka diak
Ku na ciet e piɔu yɛn
Miyar, yin bi miɔɔl pɔl.'
Magar awin miɔɔl ci deŋ jot.   5
La ye gam
Aguɔn tiam kɔɔr e mɔɔth e kol
Tiam kɔɔr ku riek wiir ci lan aŋui;
Ka ca pal, aban dul loi nɔm e pɛi ya.
Ya wien yeer aguɔn cin awany   10
Ci yenh de gon.
Ya rɔt duany ci riny thel lɔɔr
Yɛn akɔr ater.
Miɔr akol jel e wa ya lɛc nɔm ɛɛ
'E miɔr e ŋuɛt akic roŋ ke miɔl; 15
Man yen wut kuany ic
Na yen la yi weer ca Ayaŋ de Köör
Ku la joŋ de luɔc
Abin wut maan.'
Luɛɛl, 'Wa ace weŋ e miɔl   20
Ke weŋ nyimuny.'
Wa lueel, 'Dɔl ku e path
Ace weŋ e miɔl ku bin wut maan.'

Loŋ e raan ŋuɛn aca lɛɛŋ
Na ci wɛt e wa guɔ ruɔu pɛɛi tok 25
Cit e miɔl tem
Miɔl tem aguɔn wut koon ci ke lei
Ca be la wut
Ku buk wut luel ic wok Yardit kek
 Deŋ
Na jal wut luel ic   30
Miyar dit kuar wei thian.
Pɛɛi wil, pɛɛi wil
Ago Yar Deŋ Wadit Akuaar agon
 yɔk riau
Ruel Mijok du ruel pɛɛi
Ca alaany ake wo diir.   35
Ajɔk de weŋ na ke lony e weŋ
Ke bak roor, ace bak ruup
Yɔk laar e yol ic
Makuac acit kɛny de tɔŋ
Ɣnic tuŋ bi riak   40
Rɔt gɛɛŋ e tɔŋ nyin athiɔk
Kic ŋɔl Kurluak luɔk e rap
Ago biaac kuet
Ci rɛc da awan muk e laŋ.

Piny dit e Kuɔt Awet   45
Ye kuar kɔu ci yiŋ de kɔɔc
Ago duɔl ariiuriiu.
Piny de weŋ alok yok Maŋar walen
Mijok mai e Pabur
Biaac da awɔu   50
Nhiar weŋ awɔu, acɔl biaac da
    awɔu.
Mac e wut Maŋar de Tɔŋ d'Ajing
Yɛn kic lom wo raan daŋ
Yɛn kic kɔn jam adec
Thuɔu yɛn man wɛt e ŋuɛt wei ci
    bok
Ye loŋ e ŋuɛt yɔɔt kɔu ci bel   55
Ago yaany teem.
Bɛn de cier
Miyɔm de Dɔr Aguek e ya bɛ gɔk
'E ŋɔ kic e weŋ raak?'   60
Ke luɛl, 'Weŋ abi raak.'
Weŋ da ka der ee

Weŋ da ka der ago biaac mim ca-
    amal
Mijok weŋ da ka der.
Run de piny e Maŋar Ajak   65
Yen ke yɛn ajuɔŋ miɛɛt
Diët ci luŋ tuër ic ci dom ic
Akic loth cuɔɔŋ.
Ke wo diir ci duet yam e jöt.
E Yar di röl cet köör ku rum   70
Pal Adheeŋ rak
Adheeŋ ka bi la mai Bulei
Adheeŋ ka bi la mai Dɔɔl ɛɛ.
Maŋar a akic roŋ ke raan kor
Yen mane ka roŋ ke raan ŋuɛɛn.   75
Ka ca pal ee
Ce yɛn raan ŋuɛɛn?
Ce yɛn e kuet yen?
Raan ŋuɛɛn ce yen e kur cien ɛɛ?
Ku raan kor ce yen e bɛn a-raan
    ŋuɛɛn?   80

3. *Löth Mijok kɛɛt nɔm* [Dɔk]

Jur Col e gut
Kic Maŋar di löth riɔɔk ku tem diɛɛr
    kɔu
E ku dhur ka ci riaak;
Löth ka riaak
Na la Kwɔl ye piŋ   5
Ke ci piɔu bi diu?
Akuei Miyɔm Kwɔl
Kɔc luɔɔb cikki cit acuek;
Eŋɔ bi lueel?
Piŋ Kwɔl e ku thöök edɔl,   10
'Ye kenɛɛ na ca-Akuany du löth
    riɔɔk
Ku teem diɛɛr kɔu ee
Ke kee duaar da wodhie.'
Ye lönh mith ka-Aŋɔr e Bɔŋ tuɔm
    nyin ci nak de raan awɔɔk
Tom raan nyin.   15
Mabɔŋ bi löth wiiu
Mijɔŋ bi thath Jur da-Abyiem wiiu
Ye thath Rek da-Abyiem biir ic꞉i
    wun
Teŋ Maŋar ago luuŋ dhiau,
Ya-ajuɔŋ Mijo kkɛɛt nɔm ci kuer koor.

Dhien da yee ke wo guer Aŋuek kɔu
    wo wa,   20
Ago wa kek lɔɔk de,
Ayi yɛɛn wok lɔɔk dien e yɛn Makuac
    tiit.
E biak e riny da rɔt liaab wɛɛr ic
Raan bi yen tɔɔr   25
Maŋar de Jak ci wa bi kuɔc riɛɛt ci
    Deŋ
Ci min ci kol de nyin riaak alen
    nhial.
Dar de Jak aci weŋ e pɔl
Cit ken ke weŋ
Ayi yɛn ciet ken ke weŋ.   30
Maŋar ci wa ya wiic nyin ɛɛ
Kic wa ya wiic nyin ɛɛ?
Maŋar de Deŋ d'Ajak Tɛɛm
Rɔu dhien keer kän rial
Mijok cet ke cien warak.   35
Wal amai ke Mijok biɔɔr
Ago dul paac ke diu
Ca-adheeŋ ke door toc
Mɔny dit piɔu yen ke jal ke diu
Ke luel e kuc e tɛk.   40

Yany Aŋueek tony de gɔl
Maker tony la wel rɔɔl
Yuɛk yɔl ajuath
Ku wɛɛr cin e jac
Nɔm cet Makuany de rap 45
Ku la doŋ e tiŋ Rurueŋ
Cɔŋ lɔɔr ke ci pot arom aluɛɛl.
Cil tuŋ atuɔt ke dhal jaŋ.
Kuɛɛt Maŋar agon dhiɔɔp gam
Guŋ dit e Deŋ d'Aguer 50
Maŋar agon dhiɔɔp gam.
Dhor Ka thöŋ ku de ruɔb de ŋɛk;
Dhor ka thöŋ ake ruɔb de wen
  Minyiel.
Ya miɛt biɔɔth ci wen Kurluak
Athan ci nya thiaak; 55
Nya thiaak e wundit Nuɛr
Ago buɔt der go Kwɔt jai²
Na biiy buɔt ke Kwɔt jai;
Kwɔt jai, 'Na cak e jal teer
Ke weŋ e yɔl de rou na la yekɣɛn.'
Jot abɛnbɛn apiɛɛr thut 61
Aci yen lɔŋ, ken rɔt dhuɔk cien,
Na jel bɛn ke weŋ e yɔl rou
Ke Kwɔt jai, 'Ka mat keek
Yi weŋ buɔɔt ku la nyandi.' 65
Kwɔt e dɔk ci bany thɛɛr
Kɛc yen aduet kukuar nɔk;
Kukuar akuaŋ rian kic e guaŋ
Alen lɔɔk tui rian kic e guaŋ
Malual akuaar bɛny tɛɛm Myidɛɛŋ 70
Lee lɔɔk tui Nyindɛɛŋ.

Yɛn ci Madiŋ d'Aguer Kur
Ka ci bɛ dhieth akuaar Mijaŋ wɛr
  kuaaŋ;
Ci nyaaŋ piny
Ku be wa ya lɔk dhieth 75
Be wa wo lɔk dhieth Mijaŋ Paweny
  e wa ee.
Piny yɔn thɛɛr e wel niim guiik
Ci wel piŋ atuur keek
Ke mɔny ci weŋ lueel ke wa
Ke tɔc ke diɛɛr biak bi Rɔw jɛɛm thin
  rial. 80
Maŋar de Jaŋ d'Aguer
Rɔw ke thar tuŋ kareeu
Ci Maleŋ de Lual Amiɛɛk
Cen cit wa wen Gitbɔŋ
Raan mac Mijoŋ e kit ke diak 85
Mijoŋ ci kit ke rot weel ci paan e
  kuɔɔk.
Maŋar nyuath ke de yeth diɛɛr ku
  thiɔu
Ku'aweleek e ruɔp keek.
Bɛn weŋ da wut
E Maŋar di bɛn thɛɛp 90
Ci dɔu, dan cath ke thɔn.
Maŋar aci wut nööm mathɔn
Kic wut nööm thɔn yaath mith
  Pabooŋ
Thɔn e mith ke Gitjok.
Jok Matuɔŋ yen wa ya lɛc nɔm 95
Ci mɛnth e tik dɛn cɔl 'aguen'
Mijoŋ e wo diir ci din geeu.

4. *Kɔɔk nɔm piör e yom* [Ŋok]

Kɔɔk nɔm piör e yom
Kic wun Malual aniin wei.
Awai dek Mithiaŋ Nɔɔn.
Mijok bur wun Lual
Amiok Bany de Minyiel Payaath 5
Tɔr ci rɔt tuk amec
Tuɔt ka ci rɔt piic.
Wa agurbiɔŋ juɛɛr piny e tɔŋ ic
Alei lek nyin
Aturtur e gueth ka waŋ; 10
Jak alei leknyin
Aturtur e gueth ka waŋ.

Jaŋ lou ka de nyin mandhar.
Buliɔk lec atenyeny
Aci biɔŋ kuɔth ic wal. 15
Tɔ piny e lɔrlɔɔr
Yen ke kura da agatwal
Agatwal de jak.
Mɛi jɔt ke la wɛr ayot
Mɛi jɔt ke la Lɔɔl 20
Biɔŋ di ka muk theep thok e girgiir.
Aliir e rut ken tɔc rɛɛr ke muk pal
Atuuk jaŋ e muktau.
Kediit e kuaŋ

Ago Lɔl miööt atutuur 25
Ku miɔɔt adhidhɔb.
Na be akɔl nyin bɛn
Ke thoot piny Manluɛɛl.
Awat teeŋ aba
Ayual e juatat 30
Kic tuŋ thook adanyany.
Nɔm cet yɔk ke Palath
Ku la yɔk ke Nuɛr
Athan biiy akuaar Marɔl dhien wiir.
Ke diit ci nɔm kuɔc la yir 35
Ci wɔɔr akum nöök
Wor ke gadhi
Athöl yen ke baai Janub
Mijoŋ di yin ca deep e win e thilik de
    riai
Loc e yaau 40
Mithön ke Malual Nɔɔn cur ke nyiin
Cur ke nyiin e loc;
Ci tɔŋ ya-Abyor ke Manynyuar akol
    yɔn
Nyuen yin ke meei de lukuk piny.
Ka nyuan meei de lukuk piny. 45
Mijoŋ dool ka col nyin ci yoi.
Mabior dien ci ŋɛɛny thööŋ
Ka dɛp nyin ci dan de markath
Akol tuk e deec rɔt nhial
Nyin ciet many tuk deec rɔt nhial.
Ca-athok puur kuɛɛth agor ŋeek 50
Gɛrgɛɛr ka muk yem ci ther jaŋ ŋok
Aic lany ateem yɔl
Adhuny yɔl ci weŋ de biöök.
Wɔi diit a ka nak rɔt aparak nya ci
    thin akirkir 55
Woi diit a ka nak rɔt aparak de lek;
Door ke la yoi wiir Padhieu nɔm
Padhieu ka wik
Ya go tɔɔr akɔl paat.
Ka ril nyin ci Miyar de köör yɔk miit
Athan ci piny riak wun Rakayan 60
Ka dhoŋ rɔk wun Rakayan
Wun Dinbil
Jel be doŋ kek Nyɔk Adeergɔl.
Adeergɔl bany dan Jimbek Miyar.
Dool e wok nyin thok athiɔk. 65
Jal biöök roor ci buruc de Lɔu.
Math Magaŋ d'Amac Beek
Tɔŋ guut e kööt abe rieel miak.

Anyinjiëëc dien tuŋ riiëëc 70
Ci Mijok niaak
Nɔm ataŋ e Lɔl e Jekeny
Kic bioŋ ciet jur e riai
E kat ke man rɔu
Tony de Juuk muk Ajak wic. 75
Nyuɔɔp kat kek Yɔm tooc Mithiaŋ
    de Nɔɔn
Ale pieet piny paan Kondok.
Na rial miak ke wok la tooc
Aluel Tuic be yk, kua dɔk niim.
Amor ci dit 80
Anɔm nɔk aguɛɛk kek mac.
Wok ci thiit niim
Wɛk dit, Wɛk dit
Wɛk dit Agonh ci toc kuum ic awa-
    mor.
Jong de Lual apek nɔm Alal 85
Weŋ d'Alin de Nimir acath ca-amal
    e rip
Buuny cath ca-amal e rip
Apek nɔm Alal.
Alɛk Marial de Dhiendiɔr
Mɛnh e dhien de Col Tɔctuŋ 90
Kueth ci rɔt yɔɔt.
Löc arac piny e tiit cok
Kic wun Deŋ Matjak kuëëth
Ci Mijok alitit ci kuur
Win wal kan löc piaat 95
Ateer Miyɔm d'Akiec, jal akɛɛl mam
Ci Mijoŋ di kueth cuɔn kɔu
Ago tɔɔr akɔl kum nyin
Ci joŋ de Bagaar.
Yɛn Mithiaŋ yɛn dit raany 100
Acak raan bɛ göök kek e cak
Ke ka ŋoot ke ruɔɔp
Cok dan e wok niim gaau
Acak raan göök kek e cak
Ka ŋoot ke ruɔɔp. 105
Kic Dɔk Tuic ŋak nɔm e win ci bi bɛ
    tueny
Wien akut e kɔu ci wiɛɛl e guuk.
Nɔm yɛr ci lan de kuiil
Akɔɔn ke tuŋ gɔɔc ye ŋeep 110
Kic Mijoŋ di tuŋ gɔɔc ye ŋeep.
Ca ajuɔɔŋ agiu kir de Nuɛr
Tɔŋ thɛɛr ke yɔk e camal
Cik liaap ke yɔk janub

Ala kiɛɛu rot 115
Ca-akol thiok nyin kan col
Na le weeny
Ke rueet nyin ala wai ɣɔɔu.
Apuruuk ke Tuic ke ki kat
Ci Nuɛr tɔŋ riit 120
Biak bɛk tuŋ thook aliu
Piny aci guur e ŋuɛɛk

Dɛr ki ɣɔk
Kac ki door tiŋ aci ɣeet Malual
Kic ɣeet Malual Adenydɔu. 125
Wun Nyuɔl Gitbɔŋ kuëëth akɔl ic
Tëëŋ aci nɔm luiit ca-agaar
Ala kiɛɛu rot
Tɔŋ arac tɔŋ aweer e yic.

5. Apiɛɛr [Ŋɔk]

Apiɛɛr ee Apiɛɛr dit dhieth bany de
    nɔɔn
Na rɛɛc e Thiɔr ke yin acam.
Apenh dit tul e Thiɔr
Ke nyin ajac ke cam raan.
Akɔu piöl ke jɔt ci deŋ nhial abi yaau
Anyooth duɔl 5
Kedi ka nyooth duɔl ci neel kɔu
Ci rol e guak duɔl ala ke beŋ
Ci raan ci rɔt coon e mɔn col;
Ke cɛth yen ee duɔl ala ke beŋ rɔt 10
Ci raan cath e jamel
Duɔl de ala ke beŋ rɔt ci mɔny e
    jamel
Malinh akuar Arob Ajuoŋ
Ci duɔl wiik.
Deŋ de Kwɔl, Deng de Kwɔl d'Arob
    de Bioŋ ee 15
Ka cit Aciek e baai nɔm
Ke ya wec Malink amuk,
Aröl theei ke de piɔu cölöm
Biɔny aguaŋ e bɛn bur ke weŋ mac.
Wun ya Akuaar Ajoŋ de Col 20
Ka wɛɛc yɛn maguɔp athieŋ
Kic tuŋ de kuɔc wai ci kon e peth.
Malith acit piɔu anyaar
Ke kɛɛc e weŋ ke lony de dhong e
    koroom.
Wok ka riëëc wo Maleŋ de Yak 25
Tuɔŋ Awiith Maleŋ dhien Jadoor
Ke kuëëth e wut ke la tooc
Malith Anyuath nyon liɔi cit nyan
    apiɛɛr
Ke daai de kɔc diir
Ke kiiu yen, ke rol mɛɛr piny 30
Ca ariëël.

Athiëëŋ di guɔp cuɔl ci wakɔu
Akɛɛm e cɔk ci nyan cieŋ bɔu;
Malith ke juar e miöör
Akuɛɛŋ rɔt ŋuut wun e Cuɔr 35
Ateem rɔt e thɔn guɔp
Agua adaat ciet adaat ci köör la nhial
    e weŋ.
Nyaan ci cak e rin ka akaak man Deŋ
    de Bɔŋ
Ci cieŋ de rɔt caal ke kɔc thɛɛr
Abiiy Malinh diit ci guɔp ɣɛɛr bei. 40
Ci lan dit
Aköön ee cɔk e rɔt piny
Wek ci kɛɛk we jur ameer.
Ye yic nɛɛ ca bɛɛr yok?
Ye dit ke rac 45
Aca bɛɛr yok?
Cit ci wa wo nyaaŋ piny wo duet e
    ma
Go de nyaan kuc ya lɔk cieŋ.
Malith acan wel ke baai koon
Ci bi teem wei 50
Ci wun athan dök e tɔɔŋ
Ku ye mer e kuuckuuc.
Nyan dit wo niim tueeŋ
Aci nɔm e dɛɛr piny
Ka cen athieeŋ cit athieeŋ rɔu wiir;
Yɛn e mac e lai 56
Yɛn amac anyaar ke lan wiir
Ca athieeŋ kɔu tɔ e bilbil
Ayee aci toc gor
Ye nɔɔn reem ke bɛr ic 60
Ci liekliek e lan e nyiel,
Anyuath nyuɔɔp ago thoŋ de kap
Ci raan rem e bathaal
Nɔm e gɔl ci nɔm cuɔɔth.

Man Wɔɔr man Wɔɔr Mijok   65
Tiŋ dit cit man Wɔɔr akac kən yok
Dil biəny adheŋ e le ɣaac;
Ci thuuk kedit baai bei
E ŋɛk miɔr de kueet
Ku lueel tik e le ɣaac;   70
Malith acan jai
Ka ca waar ken e Man Dau e Micar
   Col

Ye run athan
Ku bɛ waar awoc dien e ca looi
Ye run athan   75
Ku bɛ peen cuĕn cuët Nyannuɛr
Ye run athan
Ya weŋ poc kɔu ci ruəŋ
Adɔŋ gɔl yaath
Alaraan man yɛn jam   80
'Cit ci Lual aköör ci wath.'

6. *Mithiang ŋɔk ci köör* [Ŋɔk]

Yɛn de Ayen dit e ŋɔk ci wut;
Yɛn de Mithiaŋ dit e ŋɔk ci köör ale
   yic tuuc.
Aba thiëëc e Bɛny Dit
Anadher, Mindir e piny
De raan e peec ke piny kic riak?   5
Raan pec adhɛŋ de Marial e Ker.
Ban piny rial ci tuŋ de deec
Yɛn bi kat rian da-Ali
Yɛn kɛɛu rɔt e Nhialic
Yɛn nin kuer   10
Na miak e dur ke wo rɛm ajööm.
Ayee kedien yɔn e ke dien thɛɛr,
'Ke duön athan
Aye cɔl ŋɔ?'
'Ce Mithiaŋ ku Miyan?'   15
Yɛn de Malɔu ku Miyan ku Malɔu
Lɔn dien athan ci wa yega.
Many d'Awun wa ka de piən de
Ke yup e luŋ babuur
Na ci ye yup Mithiaŋ ke wok ka
   lat.   20
Kamaan kaac kueer keki ya thiec,
'Malən duon na la baai no?'

La baai paan Awun wa yeo
Cɛk nyin bɛ bilbil
Ka la baai paan Awun wa yoo.   25
Man can Mabeek yup ci telepun
Ale tai juur
Na yok gaat akum ee
Gaat ke duet k'akum
Ke yi dap e nyan aben.   30
Ɛndi yuu jal wɔc adi
Ku ca dɛɛ dool
Anyaŋ dit e bur.
Wun e Tuic ke bɛ kueeth
Wun e Bol Col   35
Wun e Bol Aturjok apieet Ameth.
Ruel biic aci yen leu
Yen ken ɣai ci dhunydhuəl
Weŋ a toom abi nyin atə doidoi
Na nɔɔm tɔɔŋ   40
Ke loony kueer;
Diëët cath wanywany
Ci duet k'Alal kɔu.
Wel ke lum ka ca kek e piŋ
Ke yɛn e nɔm muk e deŋdeŋ   45
C'Ajinh ci mɔny kuɛth.

7. *Rol ic Ayaau di* [Ŋɔk]

Pagɔl e wa yiek yɛn aying lan ayaau
   gɔɔŋ
Yiek yɛn dhuɔr Maker Ɗargɔl
Mɛnh riic wok yiek yen ayiu lan
   Ayaau gɔɔŋ.
Cit ci Beek la yit ci la wok

Rɔl ke ciet ke cak kek weeu kɛɛn e
   cieŋ.   5
Diɛɛr ka ku muk Marɔl de Deŋ
Ke baak yen daar ke tiŋ yen Mijoŋ
   thɔn.
Kuɛth dan e wun thoor

Ago Beek bɛn wut ke dan agöröl
Marɔl apen wut kac.   10
Cak wal bɛ mec abik la Madiŋ
Diec yɛn ci dɔŋ piny
Tuŋ duɔna ka ba leŋ thok
Jal liaap we thɔn Deŋ Col
Ke ya puɔc Maŋar e wa   15
'Wa Deŋ jɔrɔt yɛn be kuɛth nyɔk.'
Cuɛt nɔt wiir wanh e wen Awet
Ago Beek kim ci ke rem cin
Agany wen e wa Marɔl ke liec e gik.
Ke luɛɛl e yɛn cit ke lueel Malɔu 20
Ku ke lueel Malɔu cit ke luɛɛl e yɛn
Cuk kuɛth took ke kic ku thiec
    Kuanyŋar
Kuɛth amai ace dɔɔr kɔu
Ka ŋek thok ci riny de dhɔl
Go wun Awet ke Mannyuar dɛɛ tony
    da Anyiel   25
Ku dee Beek tony dɛn athan.
Dit be kat aba ya la wil
E ŋɔ cin ic aguebeb
Ca adhɛŋ da aguek wen ci gɔɔr rɔt
    pɔɔt kueer.
Kɔr e wal le wok kuɛɛth tooc e mɔɔth
    Aduɔŋ   30
Eŋɔ cen bɛɛ mec ci kiukuar Madhɔl
    ka
Cɔl yɛn ka wai yanh de Bol ee
Cit thar e tɔŋ thɔɔth Amaath
Ku ber Mithiaŋ Akonydɛɛu
Nan ci mai bi guɔ cek ci yɔl de
    mieth   35
La piny wany ci ke ci ruw.
Jal mioc, 'Adool dit ci wa ya thɔɔn'
Na la cɔŋ ku agaar yɛn bi ya mioc,
'Wayee ye wayee
Ci Beek ayiŋ cieŋ   40
Yee
Ci rɔu ayiŋ mɔ̈r
Yee
Ci rɔu ayiŋ tueny
Jala dhuɔɔr de Mijɔŋ de wun Kon.'
Diëët kat ci biɔny leer e Nuɛr.   46
Gai e karac ke Lunhayaa!
Cen atuɔɔk rol ca akuɔɔt
La nyin yem ci ke thöök
Ɖaath nyaan e Deŋ de Maker kueer;

Ya biny kiik e luɔi de jur   51
Na cak raan alat
'Eŋon biny kiik
Cit e raan ci mɔny thiɔɔŋ?'
Aba ruuny ci dhiëër;   55
Gai e karac e tony de ruɔn!
Ago riny e Nhial e thok dök ci kir
    Acuɛɛŋ
Madool di ka kɔr tɔŋ
Cuk toc yaac ic ca ayaau
Ago Beek kim ci ke rem cin   60
Wok yok nyuɔɔp ke la ɣeer.
Marɔl ke cath e damdam
Ci Tuiny ci la ɣɔɔc awuɔw
Ake jur lat, 'Enaal abuk.'
Ku luel, 'Yaac Majoŋ Akuur   65
Abuŋ e Mawien ka ci jur ŋic.'
Thoŋ dɛɛn ci guuk ic
Ci lec ka aŋuaam
Kɛc yen kemiit cɛm.
Na wadaŋ la dhiɔp   70
Ba piɔu acɔŋ wo kɔc kuan riic wok
Yɛn bi ya mioc, 'Rol ic Ayaau di, rol
    ic Ayaau waa,
Gueŋ dit e dhuɔɔr riir!'
Jur col ke kip ci tony.
Nyan de kiec ka de piɔu ater   75
Tok dɛl e rɔu acol mɛɛc
Ci kur e wen Aŋau
Na la ke tɔɔu e guŋ biak e cam
Biak a col ɣööc ci kuiŋ de Maker ee,
Na kɛc yen ke go lec nyuɛth   80
Na ruɛc yen ye cok ke go cok nyuɛth
Dit be tɔc ci Miyɔm la cok ci makaŋ.
Agɛɛŋ cuɔth e ŋet
Nyancam cuɔth e ŋet
Cuɔth e ŋet ku ye dhuny yɔl   85
Na le rɔm ke Malinh yool
Abi kök ke löth.
Dhien da yuu cit ci Beek a ŋic
Cɛk a jö yen e dhieth Beek ci Beek
    a ŋic
Cɛk a thɔk yen e dhieth Beek ci Beek
    a ŋic   90
Cɛk a nya yen e biiy yen ci Beek
    a ŋic.
Ruɔk dit yɔu de Mijɔŋ de Buɔŋ cur
    wayaa

Jal Lueel, 'Ayi, yin adhɛŋ de cok
  dhuɔɔr cuɔt rɔt tueŋ.'
Dhuɔɔr atɔc nyan de Kiec da Awet
  ku nöök
Ago gon alieth e Borou ku nyiɛn 95
Guɔ gon a cur ku luɛɛl

'Eŋɔ cen guäk la yutut
Athan cuɛt wek Yɔm dun wek e nɔɔr
  aŋui.
Wa ye lueel bi wek akuɛt miöök?'
Kuat yɔr piɔu ci yon e kudhur oo 100
Awan, awan, yen e linh den.

8. 'Kur kony yɛn' [Ŋɔk]

Mijoŋ di ke miɛt
Acit nan e thap ke tuŋ
Na ci thap guɔ liu
Ke tuŋ thöök;
Awuur kua thoŋ kedhie waa. 5
Jel yɔk cooth ke cieŋ löth
Jur col de wen de Malek
Yen ke Mijok goor nyin ci doŋ de
  thaap
Kɛt nyin ca aduɔŋ kiik e jɔɔl
Ya go löth guɔ dhiau: 'E Kur o.' 10

Kuɛth mec Miyan joŋ de dɔu
Yen ke loth Kur cɔɔl. 'Ci piny thiɔk?'
Ku Madiŋ de Guɔt Awan
Madiŋ de Guɔt Juɔr.
Nyuɛɛth Mijok ago lɔɔm kɔu maar 15
Yɛn mac Mijoŋ yer
Yɛn mac Mijoŋ yer cit ayɔŋ de piiu
  kamol.
Yool Mijok kuuk oi thiou
Adoony loth ci raan ket jooth
Mijoŋ di ke yɛr ci thipiei. 20

10. Mɔu [Ŋɔk]

Tik meth tooc,
'Akɛnyai e ku diec e dhiim tɛɛn.'
Piŋ mɔny kuɔɔk jel e yith keet
E bith miit kek e tɔŋ ku jel cath e
  kɛnkɛɛn
Kuɛny cok biak e tul e dhiim thin 5
E biny thiic ku jel mioc,
'E yac dïëët ca lai thɔr!'

Mioc de mɔu acen kit kee.
E raan reet nɔm e thieny diit
E wil ci deŋ 10
Alarɛt ka bɔr yiëec
Athuai mat kek e luɔu
Apal kuin ariep
Ci paan e piɔt agɔk.

13. Luŋ e weŋ [Ŋɔk]

Ce ke de jur yen ci ya wieel
Na yi ke de paan da wen yin kic a
  wieel
Yɛn ci jal thou wo koŋgöör,
Akol waan paan e bɛny
Jal cam oo aba kɔu adhoŋoŋ ci cuar
  e köt 5
Ku la ke ya cem mieth athol
Ke ya ŋoot e garac ci dhöŋo de yic
  abeet

Ce ka le e dom ke wei.
Yɛn muk awerek e cin cam
Giɛk Amiɛt 10
Ci ke da-ariau
Raan e piny awek ke ŋoot thin
Ka mɔk aril, mɔk aril, abi cin di nuet
Ci bɔɔl ca acuuk ke de dep thok.
Wɛt ci nɔm juɔr ci dɛɛl akic kɔn lɛk
  yɛn 15
Ya wɛt teem ca ajuɔlac

Agon dɛ ke miit yen bany yith.
Yɛn ci Miyɔm yɔɔk, 'Wa Miyɔm, wa
   Miyɔm
Deŋ Kuei ku ce wek e dhien
Ajaŋ de Deŋ wen dhieth Deŋ Kuei
Ku ce wek e dhien?   20
Miyɔm ci wien pal e tak
Ajak acɔl raan du.
Ku ye ŋɔ? Ku na kucmuk, kucmuk,
Ku ce nyan Bioŋ Jaclek e dhöc kɛɛ?'
Weŋ di yoo   25
Ce weŋ athan yɛn rial wakɔu
Aguɔn nyin ajacejac
Ca abor de yic aturtuur
Ku bɔɔl raan ce mɔl e thiu.   30
Raan rɛm wok kueer ke ya thiec,
'Ku ye ŋɔ yin ba luk ke yin ci thou kɛɛ.'

Dhieu nyin ku ci ya leer.
Agɔk Miyar ke yɛn yɔk,
'Acuil mɛnh e ma ku yok eyi la   35
Raan cen nyan kene ke ŋiec jam
Yɛn ci thiou göök ya nhial.'
Ade paan Kolcum ke yɛn akop yɔɔc
   ci nyuɔm akɛr
Ya rɔt duɛt tɛɛm ci joŋ baai
Wum ke thiaŋ e lik   40
Naŋ kac piny
Ke jal la dïr ci nɔm de riɔc
Ya jal jor ke ya kaac.
Weŋ di yoo
Ce weŋ athan luk bɛny   45
Luk Wun Nyantiwit abi cuet arob
Yen bi köör thuany bɛn wuuk
Keci thar yɔɔny ca alɔɔl.

15. *Aguɔn ca ye nin* [Ɖɔk]

Madiŋ de Deŋ d'Awan
Yɛn de math e nyin agiir.
Yɛn kuc ken e lum gɔɔny thar
Ke cen nyuc e bɛɛ gam.
Wa Ajith ee   5
Ce yin Ajinh de Tɔŋ
Ku ye biak kikɔk?
Ku ye mɛnh nyankai
Alaraan da ci yic kith acit yany de
   rɔu ɛɛ;
Ce yin Ajinh waan yɛn col kat tim
   d'Abyei?   10

Yen bin ninar poot thok
Ca aron de dheel
Aguɔn ca ye nin.
Wa ke nhiar yɛn
Akol e bi riak   15
Ago ku la bɔŋbɔŋ;
Awet ee aci wa yek ɛn
Din dien Awet aci wa lueel dit lok
   pɔl
Ca kit noom wa nɔm
Mɔny dit ke wɛɛr bei ca acunh e
   wien.   20

17. *Nhialic rɔt miɛt wei* [Ɖɔk]

Wa ater ee wa ater athan lok bɔɔt nɔk
Ka ben dit ayok ku pɛc ŋeŋ
Ater e yom
Ater athan tem amɔɔr wien
Tok yen mor atac,   5
Lok adicool daŋ a bɛɛ nyɔk
Ajel e dit e ci jak
Akɔlkɔl e raan e path
Na ci rɔt puk aye raan

Wen acol kat e ke luel nyiin   10
Cɛk adicool daŋ e guut nyin.
Biak athan duet yen diaar nɔk
Pɛl nyin e moc
Wen kaŋ ce la yom,
Many ce la yom   15
Many ce tiŋ
Many e cien tol.
Aye ci luil guut

Luil guut dit e dhiau, 'oi oi'
Ci luil guut   20
Ke duet athut tim biak
Ku rɛɛr man ke wun e jac,
Nyal agɔk aci nɔm yɔɔŋ
Cak tiŋ athoŋ kek ber kulab
Duet athan reec wun e jaŋ   25
'Ca be la wut ke ya cen e cin.'
Thɔɔny ka dit cak ke nyaŋ piny!
Ade duet e pot arom ci wɔɔk
Cɔŋ e löör e paan dun.
Ya thiec, 'Löör paan dun ye cɔŋ
    adi?'   30
'Wok ka kuc cɔŋ e löör
Ku la nhial akuc awan.'
A yee nyan e Cɔŋ ka juec
Nyan dun ke jaŋ lueel cieŋ gaŋ
    athoŋ joŋ ci kuoc dik
Ade wɛt e luɔc lueel baai acieŋ awan.
Yɛn ci nɔm kuɔc la pil   35
Weŋ dien e baai luk
Nɔm e gɔl
Ci makam ajööm mat;

Malinh dien thoŋ ke Malinh de guuk
    dɛn wan to nhial   40
Dik e piny duon wan tueŋ
Paan duon cak nuɛɛt thok ayi guuk
Yen dil nyan a bɛny adi;
Ca amɔɔr yen dheeŋ maan
Tem awiɛi   45
Ago mɔny e ci thieek doŋ e goi
Dɔŋ thierbɔt e guuk nhial
Na la theei la akɔl tɛɛn
Ke Nhialic amac ɣɔk ke guuk
Ya go guuk adhiau, 'Gi ruw   50
Ka-ala lioi
Piny dap bak
Ka-ala lioi.'
Awan ke coot, 'Guak'
Malinh Jok   55
Dul acit adhuut köör.
Awat tieŋ ka anguɛm ke jur
Yen ki
Lan ci juur riɔk thaar
Ke dit le lec ŋuanyɛny.   60

19. *Aba luɛɛl* [Tuic]

Ye toŋ mɛɛn ca jal yok
Aŋoot ba luɛɛl
Bany eban aba luɛɛl
Cier Rian, aba luɛɛl
Laŋ Juuk, aba luɛɛl   5
Nyol Bol, aba luɛɛl
Aba luɛɛl bany kua.
Ye tɔŋ mur puk
Ka ye looi keda?
Bany kua   10
Ka ya piŋ ye puk weŋ thɛɛr.
Wen ala coot paan ya Ajoŋ dit Arob
Ke ya yok Ajɔk ɣööt
Ka cee nin
Aye reer ke piŋ e yic   15
Kak e ɣön tueŋ ku cien
Ka ye deet
Ka ya Ajɔk deet kedhie.
Ken Ajoŋ Arob keer mur lei
Na yin Akuɔl aya   20

Yeŋo pɛɛc yin Ajɔk?
Kak ɣan thii
Aye ŋɛkkede guum riɛl de
Raan dɛt ace pɔɔc;
Wek caawoc mat nhom baai Aguɛt
Yen bin we ya nyooth.   25
Ke ben cin akueen
Nyan Arob e
Yin ca luet e
Ka ye tik luet mony de   30
Ka ce luet mony dɛt ayɔk rɔt ɣöt.
Lok Jam Turalei
Ke wek bi nyiin cet miɛr cop ajuath
Ka miɛr cop ajuath.
Wok aye diak ɣööt   35
Ajɔk ku Akuɔl ku ɣɛn
Kɔc gɛm a ɣöt
Ku ɣɛn ke taŋkie
Ku atuel mabil,
Taac aba la laŋ piiny   40

Xɛn ci la laŋ piiny
Nawen la puən alei bɛn
Ke yook yɛn 'E ŋo nin yin ke mieth e?
Mɔc diit e Mɔnyjaŋ war e tɔc
Ake nin bi la wɛlwɛl   45
Riŋ ee go la wɛlwɛl.'
Wen jal awɛl
Yen Akuəl coot, 'Ajɔŋ e ma kony a

Ajɔŋ e ma kony a'
Ajɔŋ Arob e Deŋ   50
Ca dɔm e dom maan agut emen
Aca dɔm nhiaan
Ku ye ya rul ci tuk
Ku ye ya nuai ci cuɛi
Diet athɔk apayem,   55
Maγee ca Ajɔk arak ci weŋ.

20. Dɔm atuel ten e kɔc loŋ [Tuic]

Paguɛn da
Xen ci muəl
Ruan Akuəl Aduot
Ka ce yic wɛl wei
Ya raan ci doŋ wut ee,   5
Ca Ajɔk anak dhaal
Ca Akuəl anak dhaal.
Ku ce pou Dau Kuacnyiel
Yen cɔl yen ajel Lɔl kəu
Ke la yok ke dit ci pioc,   10
Ajɔŋ Arob aci pioc
Akuəl Aduət aci pioc
Ajɔŋ ce bɛ thiak
Akuəl ce bɛ thiaak,
Abik areer ke döt mɔc   15
Abi kek ten kɔc loŋ ŋic alande
Ajɔk ŋic alande
Wen ale paac
Ke dɔm atuel ten e kɔc loŋ
Ago mith kie la kuarkuar.   20
Aca kut ic
Ci wei waac,
Ajɔŋ Arob
Jal kɔ̈ɔ̈c
Ku Akuəl, nyan Aduot e dau   25
Kɔ̈c rot, kɔ̈c rot.
Wun Ater lom ku
Ka ce wek wedhie
Awek Parum
Ka ce wek wedhie   30
Nɔŋ ya Awɛk Riŋ ee
Ka ce wek;

Xɛn anoŋ thok jam Paguɛt
Ku ka ce kɔc Paguɛt kedhie
Ka nyiir ka karou   35
Kek ya dhur tɔŋ mur
Ku tɔŋ mur ka cit peeth
Ka ye pal raan tok nhom
Ku jal Ajaŋ daai.
Deŋ Kuac Nyiel,   40
Ka ya tak kedien ba gut wadaŋ
Nyaŋ Aγɛr
Yen bi yɛn jal buəc e rin Ajɔk
Ajɔk raan ŋic ten kɔc thööŋ?
Na la buəc wadaŋ ee   45
Ku la Akuəl kɔɔc
Ku la Ajɔk kɔɔc?
Piny lɛn ya akol mɛn
Ka ce piny waar tueŋ
Ka ye ŋek thuth mith ke ka rou   50
Ku mith ke ka diak;
Diak aca be leu
Ku rou aca be ŋiec rot.
Ajɔŋ e ma
Jal mɔl e dom dɔm yin wok   55
Ku mal e caat;
Ku jal adil ba rool.
Bi mith kie acath ke war piny awaar ic
Bi kac kie acath ke war piny riaŋ kəu
    ee
Xɛn ci nyan Arob la nyuən tɔɔr   60
Diɛc lɔn ban dhieth.
Nyan e Col
Yɛn ci nyan Maper Adiɛl buəc.

21. *Aca roc* [Tuic]

Rɛɛr baai ke tiɛɛl
Baai arɛɛr ke kuc rot
Rɛɛr baai ke tiɛɛl.
Na cak a Riŋ Dau
Aba gɔk,   5
Madut Riŋ
Aba gɔk,
Riin Riŋ
Aba gɔk athɛɛr.
Dan Riŋ akic a guan ye yɔu   10
Na ca guan ye yɔu ɛɛ
Wen ɣɛn akic Nyaŋ dan Kuac la reet
    ic
Kek Nyaŋ dan Aɣɛr
Ku luɔb Akuɔl tooc.
Akuɔl Aduɔt aci dön   15
Nya arɛɛr kek Ajɔŋ kɔc cot ic;
Wɛt abi Dan Riŋ cɔl apiŋ Noon
Waan can ye lueel ɣɛn bi thiek gek
    nhom
Paan Ɖɔŋ wa Marial dit,
Paan Ɖɔŋ wa Deŋ Awet ku Maper?
Ɣɛn ca Akuɔl Aduɔt la wet piny   20
Ku ɣɛn bi thiek wut ciɛl ic
Adiaŋ Maper.
Ka ye Dan Riŋ nyooth,
'Madut Riŋ buɔth.'   25
Ba ya cath ke ya kic Maper yok
Baai yen la gut kɔu ten
Nawen thuɔt Akuɔl
Ke ye gam
Akec ya kan rɛɛc Kir nhom,   30
Wen wok akec la ɣöt

Wen wok akec la bei;
Aba daŋ den cɔl Ajoŋ rocroc
Yen ale kuɛth ɣɛn.
Na ɣɛn mane   35
Ce biöök yen e nhian duut
Ku meei nhian ka liu
Ku cok e nhian ka liu
Ka ci tuɛny
Ka ca Ajɔk ke tueny.   40
Na ɣɛn mane
Ca guɔ buɔc
Ke ya kec Paan die yok;
Nyan Arob aciɛɛn
Ke lan buɔc ke ya kec paan die yok.
Tiŋ Ajɔk e ɣɛn dil   45
Cit nɔŋ ke dɛn thiin ye yen nyiir
    lööm
Aci luɔi de waan
Ka ci luɔi de woc piny
Ye dil mur nyan ci bi leu;   50
Nyiir e toc ka bi pal Majɔŋ dit
Majɔŋ dit Arob
Raan ci ŋeer Lɔl kɔu
Raan aya Akuɔl tiit.
Ka ci ɣɛn nɔk   55
Ku dɔm tik acok bi ya ɣöc
Cimen e rian bɛr.
Ku thɔɔŋe, Col Agɔth ee,
Wok aye lat nyiir Maper
Ka nyiir Maper.   60
Ala Ajɔŋ Arob ca cuɔny mac
Yen apal ɣɛn Akuɔl Aduɔt
Ka ŋoot ba lok yok Majɔŋ dit.

22. *Ke nuääl* [Ɖɔk]

Mok ki rot
Akac gut e tɔŋ
Ake nuääl, ke nuääl,
Cuk la piny nyan e Baggaar
'Mɔnyjaŋ bicheech, bicheech.'   5
Ɣɛn huc 'bicheech'
Ka dhiɛl thin,
Dam kɔu ago kiɛu ic bɛn paan
    Jabateen.

Cul di akuc nin
Ake ɣam riir,   10
Ago ku la raurau,
Nawen duet thurual agɔɔu
Ke tuɛny,
Ago ku la raurau
Taac kedi   15
Ku dak nɔm thin
Magaŋ agoot ɣɛn ci raan waac.

23. *Paan dun aca cem mel* [Tuic]

Paan dun aca cem mel
Xɛn bi ya mac won ruɛl
Paan dun aca cem mel
Xɛn bi ya la löör
Ake thuɔɔt nyiir yen aca ben ŋic. 5
Na ye baai panda

Na ye baai panda
Wen tɔɔŋ aken doŋ
Ku wen maŋan aken doŋ.
Yok nyaan won det 10
Ku ca ben a thut
Xɛn acit raan ci nhom bɛn.

24. *Aciek ic adhany* [Ɖɔk]

Aluɔny dan e dom de Tuic giir
Acuɛŋ go nyan de Tuic wok alat;
Nyankai ku dit yɛn tueŋ
Nyan e ma wok ka riec,
Yin bi rɔt tɔk alat alat dit agok ɛɛ 5
Yin bi rɔt tok alat e kedien e cɛk
   Aciek;
Na cɛk kur yin ci rɔt bi bɛ gɔk

Ka ci bi biɔn ɛɛ, acɔl ken e cɛk Aciek
Ca Aciek ya jal wil
Ago woi da tɛk ku jel akuɔc miɔc, 10
Aciek a rɔɔth Aciek ic la dhany
Wen kedi wok nyan de Tuic wen
   anyuɔth yen
Wen aca dööny e kedi
Agon cieŋ ke man Ɖɔk.

33. *Piny ice ci riak* [Ɖɔk]

Ye bɛɛny bi thuɔu
Piny doŋ kek Arob Bioŋ wa;
Mɔny dit aye thiec kathɛɛr ɣɔn
Thiec wur kathɛɛr.
Madir rɛɛr cien ca piŋ wɛt Arob? 5
Ku jɔl adhuɔk Ɖɔk
Ba piŋ wɛt lueel wɛt yi Madi.
Piny ariak akic dɔm
Nawen kic dɔm
Ke ya Arob lueel, 'Naki meth.' 10
Go nak meth jaŋ agɔi
Abi jaŋ e cin taar
'Nak e meth arɛc wɔɔt',
Arɛc wɔɔt.
Wok aci ya Ɖɔŋ e Kwɔl 15

Wadit aye bak ke cɔl loŋ
'Arɛc wɔɔt.'
Wok ka ci ya Ɖɔŋ e Kwɔl.
Ɖɔŋ e Kwɔl
Aye Tuic bɛn thiec bɛɛny; 20
Aŋoot ke buk naab thok
Cimen nɛɛb e Gagrial
Abi loony Madiŋ Awil
Ke lony Madiŋ Awil
Ace ɣeet Abyɛi 25
Ku na dhɔth ki Jokyɔm
Ke jaŋ anyuɔp
Thiec wuur ka thɛɛr
Kedaŋ arɛɛc wɔɔt
Wen ci wok a Ɖɔŋ e Kwɔl. 30

34. *Loŋar kɔc lek* [Rek]

Adut Akɔl tiŋ Akueŋ Aŋok
Madit aci tup mɛɛc cimen e yɔt
Na thou e cit keny ku bi la dhuk
Wen anɔŋ ke ye tiŋ ke mɛɛn,
Ken e nyuɛɛr e wiin wiir ka ya wɔc
   tene yin Adut   5
Tene yin Adut
Tene yin Adut Pakueer;
Adut waar cam jɛɛk ke wadit Kueŋ
   Aŋok
Nawen ale tak
Ke cɔl kemɛɛn Nhialic ee   10
Loŋ ariau ka ye Nhialic maan;
Ka ci ca la pɔk wiir
Bi cak e thɔk alɔk tuil
Kene liiu adɛm kan
Adɛm aliu gɔl e wɛt Aŋok.   15
Maluil e Kueŋ dit ale teek e nɔɔn
   ayiit
Nawen ale keny
Ke la dɛɛl e joŋ kac nhom le wiik e
   rup.
Riŋ Giir Abik dit
Wa Riŋ ale wun cɔɔl   20
Ku nyuuc piny ye lɔɔm
Ku jɔl ala ruuny nhom
Ku ye bɛn thɔn
'Manhdi Riŋ ɣɔk akak.'
Ku jɔl athɔn, 'Manhdi Riŋ ɣɔk akak
Yen ye jɛɛk; weŋ nyigɛŋ.'   26
Alɛk abi wadit dɛ wot
Baai ka ci la nyikder.
Lueek ka ci thiaŋ.

Wadit Akɔl Kuec ka ya akɔɔn   30
Ku Thiŋ Riny ka ya akɔɔn
Kiro Riny ka ya akɔɔn
Ku Riŋ wa ka ya akɔɔn
Yee ya akɔɔn
Wadit Agɔth   35
Wadit aci bith kɛɛk ke Loŋar
Loŋar kɔc alek e bith
Loŋar kɔc alek e yuai
Bi Loŋar kɔc alek atom thok
Go ariɔc jal akat   40
Go ariɔc jal anuɔk e tetui
Ku riiŋ wadit thin ku dɔm bith;
Ka ci wiik abik anoi wiir
Ku bak Mɔnyjaŋ.
Binh e bɛny aci deeb e peny   45
Ku jal muɔr muoc, 'Ala wai di
   kan.'
Go wai alueth.
Ka ci wiik abik la noi wiir e piu ic
   piiny
Ku bak Mɔnyjaŋ.
Te waar tek e riŋ thin   50
Te waar tek Loŋar Riŋ
Ku bi yek wook
Agothcithiik yen alom yuɔm e ɣɔl
Bi yen Pakuec ala tɛk ɣoi;
Yen aye wook Pakuec   55
Pakuec kuan e yuɔm e ɣɔl
Pakuec kuan e ring e ɣɔl.
Pakuec kuan e riŋ e ɣɔl
Ka coot e looŋ
Bi gal ke mac.   60

37. *Ɗɔɔŋ e nyin* [Ɗok]

Wɛt ke Kur, wɛt ke Kur
Mijoŋ de Kur Jok Yɔm
Ku la Mayol de Kur de Deŋ,
Wɛt di ka lɛk wek.
Miyan ku le cok cerem tɛɛn   5
Ke wok kabi thɔr;
Ke wok akɔl tɔɔŋ
Abuk niim arial baai.
Bɛny ka rac piou,

Bɛny arac piou wɛt e lum la ku kɛt, 10
Acol de Kuɔl,
Kony yɛn Bɛny Marial.
Weŋ dien e nɔm la wek,
Miyan aɣer nɔm ca akɔɔn.
Yee Deŋ araan ci cen wun   15
Aye luɔi amor de pei?
Yen dic yɛn bolith akum
Ke cen raan ca nɔk.

Ku lok miər lony.
Yee acik duət e nim kəu.   20
Piɛŋ thoŋ e luny e Miyan,
Ala piən di wek ci lɔər pɔk.
Wacker Marɛŋ de Malek,
Yɛn ci piən di cen ke kony ci rial ci
   baat.
Luŋ toŋa yee aba luər nəm thin,   25
Ci raan nyiy dɛɛu.
Cɛk ya cuat yinh e ruəi ic,
Miyan ka ban rət koon
Ci jur athan dəm ecin
Ku cuɛt ki rot mɛɛc   30
Ke ci wɛt di la tiŋ adik,
Abi Deŋ de Kwɔl tiŋ,
Abi Deŋ de Kwɔl caath ic ɛɛ.
Ke luŋ ci rət naai ci duŋuer;
Luŋ ci rət nyoŋ ci nyuɔŋ.   35
Marəl e Kwɔl Dorjok luk luəp cok ci
   lony,
Alen yic di yok.
Yɛn yɛn ce jam e lueth,
Yɛn Deŋ de Juacbɔŋ,
Ke dien e lueel u   40
Yen ke jaŋ guɛɛr thin
Ci biak dhiim e məu.
Ajal a raan ŋut amaan ee yen ke
   thuëëc e luŋ di.
Ku luk ade yic akɛnnyin.
Manyalkai Madat d'Akɔc,   45
Na yi lɛk,
Raan piɔc e luk,
Ace pioc amor kic kən jak ic.
Miyan di ke tai thin ke ŋuut,
Acen biak yen tɔc thin.   50
Abathɔɔk, piɛŋ ki e yith ee,
Ade wɛt ci raan lueel,
Raan ci lec lual ci tiəŋ de Tuic,
Ke lueel, 'Miyan de Deŋ guəp
Yen biy e bei ku yik Deŋ de Dau.'
E ŋɔ can jal gai adi yɛɛ!   56
Malɔn dien ci ŋuət cieŋ ke nyuath,
Adɔŋ piny ke weŋ de Rek Tooc,
Agon lec lual
Ci raan ci yik Alal Ciere.   60
Raan ci yik Alal cien guəp kamit ɛɛ,
Na cak gɔt ke nəm de gɔl
Ke tok bɛɛny adɔŋ Abyɛi

Ku le nguany e kei.
Akol lok Adöör adiec ɛɛ,   65
Alok ayok ke yɛn liu wut ic,
Akic a bɛn tiit.
Akuɔc ke ci bolith akum bɛ ya lony
Ke raan liu,
Kedaŋ ke riɔ̈ɔ̈c,   70
Ke riɔ̈ɔ̈c kuɛl yen miər guəp
Ke ya ŋoot wei.
Aguən lɔk rial miak,
Aŋoot e kuany cok,
Na cɛk bɛ la pat geeu,   75
Aca bi pɔl akuany cok.
La ku nyuɔc e tim cok,
E cuɛn d'Ayaŋ d'Ajaŋ ee,
Ajom dit ci mat eban ee,
Yɛn cen raan toŋ ya mɔɔth 'Ci yi
   bak?'   80
Aguə reer ke ya la piəu gaŋaŋ
Ca Akɔl ke yep
Diɛc ic nan can guəp dɛ amor.
Ke ya go gat wurnek e liklik
Ke ya kic e thiëëc rin   85
Podhol thok alik.
Eŋo duon gat juəp ke yi ci yɛn e
   thiëëc rin?
Dan lön di cɔɔl du ye jaŋ guə ŋɛɛny
   eban ee?
Cik yɛn bi cak laar e thijin ic?
'Ke yic, awɔc ka dit kəu,   90
Yin bi la e thijin ic.'
Ku yen e jaŋ guə ŋɛɛny eban u?
Thijin guəp de?
Ku yen e jaŋ a tuəɔk e ŋɛɛny?
Na man ban guə la thin   95
Ke yɛn ci be kuaath e bolith?
Na cɛk dɛ Nyaŋ e kɔc dəm karakoon
   ic,
Ke yɛn ala juwa.
Yɛn riit e yöt e ginyginy, karakoon e
   ginyginy,
Ago tuc wo lɛɛr nyiin,   100
Ago tuc wo lɛɛr nyiin, wen ca aniɛn
   guəp tuëi
Ci jön ci adɛɛr kiir.
Ke ci wo yok,
Wen Pakir, Mayɔn de Dan de Kir,
Jur aci cit kethɛɛr athan   105

Ciɛŋ wek piny e kök,
Dit e ŋɛɛny ke tooc e jur yin,
Yin bi dui,
Yin bi dui agua ayar nyin dit,
Ayar dui raan ŋuɛn,   110
Ku rɛɛr jööt thin,
Ku ci yi war.
Amor ace waar,
Maker de Dau,
Goku e piəth duut, wun Nyannuɛr,
Ku lok pur alath.   115
Wen kuɛth wok domic,
Yɛn e cath ke ya taŋ e nəm ci riai,
Yɛn e duet jai e reek.
Ke thɛɛr athan lueel kukuar,   120
'Thoŋ de ŋet' ke thöök yɛn piəu,
Yɛn duɛt gəl e ke gal.
Ku ya nəm ayoom,
Mijaŋ de Dak, dit cath ke yi giŋ wo
     cok,
Dit wok giŋ cok e waat,   125
Yin ci bi poth ke yi kic yup nəm
     atuel e la.
Kəc ka ci rot luəi loony
Ke kek ci gaar kekedhie.
Mijaŋ de Dak, pal e cieŋ tiŋa Dhieu,
Dhieu ke raan dɛɛn ŋut cien piəu,
E rot mat cieŋ de jur ic,   131
Ku dui ki wok.

Na nyaap ke bolith ke jur,
Ka ci raan bi jal apəl,
Ku jal raan Mənyjaŋ den nək.   135
Yɛn ci kuum, Mathac Akɛnwai,
Jal jur yɛn kuum alumar ci thou ɛɛ;
Ya nyuɔɔc akəl ic,
Ku lueel, 'Tit alumaar e din bi yen
     ŋueet.'
Din diit e wuw nhial e ban,   140
Yen ba tiit aba luəŋ ?
Aca bi luəŋ Micar Aroljok;
Din dit e paar ee,
Aci raan bi jal tiit abi leu,
Micar da Ayuel de Jöngkör,   145
Lan ci be cuet abi yaaŋ,
Yen cuəl yɛn akəl ic, akol ci la
     deŋdeŋ.
Ku luk ala e tim cok.
Ye luŋ e la tim cok ka can e diɛɛr.
Mithiaŋ wuw aguik,   150
E luŋ toŋa,
Naŋ Aciek go thiək,
Wen yɛn acəl wa,
Wen yɛn acəl wa, wen e Deŋ
Ku bi bɛn piŋ e luk ic;   155
Ke luŋ e ŋɛk bɛn ke wun,
Ku jal tim adil a tok,
Ca nyin ŋoŋ wo löŋ,
Aguən acet ke ya kic kən de wa.

II

DIƐT KE TƆC

48. *Ruan Alai* [Ɖɔk]

Ruan Alai aca wiik a tok e rɔt
Nawen jal aye liec
Ke cen raan buɔth e ɣöt.
Deŋ Aboot, Deŋ de Kwɔl,
Ye ciɛɛŋ yen can yi kuɔc cieŋ   5
Wa raan walɛn Deŋ Arialbeek piŋ
  wɛt.
Wa Majaŋ dit,
Yin e raan rɛɛr wo nhiim
Abɛɛr e ebɛn,
Na cak a tieŋ awoc   10
Ke wek ariit a ɣöt,
Na ya woc e walɛn
Ke yak ki lɛk en amaath, amaath,
Wɛt raan dit ace ruɔb ic
Thany ki piny;   15
Abi wa lɔk tak ɣööt wakɔu
Na jɛi e ruan de meth
Ke ɣɛn adhiɛu yeec.
Xɛn aci wɛt e Kwɔl d'Arob la cuet
  Ɖɔk
Cik a cuet Ɖɔŋ d'Arob   20
Abi Ɖɔk ɣɛn a lom ku lueel,
'Arob Allɔr aye raan ci cen man
Duɔk ki yik e nyan toŋ
Aye raan kuc puur muk
Duɔk ki yik e nyan toŋ   25
Duɔk ki yik Alai, Alai.'
Ka Alan cit Alan e köör aduur
Nyan Ajoŋ Payaath acak yök
Tik abi nyaŋ lööm
Na ye wa nyaŋ e Lɔl   30
Ku ye nyaŋ agör ee
E wa nyaŋ agör
Luum ke Ɖɔk cuɔt ki röt
Wek abi lai ke mak
Wek abi lai ke nɔk   35

Lai lai kek aba
Tiŋ akɔɔn ke yaac.
Xɛn ade Deŋ e Kwol, raan dit
Ajal ŋic na de ke jör ɣɛn
Ke cal apiŋ walɛn, Deŋ Arialbeek,
  bɛny.   40
Tik anhiar ater e luk.
Ka ye Deŋ de Kwɔl thany nyin kela
Aca wɛl kou mɛɛc
Aca wel cimen abaar e Kuur waar ye
  lueel.
Abaar Kuur dit ka dhiau wei ke   45
Ku lueel, 'Mɔk abaar ka rac.'
Mɔk abar ka rac ee
Xɛn raan ci wai wien.
Deŋ e Kwɔl a nyuɔth tim nhom
Tim e bɛny.   50
Aye lueel la luk
Tim e bɛny Kwɔl Arob aca jak e
  ruan Alai.
Na de ke riɔc e Ɖɔk e wɛt e Kwɔl
  Arob de Bioŋ ee
Ke tiŋ mɛɛn cɔl arɛɛr
Ku ɣɛn lök a daai   55
Xa piŋ e yith.
Ci ya ŋɔ riɔɔc e Ɖɔk ayi Deŋ d'Arob
  de Bioŋ walɛn?
Wadit Kwɔl Arob yen e thɔn la wut
  thɛɛr
Yen e thɔn ye Ɖɔk cɔɔl
E ku looi athian ten e ruan mɛnh e
  man   60
Alek nyan Ajuɔŋ e tem rim
Tem rim e dhieth e mac
Xɛn pɔk wo Deŋ de ma.
Ku dhɛl ic
Cit e ya ce mɛnh e man.   65

Na jel Alan Ajuɔŋ
Ke jel e nyan Ajuɔŋ
Ke Deŋ e Kwɔl abi riany e thööc
  nhom.
Bi ŋa bɛn yek thööc
E ŋa ben ye yek bɛɛny d'Arob de
  Bioŋ thɛɛr   70
Bɛɛny ɣɔn cuet wadit lap?
Wadit aci guup lam d'Alumaar ɛɛ
Wen dɔm yen piny e wun.
Na ye Deŋ kek e Deŋ oo
Wen e baai akic dɔm,   75
Raan kuc mɛnh de yany de
Waan cuet wadit lap oo
Ka ce mɛnh de yany de
Ka cuet e wut Ɖɔk;
Ce yen e bɛɛny akan?   80
Ce yen bɛɛny nhom tueŋ?
Xɛn ajeem a nhom
Cɔl ɣen ajeem a nhom
Ye ke rɛɛc ba thɔŋ ŋɔ
Ke pɛl e tieŋ die wei   85
Ku ye wa bɛny alath?
Xɛn ajeem a nhom wun dit Kwɔl
  d'Arob
Ke wun Deŋ Majok
Wun wa Kwɔl d'Arob ee
Atɛɛm a röl   90
Na Deŋ ku Deŋ wa
Cik ki rot bi bɛn gɔk
Wa Kwɔl Arob aŋic baai
Bɛny aŋic baai e bɛn;
Ka rou, ka rou   95
Bany waan tueŋ ka rou
Ala Bol e Nyuɔl e Tuic
Ku Kwɔl Arob Ɖɔk
Kek ake dɔm baai
Kek a dɔm baai ic.   100
Lueth aca bi mat thin.
Wa Deŋ Arialbeek
Ce wek e Nhialic baai
Mɛnh e bɛny?
Aye Deŋ mɛnh e bɛny   105
Aye Deŋ mɛnh e Kwɔl Arob de
  Bioŋ,
Kwɔl d'Arob aci rieu e Ɖɔk
Cɔk Alan Ajuɔŋ yen yok raan ke ci
  maar

Ke ci jak,
Ye ŋa ke be dɔm?   110
Ci riɔc Deŋ de Kwɔl?
Ke raan adɔm kiɛth
Ke raan adɔm mac ic
Ken Deŋ Arialbeek.
Wa Deŋ Makuen dit,   115
Duk ben mɔɔny walɛn
Wɛt alɛk Ɖɔk bi piŋ,
Wɛt anyuɔth Ɖɔk bi tiŋ,
Ku bi ganun dɔm ic akɛɛk e tik.
Xɛn aya Allɔr Kwɔl nyaŋ piny   120
Ku ben ɣɛn athɔn,
'Yin bi dɔŋ
Deŋ mɛnhe e wur
Cɔl abi thiek e tik
Deŋ mɛnhe e wur   125
Cɔl abi thiek Alai.'
Nawen jal athɛm nyan Ajuɔŋ
Ke ca leu.
Aba a luɔi abaar!
Yen jel Deŋ Makuei   130
Abi cath ke ɣɛn
Cimen ateŋ e luɔth buɔth
Ku riic rot wei
Aca riɛc luɛk.
Ku la dɔŋ luaŋ Alai.   135
Wɛt aya ŋic nyin ic
Naŋ jaam ke ye wel bi la thiek mɛnh
  e yany de
Manh e dhieth e yany de.
Deŋ Aboot ee gam wɛt.
Deŋ d'Arob yin aca wɛl kɔu wei   140
Yin Deŋ Arialbeek jɔt rot wen Arob
Ce yin e thiɛk ee
Ce yin e kur e piny;
Aba kur ee Deŋ aba kur ee
Na de ke raŋ e nyin   145
Ke ka bi Deŋ döök bi riɛl
Ku jel duɔny e we lɔm e tɛn
Deŋ de Biong Wacbeek
Aŋoot e path;
Mɛnh e raan ace pɔl bi cɔl ayuɛl ke
  jaŋ   150
Cimen macar anyaar.
Ruai guɔp ruan Alai,
Aci wec wel ka ater
Ruai aca atɛr kua wic

Tene wok wo walɛɛn kua; 155
Duɔke ben kuoc looi.
Na ye liu wa yee
Liu Allɔr wen Kwɔl
Yen Kuɔc ic
Ke ya ki lac lueel 160

Ku ba ŋic ee
Ba rot tiɛŋ akɔɔn nhom
Ba akɔɔn yiiy e rot
Na le wiik wadaŋ
Ke we mal tuɔŋ ke 165
Duɔk ke tuŋ ben thiëëc.

53. *Kedaŋ aci ya ruëëny* [Ɖɔk]

Wok ka ci ket loob wok adheŋ cɔl
  Kwɔl Akotɛɛm
Marial Kwɔl acuk dööt Kwɔl Arob
Allɔr, kua Allɔr Deŋ Manyiel yen
  cɛth wok
Ake wun tɔ Amenh Yɔr Kerjok thin;
Ajuɔŋ, Ajuɔŋ ee, Ajoŋ Yɔr Maker
  yen ci wok rɔm. 5
Ke wun mɛc Deŋ Kwɔl
Deŋ Kwɔl a bany da
Yen e ke le wok Abyɛi.
Nyibol aca mek e juɔr ic
Tewen kor yen, 10
Nyibol aca mek ke ken dit
Tewen kor yen.
Ruai ka boŋ Paguiny piny
Ruai ka boŋ cimen thɔn
Duoki ruai boŋ 15
Malual Gitjok Malual Kat
Wamuth aliep ruai ke yɔk ken thok!
E ya yɔɔk, 'Tieŋ e nya
Ke tiŋ ca guɔ maan.'
Kac ki jal tiŋ Abyɔr won da? 20
Kedaŋ aci ya ruëëny ee

Ka ye duäny Marial Jok
Yen ci wen dit looi
E ya yɔɔk, 'Tieŋ e nya
Ke tiŋ ca guɔ maan.' 25
E ya tooc e, e ya yɔɔk, 'Wic akuny'
Guɔ guɔp riɔc ku ba ya teet kede?
Ku ka kac lɛk walɛn
Ya yɔɔk, 'Wic akuny.'
Guɔ guɔp riɔc ku ba ya teet kede?
Ku ka kac lɛk yiwac 30
Ya yɔɔk, 'Wic akuny.'
Guɔ guɔp riɔc ku ba ya teet kede?
Xɛn dhiɔp gɔl ke weŋ
Arob Madiɛn Yɔm aci dhiɔp gɔl ke
  weŋ 35
Xɛn dhiɔp gɔl ke weŋ.
Xɛn e yɔɔk, 'Yin aman tik?'
Xɛn anhiar tik ee.
E ŋɔ man ajak tui?
Ke puɔth cɔl 'tik' 40
Abi yi ruany yɔu
Go yin jal yɔɔk ca guɔp naŋ ke diu?
Guɔ ruëëny jal tääu
'Xɛn adiu, diu kedi.'

55. *Awut gam* [Ɖɔk]

Awut aca ŋueet cimen e meth
Naŋ athiec wa yɛɛ
Xɛn ci ŋuɛɛt Awut.
Ya raan ci nhom adil
Kuɔc raan ba ya la yiek thöny e wa
Bi ya la rëër alaŋgereeb 6
Alaŋgerem wa kuɔc raan ba yiek e;
Ci wel tɛɛm to yɔn yen atuɔc piu
'Ku diec ayaak luɛɛk.'
Ba ke dhiɛɛl e wa nhom 10

Ken e manh ŋɛk akan.
Yen liëëp jaŋ wok
Aba ciet manh alei,
Kic wa e piɔu buɔɔk
Gɔl e wa ba ya wut? 15
Nhiar Awun e Panɔi
Abuk lueel wok e raan thiak e
Ku ba kɔc ya Awut yiek dukan
Ku ka ba yek dukan Gagrial Aguɔk;
Awut gam, 20

Kɔc e Diil
Wek ka ba yiek dukan Gagrial Aguɔk,
Awut gam,
Yakki yɛn ayiek köt
Ku yiek ki yɛn ajöm　　25
Ku bɛn ki lɔk riɔɔc,
Tik acit anyaar
Tik acit akɔɔn

Ago wa riɔɔc e luak.
Awut ee duk e jak　　30
Awut ma duk e jak,
Aba ya ŋa yen kɔn yi thut?
E ŋa yen kɔn yi thut?
Awut ee yɛn akic piɔu muɔl;
Awut dɔk athut ee　　35
Awut dɔk athut ee ye waa.

56. *Naŋ wa pir* [Ŋɔk]

Abit abit
Ca we muɔth wedhie wedhie
Ayi ma ke dhiam die
Ayi nyan waar Acai
Yok Adau ke lɛk ye　　5
Ci we bak pathuɔu die baai?
Ci we bak kɔc Abul?
Lek wa Deŋ Majok
Wa Deŋ Makuei
Ruai ace ke lɛɛŋ yɛn　　10
Wa wa Deŋ Majok
Wa wa Deŋ Makuei
Yen la luaŋ Aciek;
Na ye wa Gitbeek
Wen yɛn ace ke laŋ.　　15
Abuk lueel Abul e Maŋar kek alath,
Xɛn kuc thɔn baar yin
Xɛn ram wa ajan Alei
Xɛn ram wa ajan Abyɔr

Xɛn kuc thɔn baar yin.　　20
Ayee diet ya pɛɛr pan Abul
Ba la paar rian nhial
Bal la dööt akɔl nyin
Ku yɛn agiik rot thin
Man ajiec ku man pɛɛi.　　25
Abi dɛ mɔny tem rol:
Ajööt ace la thöŋ
Mɔny e nyaŋ
Yin agɛɛu alɛɛŋ ee.
Mɔny bi thiek mau e rut ee　　30
Mɔny bi thiek akop e rut ee
Abul ee math Abul mayuan baar
Nyan lɛɛn e Mɔnyjaŋ
Cak amaar ku ca gam.
Maŋar e ku duɔk ki riɔc wa Deŋ
　　Majok Bɛny　　35
Ca Abul meek ci tuŋ akɔɔn dhien
　　Arob.

57. *Ruan e mith ka Abun* [Ŋɔk]

Ayi yoo bi yɛn Apuk riaac
Many e yɔɔc lamba
Many e yɔɔc tharib
Cuɔt rot Ajɔŋ e Yuɔt
Bi thiak e lambaa　　5
Many duon e lamba
Ci bi ciet many e yin mer aŋuɔth e
　　riaŋ gem.
Ke yɛn anyɛɛi Ajɔk
Ca bi dhiɛl riaŋ Abyɛi.
Na yɔk muɔr e dol wec ic garau　　10
Ke ya tiŋ cit e jok
Yin ace mɛnh abun

Abun ace wur.
Male tieŋ dien Ajɔk
Dhaal e guɔp ace wic　　15
E ruan bi dhiac e tim cɔl abyɛi ku
　　ŋaap
Ruan thiin mith ka Abun
Ruai aye yom yir ic
Ruai aye yom yaak
Mal ki e nyaan de Bɛny　　20
Acak ki bi thiak.
Nyan e Giir Mayuɔt
Buk thiak wo riny e döl
Wet kui cak ki bi thaai anɔɔk.

60. *Acien thɛɛr* [Ɖɔk]

Ayee Abyiem Jok Ken aye riiŋ
Ku wic cok, 'Cak luk ee?'
'Acuk tok kou e ban.'
Deŋ Jokŋol Allər
Aye ŋɛk thuuth e wun.   5
Go bany e thook geer,
'Kur, Kur ca wɔɔc gam?
Kur na ca wɔɔc gam ee
Ke yin ayɛth ku yöt.'
Ayee dhɔŋ wun da athiec ɣɛn,   10
'Kur, Kur e tak adi?
Wa Kur e Deŋ dit
Ci yi cien dier e jaŋ
Ku na ca looi ke gam
Adhɛŋ ace riɔɔc.'   15
Cik awaac wo nyiir,
'Kur aliëëp baai
O O aliëëp baai
Ke yic aliëëp baai
Gaar wargak Bɛny dit   20
Gaar wargak Bɛny dit
Ku bi mac munayat
Ba nhom lɔk pal baai
Ɣɛth e Kur Jur Katac
Ba nhom lɔk pal baai.'   25
E Bɛny dit la 'Ɣei!'
E Bɛny dit la 'Ɣei!'
Piny ajai
Piny ajai
Piny ater thuɔu ke pir,   30

Ago wa yɛn anyooth, 'Kur'
Ago wa yɛn agɔk
'Tak Kur e nhom adi?
Tak Kur e nhom adi
Ke le yen ŋɛɛny e tik   35
Ke ye cien thɛɛr e jaŋ?'
Ye cien thɛɛr e jaŋ ee
Kuat cɔl tik
E kɔc wat nhiim liil
Ake cien thɛɛr.   40
Kur ake cien
Kur wen Deŋ paan diɔr
Maɣei manh acien
Maɣei manh acien
Kic tik aliap nhom?   45
Kic tik atuɔr nyin?
Aye lueel, 'Aloi ku.'
Aye lueel, 'Aloi ku.'
E ku le liaap ɛɛ
Le liaap e tok e rot   50
Kewen kɔn yɛn manh tui aweŋ
Ku ce ye
Nawen luɛl, 'Dek arob'
Luɛl, 'Dek arob',
Ke gam jɔk ku ci jai;   55
Ci guɔp riɔc makai?
Yin abi muɔr du nɔk.
Maɣei manh acien
Kic tik aliaap nhom.

64. *Ci nin kua lik* [Ɖɔk]

Ɖɔŋ dit e Kwɔl aci riaak
Ɖɔŋ dit e Kwɔl aci riaak;
Aye wok anak, wok agur ci thɔn,
Ayee Deŋ Bɛny anɛk paan de.
O na wa Ɣerjok dit Arob ɛɛ   5
Ba lɛk wa Ɣerjok dit Arob oo!
Ku lɛk Bioŋ Wakbeek.
Ca bi lɛk wa maɣee?
Alin e Nimir,
Ye ŋa ke loi aliap ee?   10
Raan loi aliap?

Na alanh e Kwɔl Ɣerjok Bɛny?
Lak ten Madibok Deŋ Majok wa-
    maath.
Deŋ de Kwɔl ka cieŋ alath
Acit Nhialic ee acit Nhialic Aciek.
Alin diit athan   16
Arob ba rɔt lɔk tiɛŋ baai nhom
Baai kan.
Caai ci nin kua juec,
Caai ci nin kua guɔ lik.   20
Na lök bany kueen ke ye Bol dit

Na lok bany awic ke ye Kwɔl wa.
Na loi ki liaap
Na loi ki liaap ee
Raan dit alaam athith 25
Ku ye Nuɛr e piny e wun
Ye Nuɛr e piny e wun.
Dɔŋ wa Kwɔl Arob ee!
Dɔŋ wa Kwɔl Arob.
Alin dit ke luaŋ de 30
Lony mathiaŋ tok ee
E ka wɛɛc ka Arob
E ke wɛɛc e wun wa.
Na thiëc Madibok
Ke ye guut e Dɛɛŋa 35
Raan waan ci jal yen e thɔn tiit wo
loc
Mathɔn tiit wo loc

Yen e thɔn tiit wo loc.
Jur la jal e Nuuth tan yen e thɔn tiit
wo loc?
Jur la jal e Dɛɛŋa yen e thɔn tiit wo
loc? 40
Ke ci lɔk ɣeet e ten
Ali muɔr e luɛɛl acieŋ dhoor e baai
Le ɣeet wun Arob
Aram ke ka thɛɛr ɣɔn 44
Yi kuat lɔm akajaa aci raan tok cuet
Aci raan tok cuet ku ben kerac guum
Aci raan de tem kɔu
Ku dɔm yen paan e wun.
Ke ci lɔk ɣeet e ten
Ali muɔr e luɛɛl 50
Acieŋ dhoor e baai
Le ɣeet wun Arob.

III

DIƐT K'AGAR

67. *Wɛr e loony* [Ɗɔk]

Ya gɛɛr mɔɔth wɛɛrbiak
Aŋoot piny ekic ruw?
Ajiec ŋoot piny ke tɔu
Math Col Marial
Ago theep alual acit bioŋ de jur   5
Maŋar da ka tɔc yir paan Coŋ Riak
Cen ke diik e loony waar?
Yɛn ci bi kat.
Nyielbeek dan Gɔɔrkuei tuŋ thok
Tuŋ ke muk aril ca-ajaam   10
Cuk alaŋ paan e Kuany Yaath.

Na cɛk töök, ke töök de akac yok
Adhɛŋ atɔc agon yɔu alual ci miit
Apoklek dacla tuuŋ
Nyanayen ala rib   15
Akajeeŋ dhal ke nyuɛth
Ke wai de Col Nyiel.
Tiŋ ba ke cɔŋ ruaath
Ye lueel adi kɛɛ?
Aye lueel aca guum   20
Aca guum, ke yir ɛɛ
Ɗol Akɔl ku bai e door.

68. *Piɔn ril* [Ɗɔk]

Piɛŋ thok juur
Cak Arob apeen, ke ca gam
Raal ke kut Biöök
Raan dɛɛk Kulaŋ, ke yok Adöör
Adöör kek Bol mɔnyjur,   5
Bawuut ka adhur yɛn
Ku ca la nyoŋ.
Piɔn ci rac yen tɛɛm yɛn agoth kɔu
Yɛn tɔ e cual ic
Yɛn tök rɔt aye rap dukhon.   10
Yɛn ci tic Alal
Bi looi adi?
Kic nɔm ic mum
Ya lem cop ke ya kat
Athokin ci mɔth   15
Raal aca mat ke Mabil

Yɛn la thiec Madiŋ de Yar waa
Piɔn di ka teer ee
Ya ater ci bi luɔŋ Madiŋ de Kwɔl
Aci bi luɔŋ   20
Bany ka adhur yɛn
Ka ci bi luɔŋ
Na ca ye thiɔɔny
Ka buk lueel wok e Deŋ ku Deŋ
Walɛn, walɛn, ka ca gam   25
Nyankat akat kat thɛɛr
Kat thɛɛr waan ciek yeen.
Abul acɔŋ ruaath ee
Acai acɔŋ ruaath
Gik, gik, ŋet thok wɛi   30
Mɔnydit Adöör Gagrial ee Wen
    Pajiŋ.

69. *Yɛn ci riɛɛt thijin ic* [Ɗɔk]

Ya deem mɔɔth e run e piny
Aci baak Micar Allɔr
Ca mam e doŋ e run piny ku ca gam
    ɛɛ
Aci ruw Bol Acueek
Yɛn riit yöt thijin waa   5
Ɗet ci yɔu thiɛth ci miit
Acam raal ke marɛŋ ɛɛ
Aci giɛt lany thok apet ke la giriik
Nɔm anal boŋ tem raal.
Ye runna bɛn ku ye ŋet Bol waa   10
Ariɔc abi teem juur wun Babo

Wun Maŋar Cap Kiec tan Agaar
Than Bol Athieŋ de Maŋol waa
Dit alui thök
Guir keek.   15
Guɔ nɔm alaŋ
Ɗet yɔɔt e thok
E ku be ye loor
Raal kal yen amaan
Bol abi raal kum e la miak   20
Ayang wëëth e ruw ekeŋ
Raal kal yen amaan.

70. *Many de Deŋ* [Ɗɔk]

Wok röök tɔŋ wok Deŋ ku Deŋ
    ku Agɔk Mijok,
Rinydit ka dut ci kiec kök
Ajarkööt ke ŋet pɛn akɔl nyin
Go many de Deŋ ic buw.
Tɔŋ cuk kɛɛk wok Wun Acai   5
Ajarkööt ke ŋet pɛn akɔl nyiɒ
Go many de Deŋ ic buw.
Tɔŋ cuk kɛɛk wok walɛn Jaklek
Ajarkööt ke ŋet pɛn akɔl nyin
Go many de Deŋ ic buw.   10
Bol dit aci wiic nyin
Aci cet Awɛk
Aye piny dër ke kɔt

Kiɛu nɔn ke piŋ aköök
Mɛnh Bɛny de wööt ka tɔc.   15
Jokrɔl ku la Deŋ Miyɔm
Nak ki miɔr yiŋ de Jok
Mɛnh dhien de gɛɛr bi tɔc thɛɛp.
Abyɛi acuk wɛɛl piny,
Arɛtnyuɔk Pabil akɔr Mɔnyjaŋ ye
    nɔm   20
Bi ya jur ade nyin galam.
Arɛtnyuɔk Pabil
Bi ya jur ade nyin galam.
Nya ka nööm Madiŋ de Ɗol
Bak ke kueen ci weeu ke jur   25
Bak ke kueen ci weeu dhorow.

V

DIƐT KE TOŊ

85. *Le bɛn teno?* [Atuɔt]

Athɔɔny abök dhaŋ wei ee
Aŋuala abök dhaŋ wei
Kaŋ aci rɛɛc kur nhiim
Jam aca kueeth ee
Jam e tueny ɛɛ.   5
Malual panda ci cien
Baai aci cien kun Ɣerjok aba
Ba mat ic e bi jam da ya tok
Waye Arɔl ala jam de
Cam awuuw ku;   10
Ku ɣɛn abi mɔl pei.
Ca Aciek la no?
Kuɔny wok baai.
Le bɛn teno

Anyin yeer kuɔc guɔp   15
Na ye yɛn ee,
Nyaai yi lec e ɣa guɔp.
Aɣeet kuɔi Aɣɛɛr,
Nak tuɛny
Ku nak alabiith ee   20
Bi kɔc anin e lɛi ee;
Yee athɔɔny kɔc laaŋ,
Anyim lec jɔt rɔt
Ba bɛɛ dhuk pandu.
Ayee wuth e kɔc laaŋ   25
Anyim lec jɔt rɔt,
Ba bɛɛ dhuk pandu;
Jal bɛɛ dhuk pandu.

86. *Ɣɛn e nyaaŋ wei* [Atuɔt]

Yee yɛn e nyaaŋ wei
E wet ayɔɔl ee
Cɔl ɣɛn abur cien weŋ
Ba rɔt luɔt e tuɛny ic.
Gawei ke tuɛny ee   5
Ka thɛɛr ɣɔn ka guer a guɔp

Man mur aci alual
E ku jamda wen wa
Ku tuɛny ka be bɛn
Ɣɛn e nyaaŋ wei   10
E wɛt a yɔɔl ee.

87. *Ta Abyɔr ke nyeeŋ baai wei?* [Ŋɔk]

Joŋ de Por adol
E lueel ala pal baai
Wai waa
Ke luel ku wok e joŋ adol
Kic tɔŋ wo dhal?   5

Kic joŋ de Por bob ɛɛ?
Raan lueel adi yee?
Ya mathɔn.
Alueel wɔɔt,
'Ta Abyɔr ke nyeeŋ baai piny ɛɛ?'   10

89. *Ater thɛɛr* [ᴅɔk of Upper Nile]

Bɛny Beek aci jam
Nyɔŋkuac aba mac yɛnhdi
Malual wok ci tëëŋ teem wo Nuɛr;
Ke daan ɣɔn wok Nuɛr baai
Aŋic Jekeny ku ŋiɛc   5
Miɛm ku ca luel;
Yɛn kic peec nɔn aɣɔn

Ku yɛn kic mat wut
Ci Lual jai oo
Aŋic Ajaŋ thɛɛr   10
Cak raan apeec guɔp
Ku kic piɔndi rɛɛt bic
Abi tiŋ yɛn nyin
Ruëëny die akëc peec.

91. *Yɛn rac* [ᴅɔk of Upper Nile]

Raan ya waai akeu nɔm
Guɔ ŋic aruɛi ku yoo
Duk yɛn e tɔɔr yɛn rac ɛɛ
Na la ye keeth wadaŋ
Ke yɛn bi rac   5
A yɛn ci bi tëëk lɔɔm
Yɛn bi theek guɔp e jaŋ eban ɛɛ.
Awaknyaŋ Bɛny e wut rɔt nöök
Duk diɛɛr

Yɛn tɔ ke ya ken apiɔu nyooŋ   10
Guɔ ŋic lɔn bi thau wo riɔɔk
Than ageer ce yin ci la wo rem duɔl
    waan?
Acen rem kien kɔk ŋiɛc
Guɔ ŋen lɔn bin cath yi tok
Waan yin tim thɛɛr   15
Yin bi la ku bi roor daŋ bɛ lɔk cil.

92. *Wai di ace kuuŋ e gueth* [ᴅɔk]

Aca kiir kɔu ɣɔn theei
Ku dam wai nɔm;
Ade lan dien tɔ wiir
Aci jel
Amuk Riŋ de Jiel   5
Ago mɔɔc thiab
Riny de Deŋ baai aguem lai
Aca guɔɔt ee,
Raan ɣɔb amook;
Yɛn teer lai wok e mac wiir,   10
Raan ɣɔb amook.
Yɛn ci rɔt puk aye köör
Yɛn ci la daldal wo wai
Wai di ka rem thok
Wai di ka ce kuuŋ e gueth.   15

Cuɔr ka la wiir e eyee
Malɔu ka la wiir e eyee
Malɔu abɛn wɛr e nyaany
E wɛr e yieth ɛɛ.
Ade ke ca dak ɣɔn theei   20
Aŋoot ke ba yiiy ye.
Ye wai di
Wai di ka guir weŋ yaath ɛɛ
Aye lai ka nyɛi wai waa
Lai ka nyɛi tɔɔŋ.   25
Yɛn ca cithaŋ
Yɛn ca cithaŋ ariäu e wɔɔt
Raan e yab luɔny baai
Ka ba liic amook.

93. *Lan tɔ wiir* [Ŋɔk]

Kic riny Maker awɛlwɛl
Wai ka liaab
Yap ku diët.
Lan tɔ wiir
Ka gol e bioŋ   5
Ago wai laak.
Acuɛt abeb
Wai ka di.
Cuɔr wuw ke thel wai de
Wayiyee lan dit ka ca thɔr wai mɔk
Cuɔr wuw ke thel wai de   11
Yen ŋic aŋun roor
E kɛɛc wei
O ca pal waa
Ku yɛn aŋic Aköök.   15
Ya yeep jɔt e ke roor
Dam wai nɔm
Ku dam wai thar
Cam mel Mameth ɛɛ

Mameth Alathur Ala;   20
Ara,
Ka ca guööt.
Ke wiir bɛn be de nɔm ajuaac
Guɔt e rek Mathiaŋ
Ke de nɔm ajuaac;   25
Aca keeth ke piny col
Ke de nɔm ajuaac.
Ya kiir kɔu
A go wai dhuɔŋ
Aguɔn mioc Abuk   30
Abuk nyan tɔ wiir.
Yɛn athöŋ wok e Man Aŋɛɛr.
Lan liɛny ka adual tɔɔŋ
Ku le yooi piny
Ku le yic wayee aɣɛɛc wai   35
Cuɔr anuŋnuŋ.
Ku Lal ke ke riëëc cɔl abɛk rɛɛr.

95. *Köör paar* [Ŋɔk]

Yen cuɛt abeb piny
Ku kal wai;
Köör wuw waa
Köör wuw malith.
Athokyɔm de Kwɔl ee   5
Ke lueel e cuet weŋ ee
Na guet e thim;
Wun ci riööc na guet e thim
Ka ca bi gam.
Wok luel ater wo köör miɔr,   10
Köör ba ke thol jaŋ
Ka ca nhiar.
Yɛn muny e thok waa

Maŋar da ka ce riööc c'amagiliŋ.
Wok wen Aguenbaar   15
Wok de ater;
Na ruruan can ni kɔn nɔk
Ku bɛ ebɛn
Cien e piɔu köör Aliab?
Yic mɛɛr piny ci deŋ   20
Yin ca pal ɛɛ,
Yin guɔɔt.
Na waan ca yɛn adhut thööŋ?
Wai dien mɔk e yɛn
Wen Aŋoŋ e Deŋ.   25

97. *Manyaŋ guɔ laac* [Atuɔt]

Wun e Kuer aci ɣet Ajak;
Cyer e waa
Mɔny ci kan tiem ace luel ye riööc.
Eŋan ya lɛk riööc?
Wun Apak ace riööc   5

Ca e riööc.
Cak niim maar Yom Ajɔu
Ku dam lɔu nɔm?
Weŋ dien ba luɔny böör
Wun Kuer aba yok ee waa.   **10**

Manh aɣɔl duk ben dhiau.
Kaŋ aci riak.
Yɔn ci Manyaŋ guɔ laac
Eŋɔ ben peel arom da tɔ̈ɔr
Apenh e nyin ŋuan   15
Ye guur yic juëër piny
Pel e ke ya amook lual
Ci dan e kɔryɔm.
Thöök e Mɔnyjaŋ ke kic cien.
Ye Riak thön baai geu ee,   20
'Yiek ki ya kak e wa.'
Ku cien raan biy ki
Dɔŋ kak e raan wei.

Wɛt e wa Jieŋ ake kuc ater;
Manyaŋ guɔ laac   25
Raan pel ee
Ci ɣööth yic ŋɛɛr.
Kɛɛc waar ci la de?
Aben ya ayɔɔk apal toc
Paan e wa   30
Ka ce tony kan pɔl
Aŋuɛn ci thou
Ca ki kɔc aram ke ya
Cak niim maar e Yem da Ajou
Kaŋ tiit.   35

98. Döör a riääk [Gɔk]

Lek ki Arɔl Kacuɔl
Puɔn Agaar ka ce ke cak yok
Wok aci kɛɛk ka ŋot ke kuec;
Döör a riääk, math a riääk.
Ke ɣɔn luel raan Amuk   5
'Na yok raan ke duk cok
Na yok kuɔt ke cok
Abin adek.'
Maliɛt e Tiɛny yen ca cɔk rot waar
Thar raan ago yic miööt ee   10

Cimen amal Karthum.
Liɛt e Tiɛny, raan ye cɔr ku ye ŋɔl
Wok ka ram e lol kɔu
Go raan yic wat ci kai awet;
Raan adhiau e dhien e thɔk,   15
'Ayai Padɔl duk anak ee
Wok anɔŋ ruan e thiek.'
Agar dit ɣɔr amok ci lony
Maliɛt e Tiɛny ca lec cet jon e nyuɔp
    luɛk.

99. Jeec tɔ roor [Paan roor]

Wɛt apiŋ Torit ci doŋ
Jeec e Deŋ Nhial atɔ roor;
Jeec e Deŋ Nhial adɔm Akot
Ku dɔm Rumbek;
Jeec e Deŋ Nhial atɔ roor.   5

Lak lɛk ki abib
Ci baai rɔt wel a ma ya cok ee?
Lak lek ki abib
Yɛn la wok
Ke yin adam cin.   10

100. Wok aye Mɔnyjeeŋ [Paan roor]

William ater ken e moc;
Deŋ e Nhial,
Ater ee ater ee
Ater Janub ke Mandukurat,
Ater da ace ken bi thok thɛɛr ayɔn
    da   5
Ater ee ater Janub ke Mandukurat.

Jec Deŋ Nhial kek Mɔrwel
Ake ye cɔl Nyanya
E Rek Amɔu buk biok
Bahr el Ghazal   10
Agar Marɔl buk biok
Wok Mondukuur Arab
Mathiaŋ

Bahr el Ghazal
Abuk reet ic 15
Bahr el Ghazal
Piny Mɔrwel Malɔu
Ku William Deŋ Nhial.
Wok guur ka ɣɔn,
Na guur ku guɔp 20

Ke wok abi Nhialic leec;
Na guur ku guɔp
Ke wok abi Nhialic leec
Dɔc wook
Wok ka ye Mɔnyjeeŋ Bahr el Ghazal
Ater ee, ater ee. 26

VI

DIƐT KE DIAAR

101. *Liɔi* [Ŋɔk]

Wok ci la yualyual wo mɔny de baai,
    Rialcol
Wok ci cet ajiec ke lith yualyual baai
Nyan ci gɔɔu, rɛɛra
Wa nyan nyeeng e piny e dhodot
Nyan ci gɔɔu rɛɛra   5
Wa nyan gɛɛyi.
Cit e lueel aci wen e Jok tik pɔl.
'Ka cen ke cuk lueel wo Nyantiwit
Ka cen ke cuk lueel wo nyan de
    bɛny.'
Ku dit jai   10
Micar yɛn bi kok wo ruɔɔk dit e
    paanda.
'Thithiei' ka la nhial,
Wal e Jak aci la wiir wɛr acieek
Aci jɔk la waak.
Cak jal jam wek e jɔk?   15
Mijak cak aluɔny dɛɛu wek e jɔk?
Ke kic rɔt looi
Baai many de Col yen e dhiɔp kɔc
    nɔk.
Agorot de Bioŋ kuiu
Kuiu nyan de wen e Miyar.   20
Cit e baai jal jam ee de ke dit ci wo
    yok
Wo wen Padɛɛk;
Ka looi mɔny cam de Jok Aŋueek
    dhal ki jaŋ
Ayi jur thith;
Wok ram kueer wok Deŋ Thoklooi
Deŋ de Rama de Dhakam
Jur ayɔɔk, 'E ŋɔ pal e baai?   25
Kue ŋɔ ca la wɔɔc baai ku cak
    dhieth?'
Wɛt e nyan de mɔny cam atöök
Ayi jur panɛɛr den Arob de Bioŋ; 30

Deŋ de Rama ke la ku bii
Jur la duɔmduɔm,
Acen ke diik ce bɛ riaak
Ayin Deŋ Thoklooi acen kediik ce
    bɛ riak.
Thok akuany piny e nyan de Bioŋ ka
    ci liɔɔi baai,   35
'E nyan toŋo?'
Ke nyan athan luny e mith ka adhëëŋ
    pëër ic.
Ku pal ki tiŋ da aliöör ke cath
Pal ki tiŋ de raan kuc wel
Aŋoot ke bi paan de yök.   40
Adhɛŋ kic dier ye liep
Acen daŋ e bi ye kaam,
Acɛk bɛ cath abi yet juur
Mɔny e Nyankiɛɛu,
Acɛk bɛ cath abi yet Agar   45
Mɔny e Nyankiɛɛu ka bi la,
Adhɛŋ pɔk ke nyan de bɛny.
Ka ba ya lɛk Akoŋ da
Yɛn aliei e rin ke wee
Rin ke wee ka la wo kɛɛk wok e moc;
Thiek ka riak e tuuric   51
Thiek ka riak thakit
Kalath ka ci thok
Wok ci la yuaŋ wok thɔn d'Ajak.
Yɛn kic gɔth wok kɔc ke baai   55
A nyan e aal piny e thiap.
Kac gɔth wok e mɔny ci leec
Yɛn e nyan e ɣaal piny e thiap.
Jaŋ athiec, 'Wa nyan de Bioŋ
Eŋɔ ca la wɔɔc paan du?'   60
Cuëër ka liu ya guɔp
Nyan de Bioŋ ala kualääŋ;
Kɔc kua yɛn akic e kɔɔr
Abi yɛn la laar luɛk e tim thar;

Tiŋ waan cec e dhɔɔtdhɔɔt baai 65
Yɛn acianun ci ruəu
Ke lueel acath wok e jɔk
Yɛn acath wo wal Palatha,
Raan e kɔt e wai nɔm
Ci kerac col. 70
Maboŋ de Kwɔl Dorjok,
Wɛt e jaŋ lueel ku dit gam,
Wɛt e Buŋ de Beek lueel ku dit
gam
Wɛt e Wun Arek
Jɔk ace duəi raan piəl. 75
Na ke can e nyaaŋ paan den athɛɛr
ale kuel Alei.
Wa nyan wun Milaŋ ku ba jal jäl
baai
Kic thieek rɔt rɛɛc.
Ka lueel Col e, 'Ca guə jal ke ya kic
la luɛk?'
Yɛn ci jal Maboŋ d'Ajak; 80
Ke cuk gɔɔc wok wen e wa ye
Wa Acoŋ Duɔk Luɛth Buŋ d'Awet.
Dit yɛn e kuɛn wa Marial Padɛɛk
Yɛn acit ke ci mac nyop
Dɛp baai wok e wel. 85
Buŋ de Beek yɛn ci deep adeep
Yɛn aci lɔk nyop nyin;
Wanmaath yin ca man.
Tik tɔŋ de gɔɔc ke meth ku bi moc
la cuəp.
Ka ca agonh da wo Luɛɛth 90
Ku yen nyaaŋ yɛn thɔtthɔɔt piny e
jom,

Awien lɔk mac kooth nyan e Rial
Nyan dhien Agueŋ de Kwɔl
Wok e riɛm de Mɔnydhaaŋ de Kwɔl
de Jok
Wok ci rot bɛɛr mɛnh nyaan de
Bioŋ d'Acuɔl. 95
Wok ci la yuaŋ wok e thɔn Ajak
Le piriiny ya guɔp ci raan cet kil,
Wok ka pɔk e mɔɔth de bil e karac
Bi ŋɔ cam?
Acam Yɔm de dhien Dau Coŋ Kuac
Akɔl e nyaan kai Abul. 101
Wɔc Gɔl, Abyɛi, diec e weŋ Maker
Abyɔr
Wun dit de Deŋ Koklek,
Diec e Yɔm kede mɛnh nyaan Jöök
da,
Lek e wen de Makuany de Deŋ
d'Ayuel 105
Na yik a Yɔm
Wok ci rɛɛc wok e many de Baar
Rialcol;
Dhien e Col Ayuɔt aci kɛɛc e thou
Yɛn ci many de Baar yen jɔk;
Ka jal kuc ke ca wɔɔc o 110
Ma nyan Ajiŋ Kuac Ariöök,
Arob de Mɔnytooc!
Mac dit de Bioŋ d'Allɔr aye ŋuɔt
riap
Wok e kuat jɔk thɛɛr;
Mac d'Allɔr de Mɔnydhaaŋ aye
ŋuɔt riap 115
Wok e kuat jɔk thɛɛr.

102. *Ruuw e tak* [Ŋɔk]

Ci bi thöŋ ke joŋ e mɔny cɔl Ajak
Mɛnh kai, Awet Matɛm;
Dit bɛ la tak piɔndi
Ku ŋat agööt
Ke duən athan jep yin yɛn nɔm ɣɔŋ,
Miet yin bei aba kɔɔc ci raan 6
Wen yin ɣaal e lek ku cuany yin e mac
Wen kedi wen amɛl e baai
Ayi gueer ke thok mal jaŋ.
Na ke diik athan e ŋuac miok weŋ wut
ic Mɔnymau? 10

Yen kin ke can aruuw e tak ku loi
piəu awɔc;
Wok ci rot wiiu Kerieth Pajok.
Wa Kerieth mɛnh e dhien Pajok
Mɛnh riic wek yen e jam
Mɛnh len athan gak jɔk, 15
'Gak jɔk ku ci jɔk gak'
Yin ca gak
Yin e liëëp e nɔm
Ku ba yɛn la lioi.

103. *E pial* [Ɗɔk]

Yɛn e köör e tiet keec thoŋ ke kuɔt
Ka lueel, 'Kediena ka ca bi nyool.'
Yɛn giik rɔt Malual.
Aköŋ daan e Jiel Bagat
Ke kaar cak tiŋ nɛɛ?   5
E ke la yɔɔc many e Beek
Adan Awet ka maan
Yen amaan,
Ka ba ya thiec e Deŋ,
'Ca thöŋ wa Adau wa yo?'   10
Eŋɔ ca wɔɔc kam kua wo wa?
Ka buk kɔr aluuk;
A lueel, 'Deŋ yɛn ajai paan yɛn tiŋ tɔ
   cien.'
Nyan e bɛny ŋic Ɗɔk ku Tuic
Ayi Jur ke Rek   15
Jöt Malual ci wɔɔt dhal e pol.
Abyɔr wun Kwɔl e Bioŋ yɛn mɔu
Laany agör
Akiit Man Adau, 'E kuduu
Kudu, yoo yɛn adhieu;   20
Ye raan ci tɔɔu wa ye ber
Deŋ cit e bɛɛny ke dit
Yen gɛɛm yin nyan duɔn ci bi thiëëc.
Ci looi adi e mana?
Yɛn e nyan di pëën   25
Ku ka ci la paan de mɔc tiŋ dɛn daŋ
Ku bi tɔ cien.
Yen athiëëc e week Akoŋ da ku
   Thiɔɔr
Gɔl bɛny adi?
Ku cen röök kaŋ niim?   30
Aci gɔɔc ci dany
E man cen e wiik
Ci ŋɛk bi jam e liem de?'
Jal apiŋ Deŋ, Adɔk yɛn,
'Ku dɛ e piɔu ke yi dit e thian.' 35

Ke ci bi luɔŋ athɛɛr.
Wek thiëëc akɔc manh de wen Dhaŋ
Ke ci ya guut nyin ke can e jam
Ke bɛɛny ku ke bi wa yeth maar
Wen aluɔi e yɛn.   40
Ke ci rɔt looi kac e piŋ Adau?
Yɛn e yɔɔk a la dhien e Dak
Ku dɔŋ tiŋ waar ke diu
Ku ka kic a pot
Arom dhien e Dhaŋ ku ka kic alaam
   jak e yɛn.   45
Deŋ da Akum Anadher
Ci nya la wiir a culup?
Wɛr Acai yen ci dik ke yɛn?
Ke diena ka ba kɔr aluuk
Aci rɔt bi piŋ.   50
Kuɔc nan yen Lual ku Cyer kua
   Acien de Yɔr,
Ku wa Marial, kek e Bɔl Biliu.
Ke juɛc kiith toŋ tɔ baai
Eŋɔ wan guɔp piɔ̈ɔ̈l di?
Ajal tɔ tueŋ   55
Ci kurthii e jɔt e bɛny nhial.
Paguiny yen agak
Kɔc tok nyan den abeerri
Jel abɛɛny yen e gɛɛm e nya?
Ci beer a beer ci teem?   60
Aŋoot ke cath aci doŋ ke yɛn.
Na cak doŋ ceen
Ke wɔɔc Paguiny;
Nyan e ma Acai Jur e Rial
Panɛɛr dun ade guɔp awɔc.   65
Pial ci bi waak
Wen aca la waak e Kir;
Pial ci bi waak
Wen awaak e piu ka Acai
Pial dit ci teem ci bi tɔu ke raan. 70

108. *E Kerieec thök?* [Ɗɔk]

La ku nyuɔc ee,
'Walɛn yɛn ci cen miɔɔr.'
Walɛn ya yɔɔk,
'Acen luenh ca lueel wene Jok Aŋuek.'

Ruɔk bil Micar e nyan dhieth e wook
Ke ŋuɔt yok e ku bɛr Ajëër   6
Rɔt looi aye colthaan
Mɔny cɔl Wel wen e Dɛŋ

Maŋar Pajiŋ
Adhɛŋ aŋic biöök ci köör adur 10
Ke ca Ajoŋ de Ker weŋ lony.
Jel kek adhiëëth kek e duet
Jel kaai nyaan dɛn cɔl Duɔɔt,
Ka ci lööny many yi dhien e Kir
Ruɔk Bil
Dhien e man Thɔn 15
Dhien e yɔk Nyanwiir
Wun dit agok ka di Abɛk:
Ku be dhiëëth nyan cɔl Adɛɛl
Nya ka thith ci biaar,
Aci la yɔɔc many Padɛɛk adhuɔk. 20
Ajëër Marial la yi kueet ci rɛc da awan
Dhien e Wacbeek Padɛɛk
Bil rɔt apuk aye weŋ de dhëëŋ.
Raan e yi thiëëc e, 'Wen e Mijoŋ de
Dhaŋ
Baai e miɔr teno?' 25
Aluɔny da Aliam de Maker Agaany
Duɔt toom aben nyin awoi.
Lɛk Darcol de Mijoŋ da Adol ci
tɔɔŋ e tɔɔu.
Yɛn de athuwil e nyɔŋ ajeer

Xɔk riir wen akɔu akic bɛ nin 30
Ya go Darbiak athiec,
'Awat ye ŋɔ yee? Ye ŋɔ?'
Ka Ajeer Marial biɔny e nyan Pajiŋ
Yen ci löc bɛ dhöth
Ya go raan acööt, 'Adhuɔk Bil
athuɛɛc e wiin.' 35
Jal ku tiit Tɔc Tuŋ Mijaŋ de Din Col
Wok kuëëth Gɔŋ e Thigei
Ajuɔŋ wok la luui e gek
Makor e Deng dëë buk ŋɔ looi
Kic ŋual wo yok 40
Ye runa bɛn ku ye luɔi de gek
Ajuɔŋ Malith riny de Ker e Bil
Malinh da ka wuw ke door
Loi ku dhëëŋ ram Lai de Makuei
Wok col e wiik Athokjak Burjok de
Beek 45
Na ci gek thök.
Ku ye ŋɔ e ye lueel Kerieec ke yit?
Ku ye ŋɔ ci gek e bɛ yit?
Luɔi da Akum ce thök.
Ajoŋ da ka kueth Gɔk 50
Ruw biaac e lit ke wo kuëëth Thigei.

109. *Thon Mabil* [Dɔk]

Jal reer ke ya thuc
Ace liu de miɔr yen tak
Ke ke wiik Mabil akol tok.
Jɔŋ ci Mabil laar
Ke cɔl ca bi bɛ yok 5
Mabil ke wat e ghuɔɔl.
Miɔr diena ka thoŋ rol ke kuaar wen
e bɛny
Ku Cyer e Deŋ, bɛny dit
Ku Ariath Maker bɛny e Rek
Ku la Bilkuei bany Paan Aruw yen
athoŋ ke yeen. 10
Wa Aŋueek Dorjok
Ca Ajeer lak ci ke tɔc e biöök
Raan tek tɛɛn ke liec, ci Baak kuɔc
la wek.
Thany ki luɛk, ka jai e lua
Ruɔk bil e nyaan dhien Pajiŋ ajai ci
kir 15
Thany ki luɛk e mith k'Ajoŋ de Miyar.

Aŋɔk aboor paan Abyɛi
Paan yi Dorjok
Ke git Jok d'Adol e Beek.
Weŋ kiu e yaau 20
Ago tim tɔ roor a gam
Athoŋ rol ke riai—rian nhial.
Eŋun ŋuut ke wa pɛn kac?
Yin bi rɔt ka mɛɛn mɔny e ŋuut;
Aguaŋ dien e thon wɔɔc ye tuŋ. 25
Yɛn toc Allɔr
Tuɔc Allɔr e ma
Allɔr cit Allɔr Din Col ka tuɔc,
'Yin bi Ajeer diec rial
Mac de Paan Yɔm ka maan.' 30
Weŋ de wa Aŋueek!
Luaŋ dit e Buŋ de Nyiel ke yic
athiereu ke Mithiaŋ
Micar Anyaar yen athöŋ ke yeen
Thɔn e dhëëŋ e Bil Akuei.

110. *Mijok* [Ŋɔk]

Ageer tuŋ ala ke wiëëk ee
E cit ajalwau
Ala ke duɔny piny
Ke cit ajalwau
Jok Arum   5
Kin col e Mijoŋ de wa ka nhiar
Anhiar ci bɛny
Anhiar ci bɛny dan muk wo baai.

Na cuk ku riaak
Ke yin bi gɔl nyooth.   10
Gɔl e wa
Dhien Pakuar
Amac yɛn awiɛr ci lip.
Yin ca bi waar
Acak jaŋ yi caany   15
Tuŋ kuon ka ka nhier ke yin ee.

114. *E ŋa war Deŋ* [Ŋɔk]

Ageer
Miɔr nyan e Yɔm
Nyan e Yɔm Akuengɔl.
Maŋar yin bi luääp we wɛɛŋ
Ku wur abi liaap ke Thudan.   5
Ca aten e wel ke Janub
Ke jam e wɛt ril ci tiil
Acen raan tem e nɔm wun Kwɔl.
Kic rin ki cath agut juur?
E ku ɣeet akɔl nyin?   10
Yɛn kic gɔn jam e wɛt bɛɛr e tueŋ
Kuc awet
Marial ace jam e nuɔr
Ace jam e lueth.
Ke waan Marial akac yok   15
Akac yok e wun Lual Amiɛk

Ke waan Marial akic bɛn.
Ariɔɔc e ke ca bɛ gɔl ka ci bi leu
Ku ke lueth.
Riŋ de Jok Allɔr wa ka daai wook. 20
Le wo guut nyiin
Ke dɔm Makuel Maŋöl
Athian bɛny ci dhiɔp ke wa
Ku bek ku lɔk dhiɔp wo Kuacariok.
Loŋ dɛk Makuen Ajok atiiŋ piɔu 25
Acit loŋ e math wen e Ŋöl e Jok
Makuel thoŋ ke raan e gat Wargak
Ker Anyuak e Mabek Marɔl
Cit ci paanda riaak;
Makuany e wun Pagiɛt   30
Muk ku baai.

VII

DIƐT KE NHIALIC

117. *Bɛny maar* [Ɖɔk]

Bɛny dit Madhɔl aye maar Luak
Maar Luak ca acuuk maan
E raan ci thuɔu bɛn
Bɛnydit cen piɔu tiɛl
Amat Acuuk nɔm   5
Guer baai ye cok
Ku guer ye nɔm
Micar Aduɔk, wen Deŋdit
Cɔk baai piny
Baai ka ci la wacwaac   10

Na ci piny la kirkiir
Na ci piny dɛ aliir ee
Aliir e Jɔk.
Naŋ raan nhiɛr yɛn
Ke nhiar   15
Naŋ raan mɛn yɛn
Ke maan
Aca bi maan aba dhuɔl wei
Ce yɛn e jak acuuk?

118. *Na waac yen* [Ɖɔŋ Upper Nile]

Na waac yen
Ke luɔi
Na ca ye wɔɔc
Ke luɔi
Ca bab ee   5
Ca bab ee

Ca bab Yanh Pakuɛr dan Deŋ.
Ayuel Loŋar Apinydiiŋ
Diu Nhial akuɔc.
Na ca ye wɔɔc
Ke luɔi.   10

119. *Ca tuŋ tɛɛm* [Ɖɔŋ Upper Nile]

Ayuel Loŋar, Wen Jiel.
Yin ba waac Mabior.
Mai aci bɛn
Go piny alik
Ca tuŋ tɛɛm   5
Ca be diɛr.

Mai bɛn
Guɔ rim nin
Deŋ da yoo,
Deŋ de Garaŋ,   10
Deŋ d'Abuk
Ci raan bɛn ke wei ɛɛ.

120. *Raan nhial* [Ɗɔŋ Upper Nile]

Ke dien dhala,
Abi mɛnh ba nhial bɛɛr.
Awɔl Kerjok wek Deŋ Acuny
Alaŋ Apinydiiŋ nɔm.
Nyanwiir da wek Wiɛu   5
Bak tɔu ku Deŋ rɔɔk.

Kokbɔŋ wek Loŋar
Acuuk anyin kuany run bɛt.
Awɔl Kerjok, ba piŋ ke wel lueel
Yɛn laŋ Abuk ku wen dɛɛn Deŋ.   10
Acuŋ waan cak aci lɔk ŋɔŋ
Ba röök ku Banyda.

121. *Bɛnydit, e Nhialic lɔŋ* [Ɗɔk]

Wok ci gup ŋɔŋ
Bɛnydit e Nhialic lɔŋ
Wok ci thaar juet
Bɛnydit e Nhialic lɔŋ
Wok ci nyiin ŋɔŋ   5

Bɛnydit e Nhialic lɔŋ
Bi lɔɔr aceec wakɔu
Lɔɔr acit lɔɔr e jɔk?
Duu duu duu duu
Bɛnydit e Nhialic lɔŋ.   10

VIII

DIƐT KE KÖÖR

123. Deŋ abirbiir [Ɗɔk]

Deŋ abirbiir pan Apuk ee
Mɔɔth ic,
Deŋ abir jaŋ nyin
Ku ci a bir nyin.
Jal adhëëŋ jɔt   5

Jal adhëëŋ jɔt
Aguan tɔŋ tɔk ather
Thar yɛn Maleŋ de Guil luak
Ago diar dhiau,
'Wunda acien ic adhëëŋ.'   10

130. Dhuk (a) [Ɗɔk]

Thiilim
Thilim anyom
Anyom beergo
Yeki thaabi
Thaaba yeey   5
Ya dheen
Ala thin e lek e lek

Ka la thin e nyam
Dhaan a kam
Wɛt ci lueel   10
Man Ajak
Ca piŋ u u
Dhuk.

131. Dhuk (b) [Bor]

Arɔɔl lɔ bɛn teno yoo
Yɛn la bɛn kankan kɔr wal
Ke de nyaan kec acuɛt rot piny
Ku la teŋ de Rek
Ku la gaŋ Arol,   5

Ya Arɔɔl mane acit Arɔl e gaak
Ke yin köör adök ku bin yi liet boot
Adhɛŋ lɔ dhuk cok du
Menhdu ka mɔu.

X

DIƐT KE GAT

132. *Wer e baai* [Ɗɔk]

Yɔr aci wil
Aŋic Miyar da e tuŋ thook kedhie
yee
Ɗic ric amor
Ɗic amor waa;
Miyar dan thoi amɛk Abyɛi e pɛɛi
biak   5
E tuɔm e tuŋ gat;
Miyar aŋic wel.
Ka ba wel, yen e baai
Ka ba puk, yen e baai
Kuɔr ku ya moc;   10
Yɛn nyuc e biak waan e wel la thok
Wɔr Ameer.
Ma dhiau e ban,
'Ci mɛɛth di thöök roor
Ci baai yic cien meth ee.'   15
Ca yin gak a ma
Cien ke ŋic
Cien ke ŋic.
Wɛt e piny amol
Aba ke kuany baai aköök ic;   20
Paan Karthum aye meth dhieth ku
le.

Ba yi waac e Yar e weŋ?
Na yar e thuk
Ku galam di?
Nyal wai   25
Nyal wai
Ku kiɛt door
Ku le rip;
Ku kiɛt door
Ku le rip;   30
Miyar da ka cuɛt abeb
Ku le rip.
Tim jaak thok ke kuur
Ku luɔi ker ɛɛ.
Rem ci dak, rem ci dak   35
Acen ke dɛɛn ye dhal;
Ca bioŋ guir
Ku luɔi ker
E miɛt rɔk
Ku luɔi ker;   40
Luɔi paan di yɛɛ
Luɔi paan di
Paan e mith ke pioc
Paan e wɛt mɛɛth athoot piny wɛɛr ic.
Miyar aci rɔt e nyiɛth akɔl nyinɛɛ.   45

133. *Dit gaau* [Ɗɔk]

Nyal wai nyal wai
Ku kiɛt door
Galam thok akok ke wargak di yɛɛ
Ɗuɔth nyal wai.
Athoor amuk jaŋ e piny   5
Kethɛɛr e mith ka Adam
Amuk Miyar dan e gat
Miyar e gat baai e wel.

Mɛnh ci maar, ci bi kɔɔr
Na weŋ ci kap, ci bi kɔɔr   10
Na kɔr yen, ke wok
Miyar e bɛny
Gat athoor;
Wet ba lueel
Raan muk yen ace raan e gat   15
Ka bi tiŋ e raan e gat

Ace tiet;
Tiit kuon ka ka cak kek e leec
Yɛn e raan dit
Miyar aɲic wel.   20
Mɛnh kai ci doŋ
Yin ba thɔn
Na lɔk e bɛn ke yi dit gaau
Miyar ala ke la tuɛŋ

Liec wa, liec   25
Liec e kɔu yin ci gaau,
Liec wa liec
Dhëëŋ e Miyar e Wɔr
Anak ruup kek e mac
Thabur ke la ɣam   30
Ke diit e mith ka adheeŋ.

DATE DUE

		NOV 0 1 1993		